AN ETHNOGRAPHY
of the
HERMIT KINGDOM

AN ETHNOGRAPHY

of the

HERMIT KINGDOM

THE J. B. BERNADOU KOREAN COLLECTION
(1884–1885)

by
Chang-su Cho Houchins

ASIAN CULTURAL HISTORY PROGRAM
SMITHSONIAN INSTITUTION 2004

This publication is a product of the **Korean Heritage Fund**, Asian Cultural History Program, Smithsonian Institution, and has been made possible by:

Generous financial assistance and project sponsorship by Sigong Tekku (Time and Space Tech Corporation), Seoul, Korea, with special thanks to Mr. Park Ki-seok, President, Sigong Tekku,

and by:

A generous contribution to the Smithsonian's Korean Heritage Fund for this publication, delivered on the occasion of the March 2001 visit of the President of the Republic of Korea to Washington, D.C., by Madame Lee Hee-ho, First Lady of Korea.

This book is produced and distributed by:
Asian Cultural History Program
Department of Anthropology
Smithsonian Institution
Washington DC 20560 USA

ISBN: 0-9724557-3-6 (softcover)
First printing

Library of Congress Cataloging-in-Publication Data

Houchins, Chang-su Cho, 1925–
An Ethnography of the Hermit Kingdom:
The J. B. Bernadou Korean Collection
(1884-1885) / Chang-su Cho Houchins

p. cm.
Includes bibliographical references; index.
I. Houchins, Chang-su Cho, 1925–
II. National Museum of Natural History
(U.S.). Asian Cultural History Program.

Studio photography by Kim Sungyun.
Introduction by Paul Michael Taylor.

Produced by Perpetua Press, Santa Barbara:
Jane Oliver, editor
Dana Levy, designer
Printed and bound by P. Chan and Edwards in Korea

CONTENTS

INTRODUCTION

THE JOHN BAPTISTE BERNADOU COLLECTION of nineteenth-century Korean artifacts, so thoroughly researched and presented by Chang-su Cho Houchins in this volume, represents a unique attempt by an amateur American ethnographer to record the material culture of the Korean people at a critical moment in Korea's long cultural history. John Baptiste Bernadou (1858–1908) assembled this collection from March 1884 to April 1885 as an attaché (or envoy) of the Smithsonian Institution. Since the Smithsonian, as a trust instrumentality of the U.S. government, serves as America's national museum, Bernadou was attached to the American diplomatic mission in Korea. Both Bernadou and the Smithsonian recognized that a new opportunity to record Korean cultural heritage using the methods of nineteenth-century museum science had emerged along with the "opening" of Korea heralded by the signing in 1882 of the first Treaty of Amity and Commerce between the Kingdom of Korea and the United States of America.

Long known as the "Hermit Kingdom" for its pre-1880s isolation, Korea, or at least many of the Kingdom's elite citizens, wholeheartedly began a period of openness to the outside world as a result of the exchanges initiated by this accord. Concurrently, Smithsonian scientists of the early 1880s recognized that a major cultural tradition and a previously unstudied geographical region were then available for study by the kind of systematizing sciences (including ethnology, and taxonomic studies in biology) in which natural history museums of the time excelled. Evolutionary paradigms prevailed at that time in the comparative study of cultures and civilizations; there was also considerable interest in the spread of particular technological and craft traditions through history and around the globe. Such studies required the collection and classification of a wide range of material culture objects as an essential component of any ethnography (that is, the description of a particular culture) that would be most useful for building a science of ethnology (that is, the comparative study of cultures, through the comparative study of ethnographies). Field ethnographer-collectors therefore recognized the importance of systematically collecting material culture from the widest possible range of classes or subgroups, along with documentation of local terms for objects and information about how and by whom they were used. Ethnographic collectors enthusiastically included and documented everyday village crafts within their collections, as well as aesthetic masterpieces, sacred ritual items, the paraphernalia of kingly rank, graphic arts and written works of literature, or ethnobotanical specimens (like samples of grain or ginseng). Though not formally trained in anthropology, Bernadou collected for the Smithsonian's natural history museum and seems clearly to have understood the principles of collecting that his Smithsonian correspondents always encouraged.

Yet unlike many nineteenth-century biologists collecting natural history specimens for study, those who assembled material culture collections understood very well that objects have meaningfulness within a system of symbols and uses that require study as part of a broad descriptive ethnography of the culture that produced those objects. And though Bernadou himself never wrote up a systematic ethnography, his notes and methods of collecting clearly indicate that such a systematic description of Korean culture, in all its regional and other variations, was one intended goal of his collecting. Bernadou's interest in studying Korean language and culture overwhelmed any interest in biological specimens; perhaps Smithsonian Secretary Baird expected more of the latter but Bernadou's correspondence apologetically admits he has not sent much in the way of preserved animals or plants. (In fact, this volume considers only the Korean ethnographic collections, not the relatively few natural history specimens he collected.)

The breadth of this collection, including everyday household furniture and utensils, textiles, clothing and accessories, ceramics, handicrafts, paintings, prints and drawings, books, maps, and musical instruments, allows a unique glimpse of pre-industrial Korean life. The catalog of the Bernadou Collection presented in this volume includes Bernadou's notes (and, in the Appendices, selected correspondence from him), but it reinterprets the collection based on Chang-su Cho Houchins's careful study of the objects in light of more recent methods and current scholarship in this field.

Particularly interesting is the position of the collector (and of collecting) within the early period of diplomatic contacts between the Kingdom of Korea and the United States; and the role of both collectors and those who study collections as cultural intermediaries. In fact, the Smithsonian's three major Korean ethnographic collections of this period are all by Americans associated with the diplomatic mission who integrated in unique ways into Korean culture: John B. Bernadou (whose collection is the first, and the most comprehensive); Horace Newton Allen (1858–1932), a Presbyterian medical missionary who also served as medical officer both to the American Legation (diplomatic mission) and later to the court of Korea's King Kojong; and Pierre Louis Jouy (1856–1894), who assisted with the mission that led to the 1882 treaty and who later became an advisor to the Korean civil service. These three collections formed the basis of a report by Smithsonian curator Walter Hough, *The Bernadou, Allen, and Jouy Korean Collections in the United States National Museum* (published in 1892, within the *Annual Report of the U.S. National Museum* for 1891). That report included information about Korean objects donated to the Smithsonian by five other American collectors of the period as well. Just as these collections were formed by expatriate Americans whose lives intersected in unique ways with those of the Koreans among whom they lived, the Smithsonian's study of the collection was also made possible by the assistance of the small expatriate Korean community in America, particularly Byeon Su (1861–1891), Seo Gwan-beom (1859–1897), and Seo Jae-pil (1866–1951). As Chang-su Cho Houchins notes in this volume, these Koreans in America not only exemplified the great interest of Korea's expatriate community in this project but also provided much of the information Walter Hough used for the preparation of his classic study. Already, in the nineteenth century, Korean collections at the Smithsonian took on an iconic importance to the (then small) Korean community in America.

This volume is partly a result of continuing interest on the part of a large and supportive Korean and Korean-American community in Korea's heritage at the Smithsonian. Within the Asian Cultural History Program of the Smithsonian's Anthropology Department, the Korean Heritage Fund was established in 1985 and has resulted in numerous exhibitions, lectures, performances, and other cultural activities. This volume constitutes part of a wider recent effort, underway within Asian ethnology collections at the Smithsonian, to reinterpret old anthropological collections in light of two components: what they tell about the culture that produced the artifacts, and what they tell about the collecting culture. One of our goals has also been to improve documentation of and access to the historic Korean collections of the Smithsonian. This volume was in fact initially conceived as an annotated republication of Walter Hough's 1892 report about all the nineteenth-century collections. Hough's descriptive catalog included information on nearly 400 items assembled by the above-named collectors from 1884 to 1889, following the opening of Korea in 1882. However, the "annotations" of the Bernadou Collection alone soon vastly outgrew the original work, and Bernadou's scope and mission were also recognizably different from those of the other collectors. Thus, presenting and interpreting this collection alone in the light of current scholarship required the author to start anew and produce a completely new catalog of the Bernadou Collection. Its approach and arrangement are fundamentally different from those of Hough's 1892 report, though Hough's (and his informants') contemporaneous information and insights are quoted among the sources of information in this volume.

As the author states in her acknowledgment, the multiyear preparation and publication of this volume has been made possible by generous donations to the Korean Heritage Fund, whose many donors and supporters over the years had also made possible many other behind-the-scenes improvements carried out for these collections. Thanks to the careful scholarship and dedication of this book's author along with the photography done for this project by Mr. Kim Sungyun (with the support of Mr. Sam-kyun Yoon), the Asian Cultural History Program circulated a preliminary manuscript for this book. It is significant that on the occasion of the March 2001 visit of the President of Korea to Washington, the First Lady of Korea, Madame Lee Hee-ho, delivered a donation to the Smithsonian's Korean Heritage Fund specifically toward the publication of this book, a welcome endorsement of the project. We are grateful to the primary sponsor of this volume's publication, Sigong Tekku (Time and Space Tech Corporation) of Seoul, Korea, since this volume's publication has been made possible by a generous contribution arranged by Mr. Park Ki-seok, President of that corporation and supporter of the Smithsonian's Korean Heritage Fund.

We trust that this volume not only will make this historic collection of Korea's material heritage more widely accessible but also will provide new information for the assessment of Korea's pre-industrial material culture, and of the early diplomatic and cultural contacts between Korea and the United States.

Paul Michael Taylor
Director, Asian Cultural History Program
Smithsonian Institution

ACKNOWLEDGMENTS

FIELD RESEARCH FOR THIS VOLUME WAS CONDUCTED IN KOREA in 1987 and 1988. I was helped by partial and full funding from Research Opportunity Fund grants during the early stages of the Bernadou Collection redocumentation project. These fieldtrips were mainly to study comparable nineteenth century objects in Korean museums and to consult with experts in specialized areas. I had to familiarize myself with nineteenth-century Korean material culture represented in native Korean museum holdings. I am greatly indebted to many staff members at the Seoul National Folk Museum, especially to Kim Samdaeja, whose assistance was indispensable. For over a decade, she assisted me in every possible mode, not only with her profound knowledge of traditional Korean folk and courtly objects, but with an up-to-date bibliography of published sources. To facilitate the Smithsonian Institution's Korean project, she personally sent me a number of reference works unavailable in the United States.

My gratitude goes to Brian LeMay, Assistant Director of the Office of International Relations, who contacted the American Embassy in Seoul on my behalf. He requested special assistance with my field research trips to Seoul, especially in case of illness or other emergencies, including such mundane activities as shipping books to the museum. I also thank Ambassador and Mrs. James R. Lilley and Mr. and Mrs. Charles Kartman, Political Affairs Officer, for their kind hospitality and staff members at the American Embassy for their assistance during my sojourn in Seoul.

I also received assistance, particularly regarding native terms for nineteenth century objects, from three Korean-culture experts, so-designated by the International Society of Cultural Exchanges (renamed the Korea Foundation) who were sent to the United States in 1987 as part of their mission to survey Korean cultural properties overseas. They are: Dr. Chung Yang-mo, the former Director of the Seoul National Museum; the late Ye Yong-hae, a member of the Board of Preservation of Korean Cultural Relics; and Professor Kim Gwang-eon, Director of the Inha University Museum in Incheon. I extend special thanks to Professor Yun Yong-i of the Wongang University in Seoul, a well-known expert on Korean ceramics. During his visit to the Museum Service Center in 1987, he examined our early Korean ceramic collections and provided valuable information, such as the date and place of manufacture and the use of each piece in the collections.

Thanks are due to Suh Hong K., a 1991 summer intern from the University of Pennsylvania (a doctoral candidate in Chinese art history at Princeton University), who provided extraordinary help with the then ongoing Bernadou Collection redocumentation project. She collated a mass of information on the collection from various sources: archival and published materials; collection catalog card data; the Registrar's Office accession records and list of Smithsonian ethnology accessions in the oldest ledger known as the "Anthropology Catalog Book." Excellent organizational skill together with a good knowledge of the Korean language prepared her to produce an invaluable comprehensive file relating to the Bernadou Collection.

Thanks are also due to those behind-the-scene volunteers in the early 1990s who were involved in the Bernadou project. Yun Kyung-nim, a local artist from McLean, Virginia, did a dozen or so charcoal drawings of Bernadou items, none of which, unfortunately, is used in this publication. Park Sunnae, a textile conservator at the National Museum of American History, used her knowledge of the construction of Korean costumes to provide the technical terminology to properly describe each garment. Cha Ock-shin introduced me to Korean language software and acted as a "user's guide" for me. In connection with these talented volunteers, I wish to express my gratitude to Kim Hyojung and Shin Junghwa, both from George Washington University. Busy schedules and personal reasons prevented them from long and direct involvement with the project, but all the same, I am grateful for their offer. Several years ago, I was blessed with an unusual volunteer assistant, Yook Dong-in, *Korea Economic Daily* correspondant (then a visiting scholar at Georgetown University's Department of Economics). He helped me to search for registration and bibliographic information at the library and to arrange publicity for the Bernadou Collection research project as a means of outreach to the Korean audience.

From 1998 to 2000, Yuh Junghyun, a heaven-sent (actually from the Asian Cultural History Program) research assistant proved crucial in bringing the long, drawn-out Bernadou project to near completion. Yuh Junghyun's profound knowledge of Korean history and culture, together with her facile command of Korean language software, were essential. I also wish to recognize her contribution to the sections dealing with books and maps entered in the catalog. A preliminary documentation of these items prepared by Junghyun clearly shows her research skills and careful observation of documentation methods of museum collections. Along with Junghyun, Georgia Reilly assisted me with her extraordinary skills in proofreading and editing. She also served as a sounding board for some unusually complicated descriptive text containing explanations about methods of use. If the description did not make sense to her, no Westerner would understand it. I am very grateful to Dr. Park Yong-Jean, an academic intern, whose assistance was invaluable in verifying citations by checking them against reference sources and checking each entry to ensure consistency of format. Yong-Jean's professional training in music composition did not deter her in undertaking a tedious task of checking entries and indexing, but rather enhanced precision and accuracy.

I feel fortunate to have been able to call on Randy Tims, Asian Cultural History Program coordinator, whose multilayered assistance is hard to enumerate, from computer problems to all office day-to-day crises. I thank him with much affection. Thanks to many others whose helping hands were readily extended: Margaret Dittemore, and Jim Haug of the Smithsonian's anthropology branch library; Paula Fleming and Vyrtis Thomas of the National Anthropological Archives; Jayne Holt, paper conservator of the Museum Service Center's Conservation Laboratory; Johanna Humphrey, Susan Crawford, Felicia Pickering, members of the Collections Management staff; and Winifred Weislogel and Laverne Madancy, volunteer aides whose assistance with photographic work on the Bernadou Collection was indispensable. Donald E. Hurlbert, National Museum of Natural History photographer, kindly accommodated our sporadic and urgent requests for photocopy work. I also thank Alan Bain and William Cox of the Smithsonian Institution Archives who, with professional efficiency, provided us with archival materials.

At various stages of the project, a number of Anthropology Department staff and other Smithsonian associates contributed to this project. For their help, I thank the late Carolyn Rose, Carole Lee-Kin, Joyce Sommers, especially Marcia Bakry for preparing some illustrative materials that we substituted with photographs for technical expediency; Bruce Morrison, Office of Fellowships and Grants, for internship arrangements; and Raymond Seefeld, Office of International Relations, for obtaining special visa status for Yuh Junghyun and Park Yong-Jean. My gratitude also goes to Drs. William Sturtevant, Paul Michael Taylor and Adrienne L. Kaeppler of the Department of Anthropology for reviewing a segment of the draft manuscript dealing with history of the early Smithsonian Korean collections and providing me with their critical comments and helpful suggestions. My thanks extend to Drs. Jacquelin Pak, Korean specialist at the Library of Congress and Robert Sayers of the National Endowment for the Humanities, who reviewed the final draft of the manuscript.

Several non-Smithsonian individuals greatly contributed to the project. Yoon Sam-kyun, President of the Korea Foundation, U.S.A., deserves special mention for his help in the establishment in 1985 of the Korean Heritage Fund, which provided the stipend for the research assistant position. Mr. Yoon personally paid the expenses for photographic work by Kim Sungyun, while the photographer contributed his time and expertise in photographing selected specimens for this publication. Special thanks are due to Kim Sungyun along with Yoon Sam-kyun.

Kyle Lemargie, Michel Lee and Soomin Ham, talented young members of the Asian Cultural History Program prepared the final draft. Without their great care and enthusiasm, I could not have finished this project. I thank them greatly. I extend my thanks also to Diane Dell-Loggia of the Smithsonian's Anthropology Department, who kindly applied her copyediting skills to the entire manuscript, and to Paul Michael Taylor, Director of the Asian Cultural History Program, for his support of the project and for contributing the volume's introduction.

My final comment relates to my husband, Lee Houchins. Despite suffering from ill health for the last several years, he did not resent my domestic absence and negligence but gave moral support to my singular drive to bring forth the Bernadou project to its completion. Lee Houchins died last year. He would have been very pleased that the Bernadou project had finally come to fruition.

CHANG-SU CHO HOUCHINS
Asian Cultural History Program
Smithsonian Institution

Dr. Walter Hough in Korean nobleman's everyday costume (taken shortly after the Bernadou Collection was accessioned in 1886). Outfit includes a black hat (entry 67), headband (entry 53) outer linen coat (entry 49), sash (entry 44), and black leather-lined shoes (entry 52). He holds a folding fan (entry 90).

JOHN BAPTISTE BERNADOU COLLECTION (1884–1885)

THE BERNADOU KOREAN COLLECTION deserves special attention as a combination of Smithsonian initiative and the collector's dedicated approach to his task. Professor Spencer F. Baird (1823–1887), Secretary of the Smithsonian Institution, and, concurrently, Director of the U.S. National Museum, regarded the opening of the former "Hermit Kingdom" as "a golden opportunity for exploration of all aspects of Natural History."[1] As early as October 1882, Bernadou was detailed to the Smithsonian Institution, where he was trained in methods of collecting museum specimens in preparation for special duty in Korea.[2] Under the program at the USNM, begun in 1881 at the request of the Department of the Navy, officers were trained for scientific assignments throughout the world.

Bernadou showed he was eager to undertake the planned exploration in Korea in a letter he sent to Baird on 2 November 1883, which reads in part: "As the U.S.S. Alert will leave in short time…I would respectfully request that you mention the fact in your letter to the State Department as a reason for urging speedy action."[3] Three days later, E. D. Nichols, Acting Secretary of the Navy, directed Bernadou to report to the Navy Yard, Mare Island, California, for passage to Asiatic Station in Nagasaki, Japan. He was to confer there with a senior officer "as to the best method for reaching Korea." In the letter, Nichols reminds Bernadou that he is being sent for scientific investigation by direction of the USNM and that the Smithsonian Institution would furnish apparatus and outfit him for his work in Korea. He added, "This employment on shore duty is required by the public interests."[4]

Baird provided the necessary funds and arranged for Bernadou to travel on a special passport issued by the Department of the Navy, which identified him as "Smithsonian Attaché," accredited to the American Legation in Seoul.[5] While waiting in San Francisco for passage to Korea, Bernadou wrote to the Smithsonian requesting photographic equipment as part of his fieldwork apparatus. The letter suggests that he had made the request earlier: "Your suggestion that on account of Mr. Foulk's [Lt. George C. Foulk, chargé d' affaires] having a photographic outfit there is no need of my having one I regret *exceedingly*…I will be unable to take what pictures I wish." He even offers to repay the expenses involved, and adds: "I therefore earnestly request that this apparatus be obtained for me, and I will be willing, on my return to make good any portion of expense…"[6] Because the Smithsonian failed to accommodate his needs and wishes, no photographic record of Bernadou's visit to Korea exists. Even after he arrived in Seoul, he wrote: "I cannot imagine any place where a photographic apparatus could be put to a better use than here. The costumes, buildings, memorial arches, bridges, tombs, shops, etc., would furnish work for many."[7]

Bernadou arrived at Nagasaki on 24 February 1884 aboard the *USS Alert* and transferred to the *USS Juniata* bound for Chemulp'o (now Incheon) arriving there

1. According to David S. Rubin, the author of "John Baptiste Bernadou, A Smithsonian Ethnographer in Korea." Unpublished MS, un-paginated [1982].

2. For the arrangement and for a specific reference to the case of Bernadou, see The U.S. National Museum Annual Report for 1891, pages 123–124. Hereafter, all U.S. National Museum Annual Reports will be referred to as USNM-AR followed by the appropriate year.

3. Letter of 2 November 1883, Washington, D.C. from Bernadou to Baird, Smithsonian Institution Archives Record Unit 29 (hereafter SI Archives RU) (Appendix I).

4. Letter of 5 November 1883 from E. D. Nichols, Acting Secretary, Department of the Navy, Washington, D.C., to Bernadou, SI Archives RU 29.

5. National Archives Record Group 59 (General Records of the Department of State) series: "Diplomatic Instructions from the Department of State-Korea," numbers" 28, 58, and 128 identify Bernadou as "Attaché of the Smithsonian Institution to Korea."

6. Bernadou letter of 18 November 1883, San Francisco, California to Baird, SI Archives RU 29.

S. Bernadou letter of 10 March 1884, Seoul, Korea to Baird, SI Archives RU29 (Appendix II).

on 1 March. In, he was given a house on the U.S. Legation grounds and received a warm and courteous reception from Minister Lucius H. Foote (1826–1913). Minister Foote had already received communication from the Department of State regarding Ensign Bernadou's mission and was willing to render all possible assistance.[8]

Bernadou took his Smithsonian collecting assignment very seriously. He began studying Korean with Yun Chi-ho (1865–1946), the U.S. Legation interpreter, on 24 April, meeting sporadically through early July when he ventured into the northwest region.[9] He continued to study the Korean language with various teachers throughout his one-year stay in Korea.

Bernadou's progress report of 2 September 1884 to Professor Baird outlines his intended activities: "(1) To remain in Seoul during the first part of my stay… to study the Corean language in order to become conversant with the people and thus enable myself to give my attention to Corean ethnology… (2) To visit the interior of Corea later, to make such general observations as in my power, and to incorporate such matter in my ethnographic report as might be useful to you…."[10] Bernadou learned enough Korean to travel throughout the interior of Korea to collect ethnological specimens, as well as mineralogical and other natural history specimens. He visited northern cities including Songdo, Pyongyang, Uiju, and Unsan, presumably with Korean guides. One journey covered five hundred miles. He acknowledges in a postscript the kindness extended to him by Korean officials, "affording me every facility for travelling, furnishing me horses at government rates, and giving me lodging on my way in the official buildings."[11] He also reported his plans to return to Seoul in midwinter to finish his ethnological collections and to make preparations to leave.

Included in this progress report is a brief summary of his accomplishment under the headings: pottery, painting, metalwork and inlaid work, furniture, woodcarving, stonework, and books. Despite digestion problems he suffered during the fall of 1884, he asked to be allowed to remain until the following April [1885] to continue his work.

The twenty-five pages of field notes in Bernadou's handwriting, titled "Notes on Collections of Korean Articles,"[12] include a description of each of the 156 items he collected. Each entry begins with the Korean term for the object, given in Hangul, some of which contain spelling errors, followed by the pronunciation in Roman letters. Bernadou's attempt to transcribe the Korean word used to describe each object is not keyed to an identified system of transliteration but rather is an individual attempt to codify the sounds he heard. In these efforts, Bernadou displayed his exceptional linguistic talent, which allowed him to master the Korean syllabary within a short period of time.

Also included in his field notes are illustrative drawings, which attempt to clarify the complicated descriptions of certain objects. Although each specimen he collected bears an entry number, the numbering is not consecutive; the number given to an individual object may indicate the sequence of his collecting activities. Classification of the assembled items appears random. For example, under the heading "Korean Table Ware" such unrelated items as a pillow end disk and a printing block are listed. He designates the following categories among others: "Corean Mourning Dress,""Korean Fabrics,""Men's Clothing," Women's Clothing,""Children's Clothing,""Korean Grains,""Old Korean Pottery," and "Additional Notes."

Bernadou's field notes accompanied a packing list (Appendix VI) of the Korean collection, which was formally accessioned in February 1886 as file number 16970.[13] The field notes and packing list are in the collection of Smithsonian Institution Archives designated as Record Unit 305. Other Bernadou Collection-related documents are in the National Museum of Natural History Registrar's Office, where original accession records are kept. In terms of size, content, documentation, and collection history, the Bernadou Collection is the single most important collection

8. W. Hunter, Department of State, letter of 5 November 1883, Washington, D.C., to Lucius H. Foote, United States Minister, Seoul, Korea, SI Archives RU 29; *The Smithsonian Institution Annual Report for 1883* (Washington, D.C., 1884), page 41. Hereafter all Smithsonian Institution Annual Reports will be referred to as SI-AR, followed by the appropriate year.

9. For Yun's diary entries, see *Hanguk saryo chongseo* 19: *Yun Chi-ho ilgi* (Yun Chi-ho's Diary) (Seoul 1984).

10. Bernadou letter of 2 September 1884, Seoul, Korea to Baird, National Museum of Natural History Smithsonian Institution Registrar's Office accession number 16970 (Appendix III). Hereafter, National Museum of Natural History will be referred to as NMNH.

11. ibid.

12. SI Archives RU 305.

13. NMNH Registrar's Office Accession number 16970 includes Bernadou letter of 20 April 1885, Chemulp'o, Korea, *USS Ossipee* to Baird. Originally, this file also included Bernadou field notes which were enclosed in the 20 April 1885 letter. In1976 the field notes were transferred to the SI Archives and given the number RU 305.

of Korean ethnographic material assembled on behalf of the Smithsonian Institution before the close of the nineteenth century.

On 11 April 1890, Bernadou delivered a lecture, under the auspices of the National Geographic Society on the subject of "Corea and Coreans," which was subsequently published with three maps of Korea.[14] "John Baptiste Bernadou, A Smithsonian Ethnographer in Korea," an unpublished manuscript prepared in 1982 by David S. Rubin of the International Wilson Center for Scholars, Washington, D.C., to commemorate the centennial of U.S.-Korea relations, asserts that "Bernadou's Korea episode was but the beginning of a prominent Naval career." For his many accomplishments, Bernadou was buried with full military honors in Arlington National Cemetery in 1908.[15]

HISTORY OF OTHER EARLY KOREAN COLLECTIONS

The most comprehensive documentation of the Smithsonian's early Korean ethnology collections is the monograph by Walter Hough, "The Bernadou, Allen and Jouy Korean Collections, in The U.S. National Museum," published in the museum's annual report of 1891, pages 429–488. The three collections named in the title contain the majority of the artifacts described in the catalog; however, a small number of supplementary items collected by Gustavius Goward, George Brown Goode, Captain William B. Brooks, USN, Ensign C. G. Talcott, USN, and William Woodville Rockhill were also included.

In his introductory essay, Hough writes: "The collection has been explained and studied by Ensign Bernadou,[16] three Korean gentlemen in Washington (Pom K. Soh [Seo Gwang-beom 徐光範], Dr. Philip Jaisohn [Seo Jae-pil 徐載弼], and the late Penn Su [Byeon Su 邊燧])." He also acknowledges the assistance received from Mr. W.W. Rockhill, Mr. P. L. Jouy, and Rev. W. E. Griffis.[17]

Biographies of the author and curator, Walter Hough, the collectors, and the three native Korean political exiles in Washington who served as consultants, reveal the unusual circumstances under which the catalog was compiled. In the aggregate, these personal histories also define a unique moment in the Smithsonian's collection activities and reveal the keen ethnographic insights of American diplomats, which resulted in this assemblage of a broad range of pre-industrial nineteenth-century Korean material culture. Hough's monograph on the early Korean collections and his other writings about Korea reflect the lack of depth of nineteenth-century American scholarship on Korea, as well as his personal attempt to understand Korean society and its culture using the museological approach, that is, via a thorough study of objects and associated documentation.[18]

Walter Hough (1859–1935) joined the U.S. National Museum staff in 1886 as an assistant to Professor Otis Tufton Mason (1838–1908), the curator of its recently established Division of Ethnology. The creation of this new division in 1883 demonstrated increasing reliance upon museum specimens to study diverse cultures. By the late 1880s, a considerable number of ethnology collections had come to the museum, but the division was "severely hampered by the constant flow of accessions, lack of space, and funds...." In these circumstances, many specimens were not yet properly stored, classified, or studied.[19]

Hough's first publication at his new job, the article, "The Preservation of Museum Specimens from Insects and Dampness," which appeared in the annual report of 1887, reveals that conservation was of immediate concern. His proposal to protect and preserve specimens in the museum collections is clearly the work of a natural scientist.[20] His formal training in chemistry and geology was helpful in his pursuit of a lifelong museum career as an anthropologist. Hough did both undergraduate and graduate work at West Virginia University. He earned his doctorate in geology in 1894. He became Assistant Curator in 1894, Acting Curator in 1903, and in

14. "Korea and the Koreans," *National Geographic Magazine,* vol. 2, 1890, no. 4, pages 231–242.

15. Rubin, [1982] MS, for other accomplishments; see also *Who Was Who in America,* vol. 1 (1897–1942) (Chicago, 1966), page 88.

16. Hough refers specifically to J. B. Bernadou's original field note essays, numbered 1 through 156, which accompanied his 1884–1885 collection, now in SI Archives RU 305 (MS); also to Bernadou letter of 2 September 1884, Seoul, U.S. Legation, Korea to professor Spencer Fullerton Baird (Appendix III), then the Secretary of the Smithsonian Institution and concurrently Director of the U.S. National Museum (1878–1887). The letter contains a summary of the articles collected with general descriptions, including pottery, painting, metalwork, and books. See USNM Registrar's Office accession number 16970.

17. USNM-AR 1891: 432.

18. For example, Hough's article, "Korean Clan Organization," in *The American Anthropologist,* New Series, vol. 1 (January 1899), pages 150–154. In the same issue, his note about "Korean Crossbow and Arrow-tube" appears under the section, "Notes and News," page 200.

19. Curtis M. Hinsley Jr., *Savages and Scientists: The Smithsonian Institution and the Development of American Anthropology 1846–1910* (Washington, D.C.: Smithsonian Institution Press, 1981), page 95.

20. In fact, "Mason valued highly Hough's natural science training...for Mason himself would treat a specimen just as naturalist would [with] a plant or animal." For Mason's and his assistant Hough's meticulous attention to artifacts and their methods of documentation, ibid., page 91.

1910, following Mason's death, Hough was appointed Curator; in 1922, he assumed the position of Head Curator, which he retained until his own death in 1935.[21]

COLLECTIONS

THE ALLEN COLLECTION

Horace Newton Allen (1858–1932), who led a distinguished career as a Presbyterian medical missionary and diplomat, received his B.A. degree from Ohio Wesleyan University in 1881 and became the first Protestant missionary to live in Korea after his graduation from Miami [Ohio] Medical School. In 1884, he was appointed medical officer in Seoul, first to the American Legation and later, after having saved the life of the Queen's nephew, Prince Min Yeong-ik , as a medical officer to the royal court of the Kingdom of Korea. Allen accompanied Pak Jeong-yang 朴定陽, the first Korean Minister, to Washington in 1887 where he remained as an advisor to the Korean Legation until 1889.[22]

In October 1889, before Dr. Allen returned to Seoul, where he was appointed Secretary to the American Legation in 1890, he deposited his collection as a loan in the U.S. National Museum. It was assigned a temporary accession number (22405) and was recorded as "118 Specimens of Corean Ethnologica," many of which were given to him by the King of Korea, Kojong 高宗 (1852–1919), the twenty-sixth king of the Choson Dynasty (reigned 1863–1907).[23] In 1897 Dr. Allen was promoted to the rank of Minister to the American Legation in Seoul.[24] The Allen collection was formally received by the Museum as a gift in 1928, under a new accession number (101058). The number of items accessioned at this time was reduced to 116, as one ceramic bowl and a strand of amber beads had been returned to the donor upon his request.[25]

THE JOUY COLLECTION

Pierre Louis Jouy (1856–1894) was a longtime employee of the Smithsonian Institution, who joined the museum as copyist in 1877.[26] In 1881 he was chosen to take part in a joint venture initiated by the U.S. Navy with the Smithsonian to train young Naval officers in scientific methods of collecting and in assembling information for the museum. Under this program Jouy went to Japan, but he left the program after five months. He remained in Japan to continue his collecting activities.[27]

In 1883 he accompanied the Honorable Lucius H. Foote, the first Minister of the American Legation in Seoul, to implement formal diplomatic relations between the United States and Korea. Foote and Jouy arrived in Chemulp'o on 17 May.[28] Jouy subsequently became an advisor to the Korean civil service.[29] In November [1883], he was granted the first passport issued to a foreigner for an overland journey to the southeastern part, Busan 釜山 (formerly Pusan). During two and a half years spent in Busan, Jouy made a large collection of Korean specimens. From this location he made trips to Ulsan 蔚山, Daegu (formerly Taegu) 大邱, and other cities in North Kyeongsang province 慶尙北道. He also visited the port of Wonsan 元山 (South Hamgyeong province 咸鏡南道) on the east coast before leaving Korea in 1886.[30]

The Jouy Korean collection came to the museum during 1887–1889, resulting in several separate accessions, which were assigned various numbers: 19276, 19537, 19638, and 23703. The last accession was identified as a deposit of "a collection of Corean religious objects, book, pictures, art work, weapons, etc...." In total, Jouy donated forty items, in addition to forty-three photographs.[31] Jouy's collection of photographic prints, chiefly in carte-de-visites size, depict Korean life in cities and

21. SI-AR 1887, part 2, 549–558. *The National Cyclopedia of American Biography* (New York, 1936), page 277; USNM-AR 1936: 17, announces the death of Dr. Walter Hough and his forty-nine years of dedicated work in the museum.

22. For a full account of Allen's work, particularly during the early years in Korea, see Fred Harvey Harrington, *God, Mammon and the Japanese: Dr. Horace N. Allen and Korean-American Relations, 1884–1905*, 3–84; see also Kim Won-mo, 1991, *Horace Newton Allen Diary*, Parts 1 and 2, 20 August 1883 through 25 October 1886 entries.

23. NMNH Registrar's Office accession number 22405.

24. Harrington 1994: 294.

25. NMNH Registrar's Office accession number 101058 (now combined with the accession number 22405) includes Horace Allen letter of 9 April 1928 to A. Wetmore, Assistant Secretary of the Smithsonian Institution, acknowledging receipt of the two returned items: a bowl and a strand of amber beads.

26. SI Archives RU 64, for Lists of Smithsonian employees, 1846–1904.

27. Jouy letter of 21 June 1882, Yokohama [Japan], to Spencer Baird, announcing his disengagement from the U.S. Navy program, SI Archives RU 28; SI-AR 1882: 21.

28. Jouy's reassignment to Korea is noted in SI-AR 1883: 26; SI-AR 1884: 27; Greey, compiler of an auction catalogue entitled *Hand-Book of A Unique Collection of Ancient and Modern Korean and Chinese Works of Art, Procured in Korea During 1883–1886*, by Pierre L. Jouy of Washington, D.C., 5–7, recounts his encounter with Jouy, "an attaché of the Smithsonian Institution," as a fellow passenger en route to Japan in 1881 and Jouy's collecting activities in Korea.

29. See USNM-AR 1884: 124.

30. Greey 1888: 6.

31. See USNM Registrar's Office accession number 23703.

villages, and individual and group portraits in traditional dress. A major portion of this collection of objects and photographs was published in Walter Hough's monograph of the early Korean collections.

During his stay in Korea, Jouy also made a collection of Korean mortuary pottery, totaling sixty-four pieces, an illustrated catalog of which was published in 1888 under the title: "The Collection of Korean Mortuary Pottery in the U.S. National Museum."[32] Jouy's other published work, "Korean Potter's Wheel," indicates that his interest in Korean pottery was not confined only to collecting; he actually observed Korean potters at work.[33]

In 1898 the Smithsonian Institution purchased "a large and valuable collection of Corean birds, comprising 547 specimens" from Jouy.[34]

CONSULTANTS

Accessioning the J.B. Bernadou Korean collections by the National Museum in 1886 attracted much attention, particularly among Korean expatriates, and it was only a matter of course that members of a small community would become a source of information about the Korean specimens.

Byeon Su [alias Penn Su] (1861–1891) arrived in the United States in 1883 as a member of the first Korean diplomatic mission following the signing of the 1882 U.S.-Korea Treaty of Amity and Commerce, but he is best known as the first Korean graduate of an American university. He received a B.S. degree from the Maryland Agricultural College (now the University of Maryland) in 1891. Upon graduation, Byeon Su was hired by the U.S. Department of Agriculture to compile a report on Japanese agriculture, and the report was published under the title, "Agriculture in Japan." That year Byeon was killed in a railroad accident in Maryland.[35]

Byeon's American connection began when he was sent by King Kojong to the United States in 1883. He arrived in San Francisco on 2 September, and remained in the United States until 19 November, 1883. Byeon accompanied Min Yeong-ik and Seo Gwang-beom to Europe in 1884 en route to Korea,[36] where his political activities as a member of the progressive reformist party, Gaehwa-dang 開化黨, deepened. His involvement in the aborted 1884 coup d'état, in which progressive party reformers who championed modernization attempted to assassinate conservative figurehead Min Yeong-ik, who was injured, while the head of the newly established post office, a progressive party member, was murdered by the conservative faction. Byeon Su was forced to flee Korea and returned to America via Japan in 1886.

Byeon's thirst for Japanese scientific knowledge, which he viewed as the basis of technological advancement that would eventually lead to modernization of his nation, led him to take several sojourns in Japan from 1882 to 1886 as a member of a diplomatic mission, as a student, and lastly as a political emigrÈ en route to America.[37]

Byeon presumably first met Hough in 1887, when Hough became an aide in the Division of Ethnology. Hough acknowledges Byeon's assistance in his introductory essay accompanying the catalogue of the early Korean collections, referring to him as "the late Penn Su."[38]

Seo Gwang-beom (1859–1897) came to the United States in 1883 as the third minister of the first Korean diplomatic mission. On his return trip to Korea via Europe (19 November 1883–31 May 1884), Seo, together with Byeon Su, accompanied Min Yeong-ik, head of the mission.[39] Following the aborted 1884 coup d'état, Seo fled Korea with other prominent progressive reformist party members. He escaped to Japan as others did and remained in exile for ten years, most of which were in America.[40]

Seo Gwang-beom, with Seo Jae-pil, left Japan in April 1885 for the United

32. USNM-AR 1888: 589–596, appended are twenty figures to plates LXXXII–LXXXV.

33. Jouy's article, "The Korean Potter's Wheel," *Science* (September 1888), 144.

34. USNM-AR1889: 124.

35. Byeon Su died on 22 October 1891 at College Station, Maryland. Yi Gwang-rin provides a comprehensive biography of Byeon Su in "Hangugin choecho ui Miguk daehaksaeng Byeon Su" [Byeon Su, the First Korean Who Became an American University Student], *Sin Donga* no. 218 (October 1982), 432–446; the report was published in U.S. Bureau of Statistics (Department of Agriculture) Report of the Statistician, no. 89 (1891), 563–583.

36. Byeon is said to have "gathered a mass of information on the political and progressive histories of the world from encyclopedic sources…" during his European tour. See Harold J. Noble, "The Korean Mission to the United States in 1883, the First Embassy sent by Korea to an Occidental Nation," *Transactions of the Korean Branch of the Royal Asiatic Society*, vol. 18 (1929), 15.

37. Yi 1982a: 436-439 for a full account of Byeon's activities upon his return to Korea, which led him to become a political emigré.

38. USNM-AR 1891: 432.

39. During the European tour, Seo and Byeon were said to be "infatigable [indefatigable] in compiling notes on useful subjects." They "gathered a mass of information on the political and progressive histories of the world " with the help of Ensign George Clayton Foulk, (1856–1893) who accompanied the mission, while Min Yeong-ik devoted himself to studying Confucian analects. See Noble 1929: 15.

40. Ibid., 19; see also Jang Su-yeong, "1883 nyeon ui gyeon-mi sajeoldan gwa suhaengwon Byeon Su," 1982, 51–53.

the new cabinet, but a year later in 1895 he was appointed Secretary of the Korean Legation in Washington.[41] He died in Washington in 1897.[42]

It appears that Hough had a long and close association with Seo Gwang-beom. Throughout Hough's monograph dealing with Korean collections, references to Seo are more frequent than those to the other two Korean consultants. Seo also held the rank specially reserved for those nobles in the King's personal service.[43]

Seo Jae-pil [Philip Jaisohn] (1866–1951)[44] studied abroad both in Japan and America. In 1883 he went to Japan to attend a military academy in Tokyo,[45] and, as a young military officer, he was involved in the failed 1884 coup d'état. Together with other leaders of the progressive reform party, such as Seo Gwang-beom and Byeon Su, he left Korea. These political emigrés sought refuge first in Japan and then in the United States.

Upon his arrival in San Francisco in April 1885, Seo met J. W. Hollenback, a wealthy coal-mining operator from Wilkes-Barre, Pennsylvania, who offered to finance his education. Seo enrolled at the Harry Hilman Academy in Wilkes-Barre in September 1886, where he spent the following two years. He spent another two years at the Lafayette College in Easton, Pennsylvania, before entering the Columbia Medical College (now George Washington University Medical School). He received an M.D. degree in 1892.[46]

It is very likely that Walter Hough met Seo Jae-pil while Seo was studying in Pennsylvania (1886–1888), through either Seo Gwang-beom or Byeon Su. These three must have met frequently in Washington during their years in exile and were delighted to share Hough's interests in the Korean collections. In 1896 Dr. Seo returned to Korea, where he was active in the reform movement and subsequently in the Korean independence movement. He was not only the first Korean to earn an American medical degree but also the first Korean to become a naturalized U.S. citizen. Hough refers to him by his anglicized name, "Dr. Philip Jaisohn,"[47] as one of the "three Korean gentlemen in Washington."

OTHER SOURCES OF KOREAN COLLECTIONS

Gustavus Goward was the American Secretary of the U.S. Legation in Tokyo. In 1883 he accompanied the Honorable Lucius Foote, the first Minister of the U.S. Legation in Seoul, to take up his charge.[48] Goward made a second visit to Seoul from 24 October through 23 December 1883,[49] according to Yun Chi-ho (1865–1946), the U.S. Legation's Korean interpreter. Presumably, he collected a photographic print of a painted "porcelain screen from the royal palace" (cat. no. USNM ECC 129368) sometime during these visits. Hough's 1891 collection catalog includes this item,[50] giving no date of collection, but it likely is part of the Goward collection, which came to the museum in June 1887 and was accessioned as file number 19329.

George Brown Goode (1851–1896) began his association with the Smithsonian Institution in 1872, when Spencer F. Baird, then Assistant Secretary of the Smithsonian, invited him to work as a volunteer collector for the U.S. Commission for Fish and Fisheries. The following year he was appointed Assistant Curator in the U.S. National Museum and promoted to Curator in 1877. Goode, who had become the Assistant Director of the U.S. National Museum,[51] purchased a set of ancient Korean armor (cat. no. USNM ECC 128344) from Thomas Dowling, a Washington auctioneer, in February 1888 and donated it to the museum. The armor, which was assigned accession number 20197,[52] is the only Korean item obtained outside Korea that is included in Hough's catalogue.

William B. Brooks, Captain, USN, served as chief engineer in the U.S. Navy under the command of Rear-Admiral John Rodgers, who headed the Asiatic Squadron sent to Korea in 1871. During a hostile encounter in June 1871 between the

41. *Hanguk inmyeong dae-sajeon* (Dictionary of Korean Biography) (Seoul, 1967), page 336. Hereafter, this will be referred to as HID.

42. Jang Su-yeong; "Guhan mal yeokdae jumigongsa wa geudeul ui hwaldong," 38–39.

43. HID 1967: 336. *Guksa dae-sajeon* (Encyclopedia of Korean History), vol. 1, 701. Hereafter, this will be referred to as GDS.

44. HID1967: 344. Several other historical and biographical dictionaries give Seo's date of birth either as 1863 with a question mark or as 1864.

45. He may have been one of the fourteen students sent to Japan for military training in September 1882. See Kim Won-mo (1984), *Geundae Hanguk oegyo-sa yeonpyo* (Chronology of Modern Korean Diplomacy), 106; see also Horace N. Allen's *A Chronological Index* (1901), 12. Hereafter, *Geundae Hanguk oegyo-sa yeonpyo*, and *A Chronological Index* will be referred to as GHOY and ACI. According to HID 1967, page 344, Seo attended the Japanese Military Preparatory School (Tokyo Rikugun Yōnen Gakkō).

46. Choe Bong-yeon, "The History of Koreans in America, part 1: Leaving the Land of Morning Calm"; pages 35-36 are devoted to Seo Jae-pil's early years in the United States.

47. USNM-AR 1891: 432.

48. ACI 1901: 12.

49. For Yun's diary entries, see Yun Chi-ho, '*Hanguk saryo chongseo* no. 19: *Yun Chi-ho ilgi* (Yun Chi-ho's Diary), vol. 1, 13–28.

50. USNM-AR 1891: 467. History card for ethnology collection catalog number 129368. Hereafter ethnology collection catalog will be referred to as USNM ECC.

51. *Guide to the Smithsonian Archives* (Washington, D.C.: Smithsonian Institution Press, 1983), 26.

52. SI-AR1891: 479–80, plate XXVIII.

53. For a detailed account of this encounter, see William Elliot Grifis, "Our Little War with the Heathen," *Corea the Hermit Nation,* 403–419.

54. Anthropology catalog book number 16, page 22 ledger entry date is June 1871. Hereafter, anthropology catalog book will be referred to as ACB.

55. USNM-AR 1891: 481–482, plates XXX and XXXI.

56. ACI1901: 17.

57. Allen 1991, *Horace Newton Allen's Diary.* In *Gu-Han mal gyeokdonggi bisa Allen ui ilgi* (Allen's Diary, A Secret History of the Turbulent End of the Choson Kingdom], part 4, pages 428 and 455.

58. Ibid.: 466.

59. *Dictionary of American Biography,* vol. 16, edited by Dumas Malone, (New York: Charles Scribner's Sons, 1935), pages 66–67.

60. Rockhill's arrival in December of 1886 and his departure in April of the following year are recorded in GHOY 1984: 125–270.

61. SI-AR 1889–90: 132 reports acquisition of the eighteen paintings and assigning accession; file number 22822; see also accession, in NMNH Registrar's Office. The paintings were transferred from USNM ethnology collection (USNM ECC 131315) to the National Anthropological Archives and identified now as NAA MS 7339. Hereafter, National Anthropological Archives will be referred to as NAA.

62. Rockhill, W. W., Notes on Some of the Laws, Customs, and Superstitions of Korea, *The American Anthropologist,* vol. 4, (April 1891), pages 177–187.

63. *Dictionary of American Biography,* vol. 16, edited by Dumas Malone (1935), pages 66–67.

American fleet and the Koreans, a sabre was "brought from the field by the late surgeon C. J. Stewart, USN, who was severely wounded during the engagement."[53] Captain Brooks later donated the sabre (cat. no. USNM ECC 72897), to the Smithsonian Institution.[54] In addition to the sabre, Brooks' donation includes one powder case and charger (cat. no. USNM ECC 72900) and a bullet bag (cat. no. USNM ECC 72898), all described in Hough's monograph on the early Korean collections.[55] No accession record exists, but the catalogue data give the date of accession as 1883 while Hough provides the collection dates as 1875 (sabre) and 1871 (powder case and bullet bag).

C. G. Talcott, Ensign, USN, served in Korea aboard the *USS Ossipee,* which arrived at Chemulp'o on 18 December 1884.[56] Horace Allen, the medical missionary, noted in his dairy on 11 January 1885, "U.S. Man of War, "*Ossipee* now at Chemulp'o has been here for a few days." Allen specifically mentions Ensign Talcott being at the U.S. Legation in Seoul and states that he dined with Talcott and others on 18 March 1885.[57] On 12 May, Allen visited the *USS Ossipee* at Chemulp'o,[58] after which date the ship left for Chefu, China. The women's realgar (red sulphide of arsenic) hair ornament included in Hough's monograph on the early Korean collections is noted as Talcott's gift but with no date of collection.

William Woodville Rockhill (1854–1914), an orientalist and distinguished diplomat, was born in April 1854 in Philadelphia, Pennsylvania. After graduating from the French Ecole Spéciale Militaire de St. Cyr, in 1873, he served in the French military in Algeria.[59] Rockhill served as chargé d'affaires in Seoul from December 1886 to April 1887.[60] During his brief sojourn in Korea, he collected a small number of varied ethnological objects, including eighteen original paintings by native artists that depict the traditional costumes of the Choson Period (1392–1910).[61] In 1891 Rockhill published "Notes on Some of the Laws, Customs and Superstitions of Korea" in *The American Anthropologist,*[62] and his entire collection was in Walter Hough's catalogue of that same year. Rockhill is better known as an explorer who made several scientific expeditions (1888–1889 and 1891–1892) to Mongolia and Tibet for the Smithsonian Institution. He died on 8 December 1914 in Hawaii.[63]

These collection histories and biographical sketches of collectors provide a glimpse of the Smithsonian Institution's early, unique collection activities.

LIST OF ABBREVIATIONS

The following abbreviations identify Smithsonian museums and administrative divisions, catalog records, dictionaries and technical and other special reference works cited. See Bibliography for fuller descriptions.

ACB Anthropology Catalog Book [Anthropology Department's bound ledger to register assigned catalogue number and description of each object accessioned]

ACI *A Chronological Index* [listed under Allen, Horace N. 1901]

AR Annual Report, both USNM and SI Annual Reports, followed by the appropriate year [listed under Smithsonian Instiution]

BFN Bernadou field notes, twenty-five pages of handwritten notes titled "Notes on Collection of Korean Articles" [listed under Bernadou]

DHM *Doseol Hanguk ui minsok* (The Folkcrafts of Korea) [listed under Onyang minsok bangmulgwan]

ECC Ethnology Collection [Card] Catalog [Located in the Department of Anthropology, processing laboratory]

GDS *Guksa dae-sajeon (Encyclopedia of Korean History)*[listed under Yi, Hong-jik]

GHOY *Geundae Hanguk oegyo-sa yeonpyo (Chronology of Modern Korean Diplomacy)* [listed under Kim, Won-mo]

GMB *Gungnip minsok bangmul-gwan (The National Folk Museum)*

HID *Hanguk inmyeong dae-sajeon (Dictionary of Korean Biography)*

HJM *Hanguk ui jongi munhwa (Use of Paper in Traditional Korean Culture)* [listed under Gungnip minwok bangmulgwan]

HKC Hough Korean Catalog: "The Bernadou, Allen, and Jouy Korean Collections, in the United States National Museum."

HMD *Hanguk minsok daegwan (Survey of Korean Folk Culture)* [listed under Minzok munha yeongu-so]

HMM *Hanguk minye misul (Folk Art of Korea)* [listed under Gungnip jungang bangmulgwah]

HUM *Hanguk ui mi: uisang, jangsingu, bo (Beauty of Korea: Traditional Costumes, Ornaments, and Cloth Wrappings)* [listed under Gungnip jungang bangmulgwan]

KGS *Kkum gwa sarang: maehok ui uri minhwa (Auspicious Dreams: Decorative Paintings of Korea)* [listed under Hoam Art Museum]

KJE *Kojien (Dictionary of the Japanese Language)* [listed under Shimmura, Izuru]

KLPC *Korea: Its Land, People and Culture of All Ages* [listed under Hakwon-sa]

MBM *Miguk bangmul-gwan sojang Hanguk munhwajae (The Korean Relics in the United States)* [listed under Ye, yong-hae, et al.]

MGJ *Minhwa geoljak-jeon (Masterpiece Folk Paintings)* [listed under Hoam Art Museum]

NAA National Anthropological Archives, Department of Anthropology, National Museum of Natural History

NKDJ *Nihon kokugo daijiten (Encyclopaedia of Japanese Language)* [listed under Nihon Dai-jiten kankokai]

NMAH National Museum of American History, Smithsonian Institution

NMNH National Museum of Natural History, Smithsonian Institution

RU Record Unit, Smithsonian Institution Archives

SI Smithsonian Institution.

SMI *A Study of Musical Instruments in Korean Traditional Music* [listed under The National Center for Korean Traditional Performing Arts]

USNM Former United States National Museum (not the National Museum of Natural History, Smithsonian Institution).

CATALOGUE

Each catalogue entry begins with a brief description in English. One the second line is Korean text, which may abbreviate the English title, give a short technical reading of the object, or provide a general classification for the object. Catalogue number 49, for example, has the English heading "Man's Summer Outerrobe." The Korean read *Mosi Dopo,* literally "linen travelling coat, in romanized Korean, Hangul syllabary, and Sino-Korean characters. Catalogue number 48 reads *So-Changui,* the technical term for this garment. Catalogue number 125 has the English title "Dog with Collar of Bells," whereas the Korean text reads *Munbae-do* (design hung on a gate or door), the generic name for paintings and prints of this type.

The major component of the Korean term is given in Hangul, but some elements, for their etymological considerations, are in ideographs, as Korean words are commonly grouped into two categories: the pure Korean and Sino-Korean. The object name is followed by the date of manufacture and its component materials. Given next is the collection identification, for example, USNM Ethnology collection, NAA collection, and so forth, and catalogue number. The object's dimensions are in centimeters (H=height, L=length, W=width, D=diameter). Preceding the caption, Hough's Korean catalogue (1891) page or plate numbers, if illustrated, are given as cross-references. Additional references, such as the collector's field-note number, identification of sources when previously published, and also date and location of exhibition if the object was shown in the past, is also provided.

The caption first describes the physical form of the object, component materials and method of construction, including decoration. Following the description, the object's characteristics are discussed. The description is further elaborated by providing uses for the object, identification of users and the prescribed manner and condition of use in terms of relevant traditions, symbolism, historical origin and development. In the added remarks, one mainly finds a critical review of Hough's captions and his commentaries. Often included are corrigenda for his erroneous identifications, which may be indicative of lack of reference sources or of certain misperceptions of the era. At the end of every entry, a BFN number has been added for further reference as well as the place of collection

Korean names are given following the native practice of giving the surname before the given name. The revised romanization system developed by the National Academy of the Korean Language is adopted for renderings of Korean terms as well as personal and place names. A modified McCune-Reischaur romanization system is used for the following exceptions: historical periods, dynasties, place-names, and certain Korean terms long established in published sources.

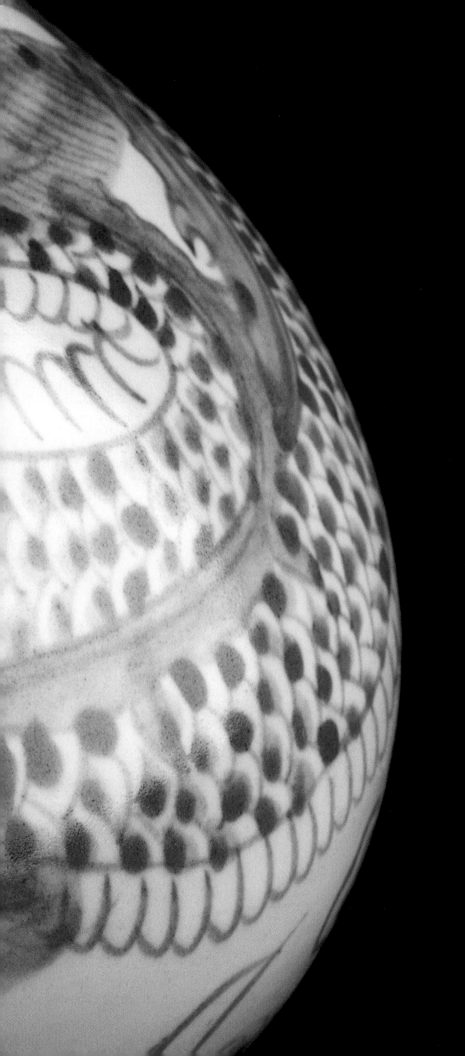

1 DISH
(*KORYO JEOPSI* 고려접시)
Koryo Dynasty (918–1391)
Stoneware with crackled grayish-green
celadon glaze
H: 3.8 cm, D: 11.8 cm
USNM ECC 121615
Ref.: HKC pl. XII, fig.1; BFN 63

This shallow dish has a low foot and body covered
with crackled, dull greenish-gray celadon glaze. It
was used as tableware.

Hough describes the dish as a saucer-like vessel,
which might be "a rude cup stand," with its glaze
corroded by long burial.
BFN 63 "Cracked dish of old pottery of very low
grade found near Songdo."
Collected in Songdo (modern Kaesong, Kyeonggi
province)

2 BOTTLE
(*BAEKJA SULBYEONG* 백자술병)
Koryo Dynasty (918–1391)
Porcellaneous ware with transparent glaze
H: 25.5 cm, D: 16.6 cm
USNM ECC 121614
Ref.: HKC pl. XII, upper fig. 2

This bulbous bottle has a porcellaneous body which
Hough characterizes as "light yellow granular paste"
applied with an opalescent glaze "showing yellow
spots and dark brown pits." He also observes that
the form of the bottle, which was thought at the
time Bernadou chose it to be four hundred years
old, does not differ from Choson-period wares of
the late 19th century.

Collected in Seoul

3 Ritual Water Sprinkler (*Kundika*)
(*KORYO CHEONGJA CHEONGBYEONG*
고려청자청병)
Koryo Dynasty (918–1391), 12th century
Stoneware with crackled grayish-green
celadon glaze
H: 31.8 cm, D: 12.2 cm
USNM ECC 121612
Ref.: HKC pl. XII, upper fig. 3; BFN 66

This Koryo celadon is a double-spouted water
vessel. The jug-shaped bulbous body projects a side
spout midway down and has an elongated tubular
neck which also has a spout near the top. This type
of vessel is commonly associated with Koryo wares
having a crackled, greenish-gray celadon glaze.

Cheongbyeong refers to a Buddhist ritual ewer or
sprinkler known as a *kundika* (Gompertz, 1963,
plate 23 A; Kim and Gompertz, 1961: 92-93, for
the term and illustrations). Hough misidentifies the
specimen as a wine bottle. The cover for the top
spout is missing.

BFN 66 "Wine bottle. Said to be about seven
hundred years old. Of a form now obsolete. The
weight of this specimen is noticeable. Of clay, covered
with a thick coating of an opaque vitreous glaze."

Collected in Seoul

4 Cup and Cup Stand
(*KORYO CHEONGJA SULJAN GWA JANDAE*
고려청자술잔과 잔대)
Koryo Dynasty (918–1391), 12th century
Stoneware with crackled celadon glaze
Cup H: 6.4 cm, D: 9 cm
Stand H: 4.4 cm, D: 14.7 cm
USNM ECC 121616
Ref.: HKC pl. XII, lower fig. 1; BFN 60-61

The lotiform, lobed wine cup sits on a flat saucer
with raised cavetto. Despite the corroded glaze, this
cup and stand are typical Koryo celadon wares,
although they were not fired together or intended as
a set.

Hough qualifies the pieces as having good "concep-
tion and general outline," and speculates that they
were probably used in ancestor worship. It is likely
that they were used for a variety of Buddhist rituals.

BFN 60-61 "... Found in a tomb near Song-do, the
old capital of Korea. Koreans say that from the
shape and design, such pieces cannot be less than six
hundred years old... This [cup] rests upon the cup
stand already described. The two pieces, however,
originally belonged to different sets. During the
long period of burial the glaze has been completely
destroyed. Shape is that of a lotus flower indicating
a Buddhist origin."

Collected in Songdo (modern Kaesong, Kyeonggi
province)

5

5. BOWL

(*KORYO CHEONGJA BOSIGI* 고려청자보시기)
Koryo Dynasty (918–1391), 12th century
Stoneware with crackled grayish-green celadon
glaze
H: 5.8 cm, D: 14 cm
USNM ECC 121618
Ref.: HKC pl. XII, lower fig. 3; BFN 62

This small bowl is of stoneware covered with a light
grayish-green celadon glaze with extensive
craquelure. Hough catalogues it as "Koreu-gi-bo-si"
[Koryo bowl], a translation of *bosigi*, a small ceramic
or metal bowl.

BFN 62 "... About four hundred years old. It will
be noticed that in this ware the bottom is never
completely glazed; but that at one or more points
where the vessel on the furnace floor [*sic*] the glaze
is absent. Also that there is no mark, character or
seal device of any kind that would indicate the place
of manufacture. In many specimens the weight,
compared with that of pottery made elsewhere, is
remarkably great." The points to which Bernadou
refers are commonly called spur marks, or small,
unglazed balls of clay applied to vessels to separate
them when they are stacked in the kiln to be fired.

Collected in Seoul

6. BOWL

(*KORYO BAEKJA DAEJEOP* 고려백자대접)
Koryo Dynasty (918–1391), 12th century
Porcellaneous ware with transparent glaze
USNM ECC 121619
H: 5.5 cm, D: 18 cm
Ref.: HKC pl. XII, lower fig. 6; BFN 64

This bowl has not been located. Hough's notes
catalogue it as white, hard paste porcelain with a
clear glaze of greenish tint due to its iron content.
His notes imply that the bowl is incised with a wave
or cloud design which shows a slightly deeper green
tint as the glaze pooled in these markings.

BFN 64 "White bowl of Korai [Japanese for Koryo]
porcelain. Of the best period of the Song-do
potteries, about five hundred years ago. Pieces of
this character are extremely rare. The wave pattern
with which the bowl is decorated is characteristic;
also the production of the pattern by cutting away
the clay and filling in with glaze, which varies in
thickness of layer to produce the pattern. On the
outer side are unglazed places, caused by long
contact with the earth in which the bowl was
buried."

Collected in Songdo (modern Kaesong, Kyeonggi
province)

7 JAR FOR COOKING
(*ONGGI DANJI* 옹기단지)
Choson Period (1392–1910), late 19th century
Glazed earthenware
H: 12.8 cm, D: 14 cm, D: 9.6 cm (mouth)
USNM ECC 121617
Ref.: HKC pl. XIII, upper fig. 1

This is a globular, reddish-dark-brown earthenware
jar. Both the inside and outside of the vessel are
glazed so as to withstand the greatest heat, as it is
used for boiling water or preparing stew-like dishes.
Hough's entry describes this bowl with a native
term, "jil-tang-quan," or *ji-tanggwan* 지탕관
(earthenware bowl for preparing soup or medicine).
From the size of the vessel, the other Korean term
should be either *ongbaegi* 옹배기 or *jabaegi* 자배기.
Tanggwan 탕관 or *yak-tanggwan* 약탕관, for brewing
herbal medicine, is usually larger in size and differs
in body form from the common bowl shape.

Collected in Seoul

8 BOTTLE WITH DESIGN OF DRAGON AND CLOUDS

(*CHEONGHWA BAEKJA SULBYEONG*
청화백자술병)

Choson Period (1392–1910), late 19th century
Blue and white porcelain with underglaze of
cobalt blue and transparent glaze
H: 31.8 cm, D: 21 cm (globe), D: 13.4 cm (base)
USNM ECC 121613
Ref.: HKC pl. XIII upper fig. 2; BFN 2

This wine bottle is decorated in underglaze cobalt
with a four-clawed dragon and clouds. Vessels
painted with dragons of five claws were restricted to
imperial use. The bottle was first given a bisque
firing, resulting in a body with the consistency of
hard leather. It was painted in cobalt glaze and
submitted to a second firing. Finally it was applied
with a thick transparent glaze and fired a third time.
Hough gives a vivid description of this bottle:
"Heavy glazed porcelain, ornamented with dragon
design in blue. Low, wide body diminishing rather
abruptly into a tubular neck. Capacity, about 5
pints." He goes on to say, "Average specimen of
modern Korean pottery. The Korean Potters were
unable to impart any color but blue to their white
ware up to the revival of color decoration ten years
ago. Used in buying and selling liquors, but not at
the table." Bernadou's field notes state, "water bottle
ornamented with dragon" and sponsor Hough's
comment about the paucity of wares with colors
other than blue. BFN 2 "Actually, stoneware
painted with underglaze iron and underglaze copper
were produced in the Koryo Dynasty and revived on
stoneware and porcelain in the Choson Period by
the 16th and 17th centuries."

Collected in Kwangju, Kyeonggi province

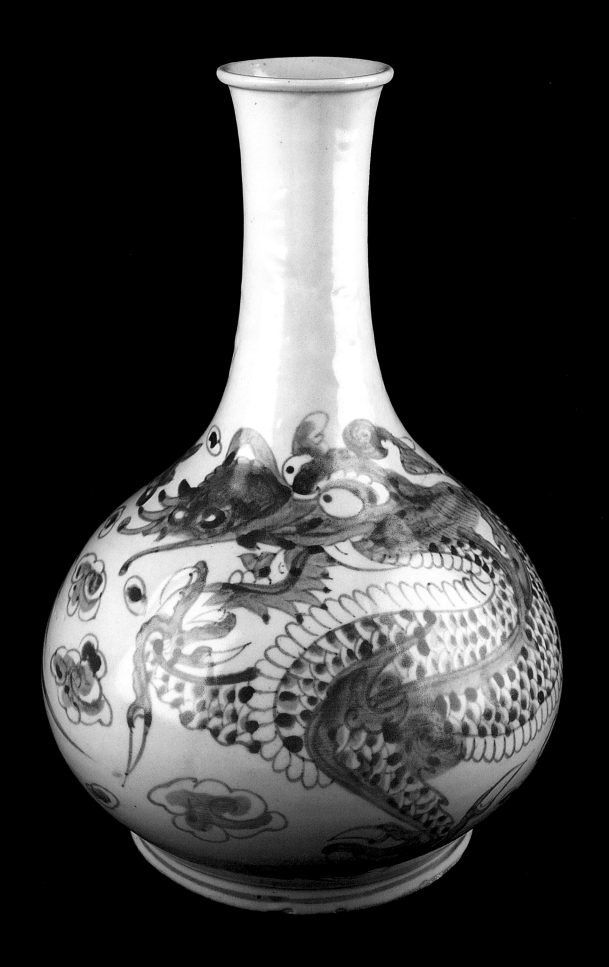

9 Tableware Set of Covered Bowls, Bowls, and Dishes

(*SA-BANSANG* 사반상;
SA-BANSANGGI 사반상기)
Choson Period (1392–1910), late 19th century
White porcelain with greenish-tinged transparent glaze; some with underglaze cobalt-blue
Dimensions per below
USNM ECC 121620-121630
Ref.: HKC pl. XIII, lower figs. 1-6; BFN 1

These are white porcelain bowls, covers and dishes, some inscribed in underglaze blue with Chinese characters. Hough describes the pieces as "heavy porcelain covered with a patchy glaze of greenish hue... the most inferior porcelain ware at present made in Korea." The greenish hue is due to the iron content in the transparent glaze applied to the vessels. Another comment, probably provided by one of the Korean experts, reads, "More pretentious vases of antique form, in white decorated with blue, or raised figures if molded, are found in every home. Ware is valued in proportion to its whiteness and smoothness and brilliancy of the glaze; weight

is a minor consideration." Porcelain was for summer use while brass was preferred for winter. Main dishes of the Choson period included rice, soup, and *kimchee* pickles, all common today. Side dishes included beef, poultry, fish and pork. The number of side dishes in an individual service was three, five, seven, nine, or twelve (Ju, 1985: 104-6). The side dishes selected reflected the formality of the occasion and the importance of the guest. The nine dish setting (*kucheop bansang* 구첩반상) was typical for family meals in an aristocratic household of the Choson Period (Ju, 1985: 104; Hwang, 1980: 419-20). The two pairs of dishes pictured here held cooked or dried

food. The two small bowls contained condiments such as soy sauce, soybean paste, or salty pickled fish. The large bowl in the lower right was used to serve soup, gruel, noodles or scorched rice tea (*sungnyung* 숭늉) taken at the end of the meal. BFN 1 "Korean table ware.
1.[entry 9: 10] Sapal [*sabal*] or rice bowl. 2.[entry 9: 1] Cover for same. 3.[entry 9: 11] Tai-tjöp [*daejeop*], for water in which rice has been boiled. 4.[entry 9: 11] Kouk-keirot [*guk-geureut*], bowl for soup or meat and vegetables. 5. Cover for No. 3. 6.[entries 9: 4 and 9: 6] Bowl and cover for tjang [*jang*] (like Jap[anese] soy [sauce]). 7.[entry 9: 7] Kim-tchi or

vegetable bowl. 8.[entry 9: 6] Small bowls for sauces. 10.[entry 9: 5] Tjopsi [*jeopsi*] or dishes for other foods. This specimen which is of a good quality of Korean chinaware as now made, is from Kyong-ki-do, the capital province. Note: No. 9 is cover for No. 4."

Collected in Kwangju, Kyeonggi province

Tableware set, USNM ECC 121620-USNM ECC 121630 consists of the following porcelain wares:

9: 1 MAN'S RICE BOWL COVER
(*BAEKJA NAMJA BAP-GEUREUT TTUKKEONG* 백자남자밥그릇뚜껑)
Choson Period (1392–1910), late 19th century
White porcelain
H: 4.5 cm, D: 16.5 cm
USNM ECC 121620

This piece was misidentified as a dish and given an independent catalog number. It is the cover of man's rice bowl (cat. no. USNM ECC 121629).

9: 2 WOMAN'S RICE BOWL COVER
(*BAEKJA YEOJA BAP-GEUREUT TTUKKEONG* 백자여자밥그릇뚜껑)
Choson Period (1392–1910), late 19th century
White porcelain
H: 3.8 cm, D: 12.6 cm
USNM ECC 121621

This small and shallow dish-like piece is the cover of woman's rice bowl (cat. no. USNM ECC 121628).

9: 3 CHILD'S RICE BOWL COVER
(*BAEKJA AEGI BAP-GEUREUT TTUKKEONG* 백자애기밥그릇뚜껑)
Choson Period (1392–1910), late 19th century
White porcelain
H: 3.2 cm, D: 11.5 cm
USNM ECC 121622

This small and shallow dish-like piece is the cover of child's rice bowl (cat. no. USNM ECC 121627).

9: 4 SMALL BOWL COVER
(*BAEKJA JONGJI TTUKKEONG* 백자종지뚜껑)
Choson Period (1392–1910), late 19th century
White porcelain
H: 2.0 cm, D: 9.5 cm
USNM ECC 121623

This is the cover of a small bowl (cat. no. USNM ECC 121625).

9: 5 DISHES
(*BAEKJA JEOPSI* 백자접시)
Choson Period (1392–1910), late 19th century
White porcelain
H: 3.0 cm, D: 9.5 cm
USNM ECC 121624

These four identical dishes are used for serving dry, sautéed, broiled or fried food.

9: 6 SMALL BOWL
(*BAEKJA JONGJI* 백자종지)
Choson Period (1392–1910), late 19th century
White porcelain
H: 5.0 cm, D: 7.0 cm
USNM ECC 121625

These two white porcelain small bowls are used for serving condiments such as soy sauce, soybean paste or salty pickled fish. The cover of one of the small bowls is entered separately with an independent catalog number (cat. no. USNM ECC 121623).

9: 7 MEDIUM-SIZE BOWL
(*BAEKJA BOSIGI* 백자보시기)
Choson Period (1392–1910), late 19th century
White porcelain
H: 4.5 cm, D: 17 cm
USNM ECC 121626

This medium-size bowl has not been located. Called *bosigi*, it is used for serving various kinds of *kimchee* 김치.

9: 8 CHILD'S RICE BOWL
(*BAEKJA AEGI BAP-GEUREUT* 백자애기밥그릇;
BAEKJA AEGI BAP-GONGGI 백자애기밥공기)
Choson Period (1392–1910), late 19th century
White porcelain
H: 5.7 cm, D: 10 cm
USNM ECC 121627

Gonggi is used for serving children rice or soup. Use of the term changed over time to refer to any small conical bowl as *bap-gonggi*, or rice bowl, for both children and adults. The cover of this bowl is entered separately with an independent catalog number (cat. no. USNM ECC 121622).

9: 9 WOMAN'S RICE BOWL
(*BAEKJA YEOJA BAP-GEUREUT* 백자여자밥그릇;
BAEKJA YEOJA BAP-GONGGI 백자여자밥공기)
Choson Period (1392–1910), late 19th century
White porcelain
H: 7.0 cm, D: 11.2 cm
USNM ECC 121628

For use and references, cf. entry 9: 8 above. The cover of this bowl is entered separately with an independent catalog number (cat. no. USNM ECC 121621).

9: 10 MAN'S RICE BOWL
(*BAEKJA BAP-GEUREUT* 백자밥그릇 *BAEKJA BAP-SABAL* 백자밥사발
Choson Period (1392–1910), late 19th century
White porcelain
H: 9 cm, D: 13.5 cm
USNM ECC 121629

This size of bowl is also known as "father's rice bowl." A man's brass rice bowl with cover is called a *jubal* 주발, while a woman's smaller and bulbous bowl is known as a *bari* 바리 (Hong and Yi, 1955: 48 for illustrations of various serving vessels with their terms). The cover of this bowl is entered separately with an independent catalog number (cat. no. USNM ECC 121620).

9: 11 SOUP BOWL
(*BAEKJA GUK-GEUREUT* 백자국그릇; *BAEKJA GUK-DAEJEOP* 백자국대접)
Choson Period (1392–1910), late 19th century
White porcelain
H: 7.5 cm, D: 16 cm
USNM ECC 121630

This large soup bowl also is used for serving gruel, noodles, and scorched rice tea, *sungnyung* 숭늉 served after the meal (Nam, 1987: 57; Hong and Yi, 1955: 48).

Please note: Items 10–16 have not been located and thus specific details pertaining to size, dimensions and color remain undocumented. Where possible, supplementary information was added to the description of the items to give the reader a better understanding of Korean cloth. Hough assigned the identification number 7907H to these pieces, but that number's origin is still unknown.

10 SILK
(*HANGNA* 항라 亢羅)
Choson Period (1392–1910), late 19th century
Medium weight figured silk
No. 7907H
Ref.: HKC p. 439; BFN 36

This item has not been located. It is medium weight, figured silk. Though medium weight, the silk is almost transparent, and it "has paralleled lines created by means of skipping the weft at intervals" (Yi, 1992: 13). The fabric is used for spring and autumn garments (Kim, 1988b: 524).

BFN 36: "... One of the best [illegible]. Pyong-an do, and especially from the town [illegible] that neighborhood. Worn by nobles and the rich, for light summer garments."

Collected in Anju, South Pyeongan province

11 SILK GAUZE
(*SAENGCHO* 생초)
Choson Period (1392–1910), late 19th century
No. 7907H
Ref.: HKC p. 439; BFN 37

This open-weave raw silk is nearly transparent fabric used for summer garments. Its lightness, combined with a slight stiffness, is ideally suited for summer wear.
This fabric also is used for making official headgear for traditional military uniforms (Kim, 1988b: 293). Hough describes *saengcho* as silk woven with nettle fiber, following Bernadou's description.
BFN 37 "... Of silk combined with the fibre of the plant from which the mosi a grass cloth is made. Made principally in Chol-la-do, the S. W. province and most of it around and at the town of Chon-tjou. Made for light summer clothing."
Collected in Jeonju, North Jeolla province

12 RAMIE CLOTH
(*MOSI* 모시)
Choson Period (1392–1910), late 19th century
No.7907H
Ref.: HKC p. 439 BFN 38-39

This is woven nettle-fiber fabric, or ramie cloth. Because this fabric is especially thin, light, and airy, it is used for summer clothing, second only to silk. The bark of the rami perennial, is harvested three times a year in spring, summer, and autumn. Harvesting begins with a one-year-old plant. After peeling the bark from the tree, the bark is split with hands and teeth. Ramie fibers are acquired by chewing the tip of the split bark into hair-thin

strands and twining them for length by rolling the ends together on the knee (Kim, 1995: 33). To achieve a desired finish of the fabric, the weaver's choice of numbers of warp strands varies from seven to fifteen.
BFN 38-39: "... grass cloth made of the fibre of the Urtica nivea ... or Bachmeria nivea. Chiefly from the southern provinces, Chon-la-do [Jeolla-do], and Ch'ong-chong-do [Chungcheong-do], the best from Ch'ong-chong-do near the town of Hansan, whence this specimen."
Collected in Hansan, South Chungcheong province

13
WOVEN CLOTH OF COTTON AND SILK
(*GYOJIKPO* 교직포 交織布)
Choson Period (1392–1910), late 19th century
No. 7907H
Ref.: HKC p. 439; BFN 40

This fabric is woven with cotton and silk yarns. Silk is used as fixed threads, the warp, and cotton as the woof (Kim, 1988b: 64 for an explanation of the term).
BFN 40 "Tjo-tjok [*gyojik*]. A mixed fabric of cotton and silk. Made in both north and south, but the best in the S.E. province of Kyong-sang-do, whence this specimen."

Collected in Kyeongsang province

14 UNBLEACHED HEMP CLOTH
(*BUKPO* 북포)
Choson Period (1392–1910), late 19th century
No. 7907H
Ref.: HKC p. 439; BFN 41

Here the cloth is woven with very fine warp thread thus producing a smooth textured, highest-quality hemp fabric (Kim, 1988b: 257). The weaver prepares threads of different density. One *sae* 새 (a unit measuring the density of warp threads in cloth) consists of eighty strands. Five-*sae* fabric is usually for work clothes, seven for ordinary, regular clothes, and three *sae* for mourning costumes (Jo, 1995: 14). The term for hemp cloth varies depending upon the region in which the cloth is produced. For example, *yeongpo* 영포 is from Kyeongsang province, and *gangpo* 강포 from Kangwon province. Hemp is planted in the third lunar month and harvested in the sixth lunar month. Hough also notes three different densities in the woven hemp cloth by alluding to "three grades of serviceable cloth."
BFN 41 "... a species of poi [be 베], or grass cloth from the northern province of Ham-kyong-to. The above is a specimen of very good quality. Used for

mourning garments by the better class."
Collected in Hamgyeong province

15 COTTON CLOTH
(*MONGMYEON* 목면 木棉 ; *MUMYEONG* 무명)
Choson Period (1392–1910), late 19th century
No. 7907H
Ref.: HKC p. 439; BFN 43

This hand-woven, plain, cotton cloth is not only for clothing, but for various other items, including armor, banners and tents.

A Koryo-Dynasty official, Mun Ik-jeom 文益漸 (1329–1398), is said to have smuggled out ten cotton seeds from Yuan China in 1367. King Sejong 世宗 (r. 1418–50) encouraged its cultivation in the southern provinces, as the climate of the northern region was unfit (*GDS*, 1962: 481–482; Choe, 1943: 132). The Koreans mostly used home-spun cotton until 1919 when the first machine-woven cotton fabric was produced (Kim, 1995: 32 for the history of cotton farming and weaving). Hough states that cotton cloth is "made in four of the eight provinces." According to Bernadou, the cotton fabric was produced in five provinces.

BFN 43 "Korean native made cotton cloth, good quality. Made in large quantities in the provinces, Pyong-an-do and Hwanghai-do. Also in Kyong-ki-do, the capital province and in the southern provinces of Chung-chung-do and Chol-la-do."

Collected in Seoul [?]

16 OPEN-WEAVE SILK CLOTH
(*SA* 사 紗; *SAJIK* 사직 紗織)
Choson Period (1392–1910), late 19th century
Creamy yellow open-weave silk
No. 7907H
Ref.: HKC p. 439; BFN 45

This open weave, lightweight, creamy-yellow silk is called *sa*, similar to gauze. *Sa* are nearly transparent and, in many instances, patterned (Yi, 1992: 13). Hough calls this type of silk "pongee-like," and "made in all parts of Korea." Added to this statement is a reference to the man's robe (cat. no. USNM ECC 77099, HKC, page 452) made of *sa* silk.

BFN 45 "Corean silk, good quality. Made in all parts of Korea. Probably more is made in Pyong-an-do, the N.W. provinces, than anywhere else. The best is from Yong-pyon in Ham-kyong-do [Hamgyeong-do] province."

Collected in Yeongpung, South Hamgyeong province.

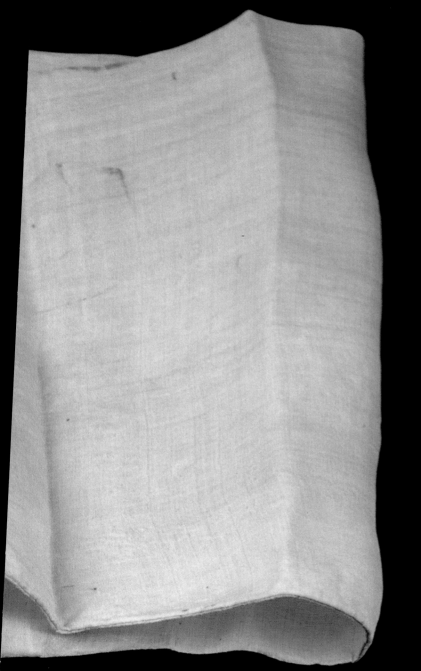

III

CLOTHING AND ACCESSORIES

17 Boy's Outerrobe
(*AEGI DURUMAGI* 애기두루마기)
Choson Period (1392–1910),
late 19th century
Red cotton
Overall L: 72 cm, W: 90 cm
Sleeves L: 29 cm, W: 17.5 cm
USNM ECC 77072
Ref.: HKC p. 447; BFN 144; Published (*MBM*,
1989: 138)

This long-sleeved, red cotton overcoat has a white-striped collar called a *git* 깃. It is sewn onto the garment creating a V-neck effect. Attached to both sides of the upper front are two blue tie-ribbons, *goreum* 고름, to be tied in a slipknot on the right side, letting part of the ribbons trail downwards. Long gussets added from the armpits to the straight body make an A-line.

After the 1884 dress-code reform (Kim, 1988b: 168), the narrow-sleeved *durumagi*, also known as *juui* 周衣, became part of the formal dress of men, women, and children of upper-class families in the late Choson period (1392–1910). This outerrobe continued to be in fashion until around 1950. Fabric, colors and other features such as lining and padding varied, according to the season, and the age and social status of the wearer (ibid., pp. 169–170).

BFN 144 "Tou-rou-maki 두루마이 [두루마기] of red cotton stuff. This is put on over the small jacket with striped sleeves...."

Collected in Seoul

18 Boy's Vest
(*BAEJA* 배자)
Choson Period (1392–1910), late 19th century
Blue silk with linen lining
L: 36 cm, W: 24 cm (top), 41 cm (bottom)
USNM ECC 77075
Ref.: HKC p. 447; BFN 145; Published (*MBM*,
1989: 139)

The blue-silk vest has red lining and wide armholes. It is worn over a jacket, *jeogori* 저고리, by young boys of aristocratic families. The front of the vest is designed shorter than the back. A band of red brocade silk across the back bears gold-embossed (*geumbak* 금박 金箔) ideographs, which read figuratively *yeui yeomchi* 禮義廉恥 (May you be proper and gracious in conduct, bringing honor and dignity to yourself). While a conventional *baeja* calls for tie-strings together with a fastening device similar to "hook and eye" in front, this vest has only the latter. The blue and red combination in clothing and other objects is considered auspicious, representing heaven and earth, male and female, the sun and moon, the duality of nature. Variations in fabric, color and style are determined by season, age, and social status (Yi, 1983: 389; Kim, 1988b: 220–221; *HUM*, 1988: 19; Jang, 1999: 169, illustration number 190).

BFN 145 "Pai-tja [*baeja*]. The characters on the ribbon at the back signify "have consideration for others; be just; be moderate in your desire."

Collected in Seoul

19

19 BOY'S OUTERROBE

(*AEGI JEONBOK* 애기전복; *AEGI KWAEJA*
애기쾌자)
Choson Period (1392–1910), late 19th century
Blue Chinese silk brocade
L: 66 cm, W: 23 cm (top), 74 cm (bottom)
USNM ECC 77077
Ref.: HKC p. 447; BFN 146; Published (*MBM*,
1989: 138)

This sleeveless and unlined robe is of dark blue silk
and has a red-silk sash.

Another red-silk band is sewn across the upper back
of the robe. Three small, embroidered, stuffed ball-
like bags with tassels, called *hyangnang* 향낭 (literally, scented bag), hang from the center of this
band. Choson-period upper-class families let their
male children wear *jeonbok* or *kwaeja* on special
festive occasions (Kim, 1988b: 426 and 490; *HUM*,

1988: 18; Jang, 1999: 170–171 for varied styles,
uses, and illustrations). *Jeonbok* are normally mili-
tary-officials uniforms and *kwaeja* everyday
outerrobes worn by civil and military officials. This
piece of clothing is identified as *su doltti jeonbok*
수돌띠전복, a sleeveless outerrobe with a sash decorated with embroidery to be worn at a child's one-
year-old birthday celebration (*MBM*, 1989: 138,
illustration number 22).

BFN 146 "Outer garment... of a Chinese fabric.
The Koreans say that there are three spirits who
enter the world at the same time as a child [is born]
and who guard him during his childhood. Account
of these are shown [with] the three little bags sewn
on the waist band. They contain cotton and sometimes a piece of the child's hair."

Collected in Seoul

20 BOY'S LEGGINGS

(*AEGI HAENGJEON* 애기행전)
Choson Period (1392–1910), late 19th century
Red cotton
L: 10 cm, W: 12 cm, stripe L: 21 cm
USNM ECC 77074
Ref.: HKC p. 447; BFN 143

Each part of these tubular leggings has two strings
attached to its diagonally cut upper end. The
leggings are worn over a pair of *baji* 바지 (baggy
trousers) to reduce bulkiness by tying the trouser legs
below the knees and allowing them to hang over the
socks. Color and size variations are determined by
the wearer's age and the color of his outerrobe.

Leggings were for full formal dress of upper-class
men and young boys (Kim, 1988b: 526).

Collected in Seoul

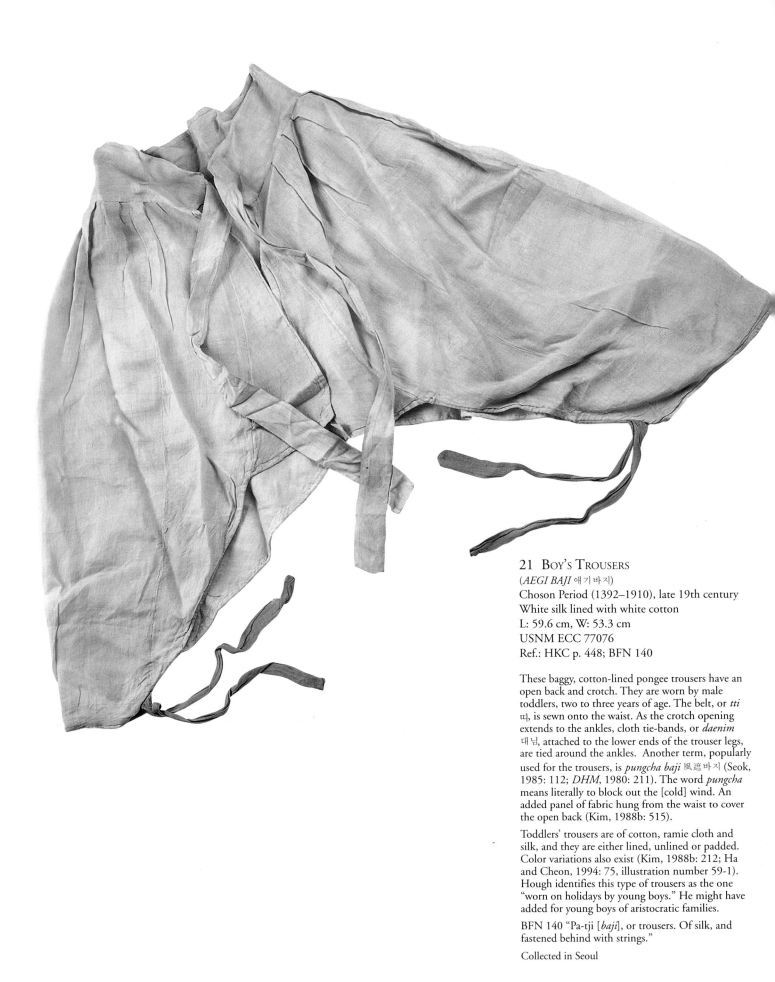

21 BOY'S TROUSERS
(*AEGI BAJI* 애기바지)
Choson Period (1392–1910), late 19th century
White silk lined with white cotton
L: 59.6 cm, W: 53.3 cm
USNM ECC 77076
Ref.: HKC p. 448; BFN 140

These baggy, cotton-lined pongee trousers have an open back and crotch. They are worn by male toddlers, two to three years of age. The belt, or *tti* 띠, is sewn onto the waist. As the crotch opening extends to the ankles, cloth tie-bands, or *daenim* 대님, attached to the lower ends of the trouser legs, are tied around the ankles. Another term, popularly used for the trousers, is *pungcha baji* 風遮바지 (Seok, 1985: 112; *DHM*, 1980: 211). The word *pungcha* means literally to block out the [cold] wind. An added panel of fabric hung from the waist to cover the open back (Kim, 1988b: 515).

Toddlers' trousers are of cotton, ramie cloth and silk, and they are either lined, unlined or padded. Color variations also exist (Kim, 1988b: 212; Ha and Cheon, 1994: 75, illustration number 59-1). Hough identifies this type of trousers as the one "worn on holidays by young boys." He might have added for young boys of aristocratic families.

BFN 140 "Pa-tji [*baji*], or trousers. Of silk, and fastened behind with strings."

Collected in Seoul

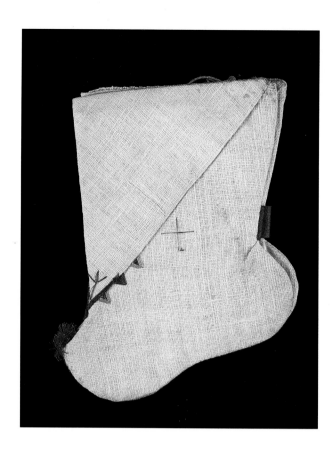

22 PAIR OF BABY SOCKS

(*TARAE BEOSEON* 타래버선)
Choson Period (1392–1910), late 19th century
Padded and quilted white muslin with
embroidered silk
L: 15.3 cm, W: 12 cm (top), 14 cm (bottom)
USNM ECC 77073
Ref.: HKC p. 448; BFN 142; Exhibited, S. Dillon
Ripley International Center, Smithsonian
Institution, "Generations: A Universal Family
Album," 11 September 1987– 31 March 1998

The upper section of each sock has diagonal
stitching, the lower section has vertical. They have
deeply cut insteps, rounded heels and sharply turned
toes curving upwards. Pink tying ribbons are
stitched midway up the back for tying around the
ankles. Red, blue, and green floral decoration on the
lower front symbolizes long life, and the blue silk
sangmo 象毛 (pompons or ball tassels) attached to
the tip of the toe represent prosperity. Red pompons
signify a girl child. These types of socks are worn on
the baby's first birthday or on holidays.

Oversized baby socks, like these, symbolize growth
and long life (Kim, 1988b: 492 for symbolism
connected with decorative motifs; Jang, 1999: 172–
173, illustration numbers 194–196, for varied
modes of decoration and quilt patterns applied).
Hough notes the socks are constructed with regard
to shape of the shoe and not of the foot.

BFN 142 "... stockings."

Collected in Seoul

23 GIRL'S HAIR RIBBON

(*DOTURAK DAENGGI* 도투락댕기)
Choson Period (1392–1910), late 19th
century
Silk gauze
L: 35.6 cm, W: 8 cm
USNM ECC 77078
Ref.: HKC p. 448; BFN 147
The two panels here are folded to a point
at the top and sewn to form a single
paneled ribbon.
Geumbak 金箔, or gold embossed,
inscriptions and seven circled dots,
symbolizing the *chilseong* 칠성 (the seven
stars of the Big Dipper), decorate the
ribbon. The inscriptions read: *su bugwi*
壽富貴 (long life, blessings, wealth and
nobility), and the seven stars are believed to
have amuletic power. The purple ribbon is
reserved for royal children. It is tied to the
hair plait at the nape of the neck, letting the
ribbon hang down the back.

BFN 147 "... ribbon made fast to the end of
the plait with which the hair is done up. The
characters signify 'long life, riches be be-
queathed.' The circular device contains seven
dots representing the seven stars of the Dipper. They are supposed to insure the wearer's
having many children."

Collected in Seoul

24 Girl's Multicolored Sleeved Jacket

(*AEGI SAEKDONG JEOGORI* 애기색동저고리)
Choson Period (1392–1910), late 19th century
Blue, red, green, and yellow silk with muslin lining
Overall L: 39.3 cm, W: 94.9 cm
Sleeves L: 30.1 cm, W: 13.9 cm
USNM ECC 77111
Ref.: HKC p. 448; BFN 141; Published (*MBM*, 1989: 137)

The lining of this green silk jacket is of coarse muslin. The collar base and one side of the front panel of the jacket are blue. The sleeves are made of nine alternating colored bands in combinations of red, green, blue, and yellow. Two red sashes are attached—one to the upper front of the jacket, and one to the right armpit seam. They are tied in a slipknot on the upper front of the jacket.

This jacket was worn by both male and female children on celebratory occasions, such as a child's first birthday and during the New Year festivals. The jacket with purple sash is for a female child, the blue is used for a male child (Kim, 1988b: 290). The multicolored sleeves derive from the Taoist concept of five basic colors: yellow representing the center; blue the east; red the south; white the west; and black the north. Spirits move in all five directions, thus becoming protective and auspicious (Legeza,

1987: 27). The five colors also are the symbols of the five elements of nature: water, fire, wood, metal and earth. Green, used interchangeably with the color blue [the Chinese character for blue and green is the same] replaces the color black on this type of child's festive jacket. Silk is the standard fabric, but the ornamentation is variable. This jacket may also be called *dol saekdong jeogori* 돌색동저고리 or a multicolored sleeved jacket for a child's first birthday (*MBM*, 1989: 137, illustration number 21; Jang, 1999: 168, illustration numbers 188–189).

BFN 141 "... a jacket with striped sleeves. All the holiday dresses for children, both boys and girls are made [with] sleeves like this."

Collected in Seoul

25(front)

25 CHILD'S ORNAMENTAL HEADDRESS
(*GULLE* 굴레)
Choson Period (1392–1910), late 19th century
Silk with embroidery and applied wax and clay
beads and Chinese artificial pearls
L: 45.7 cm, W: 22.8 cm
USNM ECC 77079
Ref.: HKC p. 448; BFN 148

The headdress is decorated with embroidery, beads
and artificial pearls. It is made of three bands: two
criss-crossing over the head, and the third headband
serving as a frame. Attached to the frame is a ribbon
embossed with gold ideographs that read: "*subu
gangbok* 壽富康福 (May you be blessed with long
life, wealth, health and peace)." A *Gulle* is worn
with tying ribbons around the neck with a bowknot
in front or worn with a back hair ribbon known as
doturak daenggi 도투락댕기 (cat. no. 23).

This ornamental headdress was designed strictly for
the children of the Choson *yang ban* 兩班, or aristocrats. Local variations in hood design and ornamen-

tation exist according to season, age, and sex of the
wearer (Jang, 1999: 58, illustration number 65;
GMB, 1980: 104, illustration number 151). Purple
tying ribbons are for royal girls and black for boys
(*DHM*, 1980: 186). Hough's description of the
headdress reads in part: "Ornamental ... skeleton
hood of colored silk," and the translation of the
inscription: "Long life, riches, health, and happiness." A notation states, "the black ribbon is re-
moved when the child becomes able to speak,"
which was then a customary practice. BFN 148 "...
Head ornament worn by very small children. Ornamented with embroidery, gilding, beads of wax and
burnt clay and artificial pearls (from China)."

Collected in Seoul

26 GIRL'S DECORATED SHOES
(*KKOT DANGHYE* 꽃당혜)
Choson Period (1392–1910), late 19th century
Red silk with green and yellow leather
L: 16.5 cm, W: 5.8 cm
USNM ECC 77081
Ref.: HKC pl. XX, lower fig.2

These shoes are decorated with green and yellow
trim on the upturned fronts and backs.

Kkot danghye 꽃唐鞋 literally means Chinese [style],
flower-decorated shoes, shoes worn by young girls
of the upper class.

Collected in Seoul

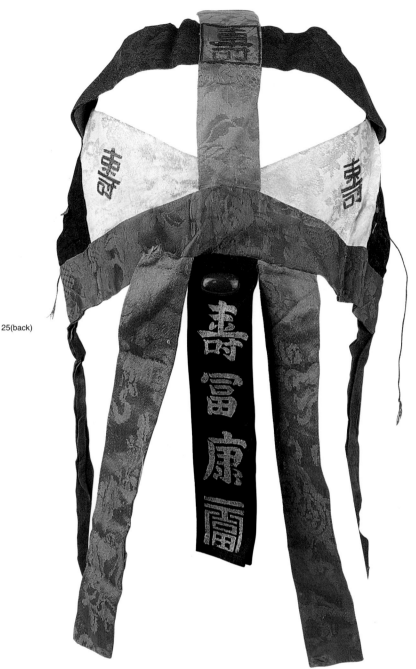

25(back)

27 TRICOLORED BAG
(*SAMSEONG JUMEONI* 삼성三聖주머니)
Choson Period (1392–1910), late 19th century
Yellow cotton with blue silk lining
L: 15.5 cm, W: 14 cm
USNM ECC 77023
Ref.: HKC p. 449; BFN 105

Attached to the folded mouth of this tricolored bag or pouch is a green string used for opening or closing the bag and for hanging it from the waist. This bag held money and a variety of small personal articles. It is sometimes called *bok jumeoni* 福주머니 (the bag that brings luck), as it became a popular vehicle for gift exchange (Seok, 1992a: 192). There is a special type of *bok jumeoni,* which is a round, colored silk pouch with embroidered decoration and tasseled tie string. This gift pouch contained a single roasted bean wrapped in paper. Originally, *bok jumeoni* was used as a royal gift on the new year's first "day of the boar," considered auspicious according to the sexagesimal cycle. Wearing a *bok jumeoni* on the "day of the boar" was believed to

ensure good luck all year long (Choe, 1993: 190–191; Jang, 1992: 62, illustration number 57; Jang, 1999: 110–111).

Jumeoni means bag or pocket. *Samseong,* which Hough uses in his entry, refers to the meaning of the three colors used for the bag: yellow representing the earth, blue the heavens and green the water. Embroidery is the dominant feature of these bags and corresponds to the background material, age and sex of the carrier or the circumstances of gift exchanges (Seok, op.cit: 193).

BFN 105 "... Small bag hung at the waist—the Koreans having no pockets. This article is carried by the poor and middle classes. With the better class the pocket formed in the long sleeves serves as a receptacle for pipe and toilet articles."

Collected in Seoul

28

28 WOMAN'S QUILTED JACKET

(NUBI JEOGORI 누비저고리)
Choson Period (1392–1910), late 19th
century
Quilted orange-yellow silk with cotton
lining
L: 25.3 cm, W: 38.2 cm
USNM ECC 77107
Ref.: HKC p. 449; BFN 137; Published
(*MBM,* 1989: 139)

This is a woman's yellow bodiced jacket, with either
purple or dark blue lapels, cuffs, and tying ribbons.
It is worn with a blue skirt. The ensemble was
formal attire for ladies (Kim, 1988b: 279). Another
feature is the triangular armpit gusset, which
extends to part of the sleeve and the bodice. It
matches colors of the collar, the cuffs, and the
ribbons.

Hough states that the jacket is "worn by women in
the spring," but quilted clothing is customarily for
winter use. For an identical type of yellow quilted
jacket see *HUM,* 1988: 35, illustration number 46;
Jang, 1999: 167, illustration number 185.

BFN 137 "... quilted jacket as worn by young
women. [It] is the same garment as the tjuk-sam
[*jeoksam*], and takes its place."

Collected in Seoul

29 WOMAN'S LINEN JACKET

(MOSI JEOKSAM 모시적삼)
Choson Period (1392–1910), late 19th
century
Linen
Overall L: 26.3 cm, W: 118 cm
Sleeves L: 40 cm, W: 15.5 cm
USNM ECC 77108
Ref.: HKC p. 449; BFN 119

This summer jacket has a knot and loop to be
fastened at the chest. *Jeoksam* refers either to an
unlined underwear jacket (*sok-jeoksam* 속적삼) or
to an unlined summer jacket. Common fabrics for
jeoksam are linen, hemp cloth, and cotton.

BFN 119 "... or short upper jacket of mosi [linen].
Women who are nursing children, and in general,
among the lower classes, all except very young or
quite old women, wear the ho-ri-tteui [*heoritti*] or
girdle low so as to leave the breasts uncovered.
When the girdle is very wide and the tjok-sam
[*jeoksam*] or jacket laps over it, the breasts are not
exposed. Among the better classes a short light
jacket of silk, longer than the tjok-sam [*jeoksam*],
but caught in at the waist is worn over these; but
this is not common."

Collected in Seoul

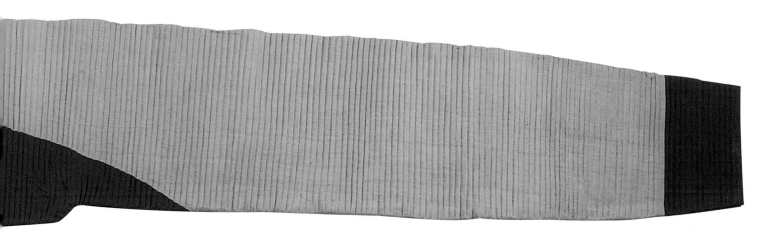

30 WOMAN'S SASH
(*HEORITTI* 허리띠)
Choson Period (1392–1910), late 19th century
Cotton
L: 95.4 cm, W: 24.1 cm
USNM ECC 77103
Ref.: HKC p. 449; BFN 122

This wide, lined cotton band is not a waistband in a strict sense, because it is worn over the breasts, and then covered by a skirt. Wearing this type of sash was practical during the latter part of the Choson Period when a woman's jacket became markedly short.

Heoritti are either lined or unlined and padded for winter use. The color is invariably white and common fabrics used are fine cotton or bleached pongee (Kim, 1988b: 529).

BFN 122 "… girdle. Holding up the sok-sok-ket [*sok-sokgot;* cat. no. 33]. This wide strip is fastened around the waist. The ends of it meet in front; the short string coming on the right side. The left or long string is taken once around the body and fastened to the short string on the right side. This band is placed so as not to lap over at the hips, but to extend well up under the breasts, and serves as a support for the strings fastening the other garments."

Collected in Seoul

31 WOMAN'S UNDERTROUSERS
(*GOJAENGI* 고쟁이)
Choson Period (1392–1910), late 19th century
Cotton
L: 105.3 cm, W: 40 cm (waist), 124.4 cm (hip)
USNM ECC 77100
Ref.: HKC p. 449; BFN 118

The undertrousers have a gathered waist, tying band, and open crotch. They are worn between the *sok-sokgot* 속속곳 (cat. no. 33) and *dan-sokgot* 단속곳 (cat. no. 32). They are not lined.

Hough's entry for this item reads "outer drawers," and adds: "Every Korean lady wears not less than four body garments." He means three layers of undergarment in addition to a skirt. The fabrics used for this type of undergarment are cotton, hemp, and linen. In modern usage, a *gojaengi* is a burial garment (Kim, 1988b: 45).

BFN 118 "… outer drawers. Put on over the sok-sok-kot [*sok-sokgot*] and girdle. The strings fasten on the left side under the arm. Of cotton cloth."

Collected in Seoul

32 WOMAN'S LINEN UNDERSKIRT

(*MOSI DAN-SOKGOT* 모시단속곳)
Choson Period (1392–1910), late 19th century
Linen
L: 81.2 cm, W: 39.3 cm (waist), 64.4 cm (leg)
USNM ECC 77101
Ref.: HKC p. 449; BFN 120; Published (*MBM*, 1989: 140)

This divided skirt, equivalent to a slip, is worn directly under the outerskirt, *chima* 치마. It has four large pleats on each side, front and back, totaling sixteen. The waistband has two tying ribbons, one long in the front and one short in the back, attached near an opening on the left side. The long and short ribbons are crisscrossed and tied on the left.

Fabrics vary according to the season, and are of various colors; mainly white, light blue and gray (Kim, 1988b: 139).

BFN 120 "... Outer drawers, of mosi or grass cloth. Tied at the waist with strings—at the left side."

Collected in Seoul

33 WOMAN'S DRAWERS

(*SOK-SOKGOT* 속속곳; *NAECHINUI* 내친의)
Choson Period (1392–1910), late 19th century
Bleached cotton
L: 81.5 cm, W: 44 cm (top), 136 cm (bottom)
USNM ECC 77102
Ref.: HKC p. 449; BFN 121

These are unlined underwear which are similar to *dan-sokgot* 단속곳, outer drawers (cat. no. 32). They are less bulky, have tying strings fastened on the left, and have longer legs.

Naechinui usually are made of calico, cotton, or cotton broadcloth (Kim, 1988b: 124). *Naechinui* clarifies that the garment rests against the skin.

BFN 121 "... Inner drawers of cotton. Resemble somewhat the 'divided skirt'... Fastened at the left side at the hip."

Collected in Seoul

34 WOMAN'S LINEN SKIRT

(*MOSI CHIMA* 모시치마)
Choson Period (1392–1910), late 19th century
Linen
L: 122 cm, W: 84 cm
USNM ECC 77104
Ref.: HKC p. 449; BFN 123

The skirt is blue and the waistband and the tying string white. *Chima* may be long or short, narrow or wide requiring fewer or more pleats, lined or unlined and varicolored, depending upon the prescribed styles associated with certain occasions, seasons and age of the wearer. A dress skirt can have gold-leaf stamped decorations along the hemline (Kim, 1988b: 482 for style variations). This wraparound skirt has a full-length opening and overlaps on the left side, with only a small amount of the material tucked into the waist band. Hough makes the curious observation that: "The appearance of this garment has led Korean women to say that they dress like western women."

BFN 123 "... Tch'ma [*chima*] or dress of blue cotton stuff. This is put on like a long apron, the strings taken around the waist and fastened behind. In walking, the folds are generally gathered by hand and tucked under the waistband."

Collected in Seoul

35 Woman's Mantle

(*JANGOT* 장옷; *JANGUI* 장의長衣)
Choson Period (1392–1910), late 19th century
Green silk brocade with muslin lining and cotton
collar and cuff facings
Overall L: 129.6 cm, W: 135 cm
Sleeves L: 51 cm, W: 17 cm
USNM ECC 77094
Ref.: HKC p. 450; BFN 117

This mantle has red *git* 깃 (lapels), two pairs of long
ribbons in front and a white-cotton *dongjeong* 동정
(narrow striped collar). Both lapels and collar
detach for laundering. For use outdoors, the mantle
covers the head and leaves only the eyes and nose
exposed. The sleeves dangle on both sides of the
head. One pair of the ribbons is for tying, and one
trail as a decoration.

Originally this was worn by middle and lower class
women, as women of the upper class were not seen
on the street. On outings, they were carried in a
palanquin or covered chair. By the close of the
nineteenth century, it became part of noble
women's outdoor apparel (Seok, 1992a: 510-511,
including illustrations). Types of fabric used for

mantles vary according to the season and social
status of the wearer, but green is the requisite
(*HUM*, 1988: 31 for illustrations; Kim, 1988b:
412-413).

BFN 117 "... a long coat. Of green figured silk and
trimmed in white, red and purple according to a
fixed pattern. This garment is invariably worn by
women of the middle and often by women of the
lower classes when in the street. It is then thrown
over the head, and the sleeves which are never of
any service hang down at the sides. By drawing the
folds closely together, the women conceal their faces
upon the approach of a stranger. The Koreans say
that once a wise king ordered that all the women of
the people should wear an outer garment in the
form of a soldier's coat, so that upon the approach
of an enemy the men could seize these [long coats]
and at once become soldiers. But after the king's
death the law was disregarded and the garment was
changed from a blue cotton gown to a gown of
green silk; and this has always remained of a fixed
pattern."

Another western observer commented that the
practice of closing the mantle under the chin with
both hands gave Korean women "an ungainly gait"
(Carles, 1886: 294). Bernadou appended an illustration showing how to wear the mantle in the street.

Collected in Seoul

Woman's Street Dress

Watercolor on paper
L: 35 cm, W: 30 cm
USNM ECC 131, 315: 13, William W. Rockhill
Collection, 1887

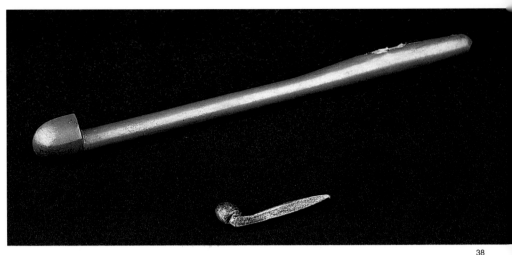

36 WOMAN'S LINED SUMMER SOCKS

(*GYEOP-BEOSEON* 겹버선)
Choson Period (1392–1910), late 19th century
Cotton
L: 27.5 cm, W: 14.8 cm
USNM ECC 77106
Ref.: HKC p. 450; BFN 129

Boot-like, these socks have deeply cut insteps, rounded heels, and sharply turned toes. Small and narrow feet were considered an essential part of high-born feminine beauty, and the socks are made to fit tight.

Korean socks are invariably made of bleached or unbleached white cotton. The only exception is colored silk socks for Choson royal dress (Kim, 1988b: 234–235). The unpadded, lined socks are for summer use.

37 PAIR OF WOMAN'S MATCHING FINGER RINGS

(*GARAKJI* 가락지)
Choson Period (1392–1910), late 19th century
Pewter
D: 2.45 cm
USNM ECC 77109
Ref.: HKC p. 450; BFN 139

These rings were worn by commoners as a pair on one finger. Finger rings were gold, silver, nickel, cloisonné, amber, coral, agate, or jade. Metal rings can be with ornamentation, such as incised or enameled bats or flowers, or without ornamentation. Undecorated rings were usually worn by older women, while colorful types like cloisonné rings were designed for young ladies; especially brides (*DHM*, 1980: 166; Kim, 1988b: 450–451 for methods of decoration, decorative design motifs, and customs relating to age; Seok, 1981: 95–98, 170,

illustration numbers 79–82; Jang, 1999: 128–131). Materials of rings distinguish not only the wearer's social status, but seasons, outings and special occasions. Metal rings are for winter. Rings as gifts, memorials, commemoratives, and for friendship are symbolic: a circle without end is eternal. Bernadou demurs slightly: "... finger rings. Of pewter or silver; rarely gold. Are worn in pairs. Such rings are worn both by married and single women and have no significance" (BFN 139).

Collected in Seoul

38 WOMAN'S HAIRPIN

(*BINYEO* 비녀)
Choson Period (1392–1910), late 19th century
Pewter
L: 18.3 cm
USNM ECC 77046
Ref.: HKC p. 450; BFN 138

An unornamented everyday hairpin for the chignon was worn by married women until the mid-twentieth century. *Binyeo* are gold, silver, jade, nickel, wood, bamboo, horn or ivory. Pearls and coral ornament long silver or other metal pins. Enameled phoenix or dragon motif heads were strictly for royal court ladies' ceremonies. In later years, lower-class women popularized such pins by wearing them at their weddings (for illustrations and nomenclature, see Kim, 1988b: 258; *DHM*, 1980: 174–175; *HUM*, 1988: 72; Jang, 1999: 18-33). A long pin with plum blossom and bamboo symbolizes chastity. An unornamented willow or bamboo hairpin represents widowhood and mourning (Adams, 1987: 35).

BFN 138 "... pin for fastening the hair. Of pewter, but often made of silver and sometimes gilt. The hair is done up in a plait, but the end is taken up and back and plaited in."

Collected in Seoul

39 MAN'S HAIRPIN

(*DONGGOT* 동곳)
Choson Period (1392–1910), late 19th century
Pewter
L: 4.1 cm
USNM ECC 77114
Ref.: HKC p. 450; BFN 99

The pin is slightly bent in the middle with a ball-like head and pointed end. Men insert this type hairpin in a *sangtu* 상투 (topknot) to hold it in place. They can be gold, jade, amber, coral or wood (Kim, 1988b: 164; Seok, 1992a: 228; Jang, 1999: 66-67 for illustrations including a wooden case for hairpins).

Hairpins express one's social status and taste. Some are longer than others, and the pointed ends are either straight or slightly curved (*HUM*, 1988: 78 for illustrations of men's hairpins in varied forms, sizes and materials; also Jenings, 1904: 151). One used a black-horn pin when in mourning (Seok, 1992a: 228). The 1895 reform laws decreed that all Korean men cut off their topknots and wear their hair in western fashion.

BFN 99 "Tong-kot [*donggot*] pin, stuck in the top of topknot worn by men. These pins are commonly of silver and sometimes of gold."

Collected in Seoul

40

40 PAIR OF WOMAN'S DECORATED SHOES
(*UNHYE* 운혜 雲鞋)
Choson Period (1392–1910), late 19th century
Silk uppers lined with donkey skin and with
leather trim and scrollwork and rawhide soles
L: 21.6 cm, W: 6.7 cm
USNM ECC 77016
Ref.: HKC pl. XX, lower fig. 1; BFN 94

The white trim on the toes and heels of these shoes
is ornamented with cloud scrolls. Rawhide sole and
cloth uppers are joined with leather stitching. These
shoes may also be called *jebi-buri sin* 제비부리신
(swallow bill shoes), as the toe resembles the bill of a
swallow.

Hough remarks that these shoes are
"neatly finished and ornamented" and "worn

by all ladies, except widows." (see Kim, 1988b: 375-
376 for term variants; for illustrations, see *HUM*,
1988: 49, illustration number 83; Ha and Cheon,
1994: 96–97).

BFN 94 "Woman's shoes. Similar in make to those
of men, but covered on the outside with blue cloth,
the common color."

Collected in Seoul

41 WOMAN'S WINTER HOOD
(*NAMBAWI* 남바위)
Choson Period (1392–1910), late 19th century
Silk brocade with red felt lining and black rabbit-
fur trim and applied tassels and beads
L: 28 cm, W: 17 cm
USNM ECC 77080
Ref.: HKC p. 451; BFN 149

Purple here, the hood is lined with red felt and
trimmed with black rabbit fur. Tassels and beads
decorate the hood. The hood covers the forehead
and the ears, and the rounded V-shaped back
protects the neck.

At the end of the Choson Period, this hood would
have been worn by a woman of any class. Fabric,
color, ornamentation, and other features such as
lining and padding were determined by sex, age,
and social status of the wearer (Kim, 1988b: 120;
for illustrations, see *HUM*, 1988: 47, illustration
numbers 72 and 73). Bernadou and Hough state
that a "similar hood is worn by men under the hat."
Conventionally, men wore a black hood lined
with green.

Collected in Seoul

42 Man's Underrobe

(*SOK-JEOKSAM* 속적삼)
Choson Period (1392–1910), late 19th century
Cotton
L: 80 cm
USNM ECC 77110
Ref.: HKC p. 451; BFN 127

Hough catalogues this jacket as having inside
sleeves, two pairs of tying strings and armpit gussets.
It was worn under the regular outer jacket, *jeogori*
저고리. It was not found in an inventory of the
collection.

Bernadou describes a "... Short inner jacket of white
cotton stuff worn as inner garment. It is not caught
in at the waist by the girdle but hangs loose over the
upper part of the trousers" (BFN 127).

Collected in Seoul

43 Man's Lined Trousers

(*GYEOP-BAJI* 겹바지)
Choson Period (1392–1910), late 19th century
Cotton with cotton lining
L: 129 cm, W: 67cm (waist), 130 cm (hip)
USNM ECC 77097 [Hough misidentified it as
77197]
Ref.: HKC p. 451; BFN 126

These wide-waist, baggy trousers taper toward the
hems. They are worn with a waistband, *heoritti*
허리띠, a cloth sash and tying ribbons, *daenim* 대님,
around the ankles over the trouser hems (cat. nos.
USNM ECC 77095, USNM ECC 77092).

Hough describes them as "...Very large. Held up by
the girdle, over which the superfluous upper part of
the garment falls." Bernadou comments: "... Trousers, of white cotton cloth. These are of the average
size and shape worn by the Koreans and are in no
way exaggerations; the specimen having been obtained at a store where ready-made clothing was for
sale. These are held up by the... girdle" (BFN 126).

Men usually wear white trousers or sometimes other
light and subdued colors such as beige or light blue
and gray. Different fabrics are used to accommodate
seasons and occasions and indicate social status and
age of the wearer (Kim, 1988b: 212).

Collected in Seoul

44 MAN'S SASH
(*HEORITTI* 허리띠; *YODAE* 요대 腰帶)
Choson Period (1392–1910), late 19th century
Cotton covered with green silk grosgrain
L: 152.4 cm, W: 7.3 cm
USNM ECC 77095
Ref.: HKC p. 451; BFN 135

Heori 허리 means waist and *tti* 띠, belt or sash.
Heoritti refers to various belts holding either inner
or outer garments (for dimensions of sashes see
DHM, 1980: 203, illustration numbers 323 and
324; Seok, 1992a: 559-561).

BFN 135 "...or girdle, a round cord (or narrow
band), generally of cotton, covered with silk. This is
fastened around the waist just above the hips. The
upper loose position of the trousers, from about a
foot from the upper band, is allowed to hang down
over this loosely."

Collected in Seoul

45 PAIR OF MAN'S GARTERS
(*DAENIM* 대님)
Choson Period (1392–1910), late 19th century
Silk grosgrain
L: 61 cm
USNM ECC 77092
Ref.: HKC p. 451; BFN 136

This pair of green grosgrain ribbons wrap twice
around the ankles over the folded trouser hems and
tie in front (Kim, 1988b: 149). Commonly they are
dark blue, aquamarine, or brown (ibid).

BFN 136 "The trousers are fastened below the knee
at the bottom by the tai-nim [*daenim*] or garters,
generally of green cotton or silk."

These garters have not been located.

Collected in Seoul

46 PAIR OF MAN'S WINTER SOCKS
(*SOM BEOSEON* 송버선)
Choson Period (1392–1910), late 19th century
Cotton with cotton padding
H: 30.5 cm, L: 23.5 cm
USNM ECC 77098
Ref.: HKC p. 451; BFN 128

Bernadou and Hough call these socks "stockings."
Hough adds, "padded with raw cotton; the rigidity
of the Korean shoe renders this necessary." Padded
socks (*som beoseon*) were worn by men and women
in the winter (cat. no. 36).

BFN 128 "... Cotton padded stocking, worn by
people of the middle and upper classes. The trousers
are folded at the bottom over the tops of the po-syen
[*beoseon*]; and held in place by the garters...."

Collected in Seoul

47 PAIR OF MAN'S LEGGINGS
(*HAENGJEON* 행전)
Choson Period (1392–1910), late 19th century
Cotton
L: 29.5 cm, W: 20.5 cm
USNM ECC 77096
Ref.: HKC p. 452; BFN 131

Bernadou and Hough catalogue a pair of white-
cotton leggings, now missing. Leggings are worn
over a pair of *baji* 바지 (baggy trousers) to reduce
bulkiness. Color and size are determined by the
wearer's age and the color of his outerrobe.

BFN 131 ".... These are provided with strings at the
top, and...are fastened around the calf of the leg
covering the juncture of the trousers and padded
stocking."

Collected in Seoul

48 MAN'S OUTERROBE
(*SO-CHANGUI* 소창의)
Choson Period (1392–1910), late 19th century
White silk
L: 137 cm
USNM ECC 77099
Ref.: HKC p. 452

This wide-sleeved, white pongee silk robe has a set-in collar, a straight slash from the armpits down and a pair of tying ribbons. The ribbons are tied in a slipknot at the right side of the breast. This robe was worn by a scholar-official at home.

Collected in Seoul

49 MAN'S SUMMER OUTERROBE
(*MOSI DOPO* 모시도포 道袍)
Choson Period (1392–1910), late 19th century
White linen
Overall, L: 144 cm
Sleeves, L: 68.7 cm, W: 56 cm
USNM ECC 77105
Ref.: HKC p. 452; BFN 124

This is a wide-sleeved, white-linen outer coat with back panel gored up to the shoulder blades.

The outer coat (*dopo*) was a scholar-official's every-day attire. Standard colors are white or light jade green; white, usually for mourning, and blue-green especially for celebratory occasions. Coats made of linen or ramie are for summer and cotton or silk for winter (Seok, 1992b: 21, and 41, illustration number 16). The outer coat is worn with a narrow tas-seled belt (cat. no. 44), leather-lined silk shoes (cat. no. 52) and wide brimmed hat (67). Following the 1884 dress-code reformation, the *dopo* was no longer required (Kim, 1988b: 162).

BFN 124 "... outer coat. This specimen is made of mosi grass cloth. To this there are two sets of strings. The inner ones are tied under the left arm. The left side of the garment is then wrapped over the right and the outer strings tied under the right arm in a long bow, the ends being allowed to hang down..."

Collected in Seoul

50 CORD BELT
(*TTI* 띠)
Choson Period (1392–1910), late 19th century
Green silk cord
L: 245.8 cm
USNM ECC 77082
Ref.: HKC p. 452; BFN 150

This belt, now missing, is worn with a man's outerrobe. Bernadou describes "... a long round silken cord with a tassel at each end. This is fastened so as to let the tassels hang down in front" (BFN 150).

Collected in Seoul

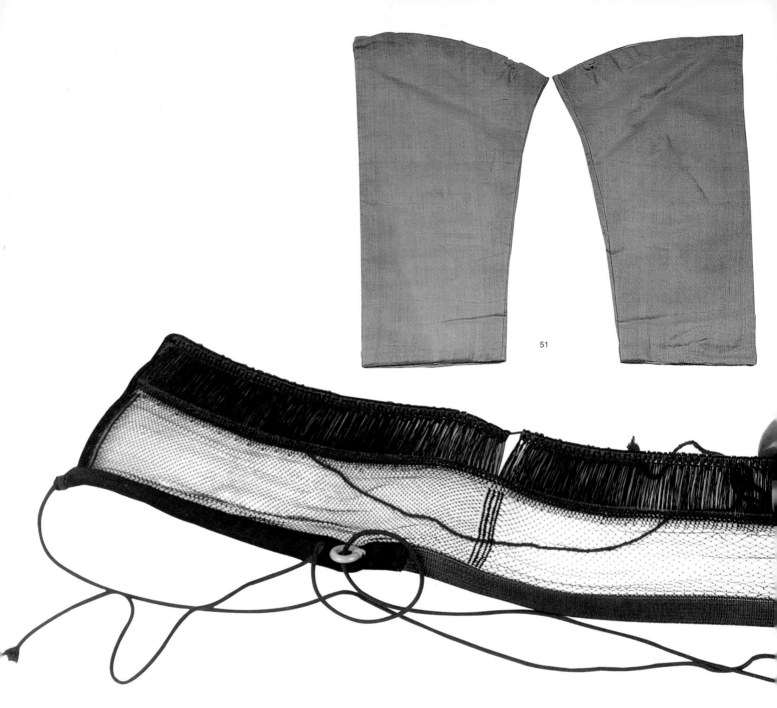

51 MAN'S WINTER WRIST CUFFS
(*TOSI* 토시 吐手)
Choson Period (1392–1910), late 19th century
Green silk with cotton lining
L: 27.8 cm, W: 15.8 cm (top), 10.7 cm (bottom)
USNM ECC 77093
Ref.: HKC p. 452; BFN 100

Originally, cuffs of this type were worn only by men, but eventually women also used them in winter. Silk or cotton cuffs are lined, and the preferred colors are white, gray, light brown and black. Woven wisteria or bamboo cuffs are for summer. They keep the sleeve ends away from perspiration (Kim, 1988b: 496). The pair Bernadou collected is green silk. Hough points out the excellent needlework.

BFN 100 "... These entered beyond the sleeves of the to-pou [*dopo*] or outer garment. Are simply slipped over the wrists."

Collected in Seoul

52 PAIR OF MAN'S SHOES
(*TAESAHYE* 태사혜 太史鞋)
Choson Period (1392–1910), late 19th century
Felt uppers with leather lining and cotton padding and leather soles
L: 24.8 cm, W: 8.5 cm
USNM ECC 77014
Ref.: HKC pl. XX, middle fig. 1; BFN 93

Shoes with silk or felt uppers lined with leather were called *taesahye* and were worn by noblemen or boys with everyday attire. White linear decoration appears on the edge of the sole (Kim, 1988b: 494; for illustration, see Seok, 1992b: 46, illustration number 28).

Similarly constructed shoes with black leather uppers were also worn by upper-class men and women. (Kim, 1988b: 572; *HUM*, 1988: 49, illustration number 81). Hough points out the similarity to Chinese shoes where, as Bernadou also writes, layers of cloth are filled between the sole and insole. "Men's shoes of leather. The space between the inner and outer leather on the sides and soles is filled in with layers of cotton cloth" (BFN 93).

Collected in Seoul

53 MAN'S HEADBAND
(*MANGGEON* 망건 網巾)
Choson Period (1392–1910), late 19th century
Woven horsehair
L: 49.5 cm, W: 7.7 cm
USNM ECC 77112
Ref.: HKC pl. XIX, lower figure 1; BFN 103

This rectangular headband has two tying strings attached to each corner of the right-hand side of the band. The ends of the strings pass through two small rings fastened on the opposite side of the band to tie around the topknot. Men wear the headband to push the strands of hair securely up under the band before wearing a hat (cat. no. 67).

The pairs of rings, for high-ranking officials, are of gold, jade, agate and coral. One finds them in foliate, round, hexagonal and octagonal shapes, plain or with applied or incised decoration. Gold is reserved for first or second in rank, white jade for third (Jang, 1999: 68–69 for commentaries and illustrations). Those officials lower than third grade wore headband rings made of animal bone or horn, amber, agate, or tortoiseshell. Mourners wore headband rings made from the hooves of oxen (Kim, 1988b: 59). A short note, titled "Korean Curios," appearing in the 29 August 1884 issue of *Science*, includes a description of rings worn by Min Yeong-ik, who headed the first Korean diplomatic mission to the United States. "A curious button is...also used by them [members of the mission]. It is worn on each side of the head, behind the ears, sewed to a velvet band.... When made of gold, they denote the highest rank, and are worn only by the prince" (Kunz, 1884: 173). High ranking officials fastened an additional headband ornament onto the center of the band called a *pungjam* 風簪, made of gold, jade, amber, tortoiseshell or agate. Commoners used *pungjam* made of bone or horn (Kim, 1988b: 514).

BFN 103 "... a head band. Passed around the head as shown per sketch [two sketches of man's head showing the front and back]. The ends of the strings are first passed through the small bone rings several times and twisted together. They are then brought up around the topknot and back made fast. This band is the support for the gat [갓] or stiff black hat.... In front of the band at the center of the forehead may be noticed the p'oun-tjam [*pungjam*] or knob of horn. Its purpose is to steady the hat and prevent it from dropping down over the eyes. The bone rings just referred to are replaced in the case of nobles of high rank by buttons of gold or jade. This is the only indication of high official rank as shown in the dress of Koreans. And this indication is not a sure one as certain nominal offices of very low grade give the holder the privilege of wearing these buttons also."

Collected in Seoul

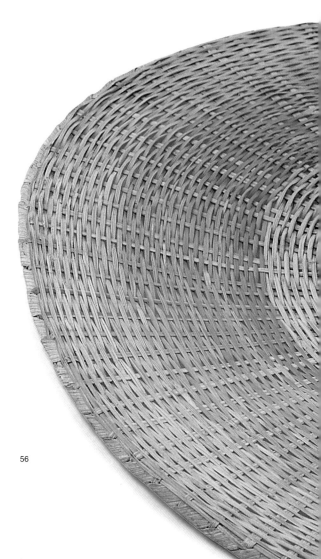

56

54 MALE MOURNER'S HAT
(*DUGEON* 두건; *HYOGEON* 효건 孝巾)
Choson Period (1392–1910), late 19th century
Hemp
H: 19.8 cm, D: 19.0 cm
USNM ECC 77089
Ref.: HKC pl. XVIII, upper figure 1; BFN 152

A *dugeon* is a head kerchief and a variant, *hyogeon*, a filial head kerchief. These head kerchiefs are worn only by male mourners together with *gulgeon* 屈巾 (cat. no. USNM ECC 77085) and *sujil* 수질 or head ring (cat. no. USNM ECC 77088).

Hough's interesting description of the item reads: "Wedge shaped; made somewhat like a grocer's paper bag of a single piece of coarse stuff." He adds that it is "worn on special mourning occasions." These are now missing from the collection.

BFN 152 "... Of hemp cloth."

Collected in Seoul

55 MALE MOURNER'S KERCHIEF
(*GULGEON* 굴건 屈巾; *GULGWAN* 굴관 屈冠)
Choson Period (1392–1910), late 19th century
Plaited and stiffened hemp
L: 33.1 cm, W: 30 cm
USNM ECC 77085
Ref.: HKC pl. XVIII, upper fig. 2; BFN 29

The band is lined with paper and stiffened to form a crown-like peak. The folded stiff band is worn over a mourning hat and the *sujil* 수질, a plaited hemp cloth ring worn just above the forehead.

Hough clarifies the manner and occasions of wearing the *gulgeon*: "the day of death, after decease of parent, at the time of burial and expiration of the first and second year after death."

Bernadou includes a drawing of the head ensemble with BFN 29.

Collected in Seoul

56 MALE MOURNER'S HAT
(*PAERAENGI* 패랭이;
PYEONGNYANGJA 평량자 平凉子)
Choson Period (1392–1910), late 19th century
Split, woven and bleached bamboo
H: 12.1 cm, D: 39 cm
USNM ECC 77064
Ref.: HKC pl. XVIII, fig. 3; BFN 12

This hat is of woven split bamboo with cylindrical crown and narrow brim. A *paeraengi* is worn by mourners, lowly persons like coolies, butchers, and members of *bobusang* 褓負商, the Peddlers Guild (Kim, 1988b: 505; *DHM*, 1980: 194; Seok, 1985: 74). When members of the Peddlers' Guild wore this type of bamboo hat, a cotton ball was fastened on either side of the hat brim, each with a string to tie under the chin. The coolies blacken the bamboo hat (Kim, 1988b: 243).

BFN 12 "Pyo-rang-i [*paeraengi*] Made of split bamboo. Worn as mourning by a son before the burial

of a deceased parent;
worn also by adopted sons in
mourning for their real parents. Otherwise
in common use among chair coolies, and worn by
government slaves. The members of the peddlers'
guild pow-syang-pei [*bobusang*] fasten small pieces
of raw cotton at intervals around the base of the
crown. Manufactured in the district of Tai-my^ng
[Damyang] in the southern province of Chun-la-do,
where also many articles of bamboo ware are manufactured."

Collected in Damyang, South Jeolla province

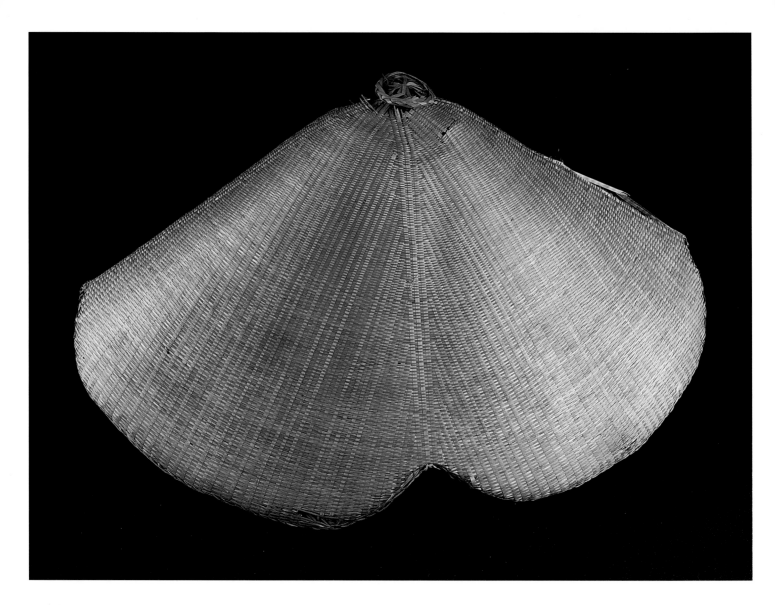

57 MOURNER'S HEAD RING
(*SUJIL* 수질)
Choson Period (1392–1910), late 19th century
Rice straw covered with twisted hemp
D: 16.6 cm
USNM ECC 77088
Ref.: HKC pl. XVIII, fig. 1; BFN 30

The straw ring is covered by twisted hemp cloth. It is worn by male mourners with their caps, *dugeon* 두건 (cat. no. USNM ECC 77089) and crown-like headdresses, *gulgeon* 屈巾 (cat. no. USNM ECC 77085). Female mourners also wear the *sujil*.

Collected in Seoul

58 MOURNER'S HAT
(*BANGNIP* 방립 方笠; *BANGGAT* 방갓; *SANGNIP* 상립 喪笠)
Choson Period (1392–1910), late 19th century
Woven bamboo with braided edges
H: 37 cm, D: 63.5 cm
USNM ECC 77066
Ref.: HKC pl. XVIII, fig. 1; BFN 106

A bamboo disk sits on top of this hat. Inside is a bamboo frame, to cradle the head, from which hang strings of twisted paper.

This hat originally was worn as protection from the sunlight or rain but came to be exclusively a mourner's hat in the late Choson period. Hough remarks "... it is considered a grievous breach of etiquette to look into the face of the mourners. Taking advantage of this custom before Korea was opened to foreigners, missionaries disguised themselves as mourners and lived and taught there for a long time without detection."

BFN 106 "... the pang-rip [*bangnip*] or mourning hat. This is a huge conical structure of split bamboo, the edge being of a quadrilateral shape. It rests upon the head by means of a light frame [included is a drawing] of this shape... the frame being tacked to the hat on the inner side. This huge affair nearly reaches the face; and with it and the poson [*poseon* 布扇, mourner's rectangular cloth fan], the face is completely concealed."

Collected in Seoul

59 MOURNER'S HEADBAND
(*POMANG* 포망; *POMANGGEON* 포망건 布網巾)
Choson Period (1392–1910), late 19th century
Woven hemp
L: 58.4 cm, W: 5.2 cm
USNM ECC 77091
Ref.: HKC p. 454; BFN 31

This headband is customarily worn with white mourning hat and robes, and wooden shoes by those wishing to express grief for the death of parents and members of the royal family (see Kim, 1988b: 511; Seok, 1992a: 143 for designees allowed to wear white mourning costume). The ties are matching white cotton.
BFN 31 "P'omang or mourning band worn about the head. This is worn during the period of mourning in place of the mang-kon [*manggeon*]: both at home and when in the street, taking the place of the black head-band the mang-kon [*manggeon*] otherwise invariable." Bernadou appended two drawings showing the front and back views of the head. The rear view shows the string drawn up and around the topknot and passing through the bone rings behind the ears.
Collected in Seoul

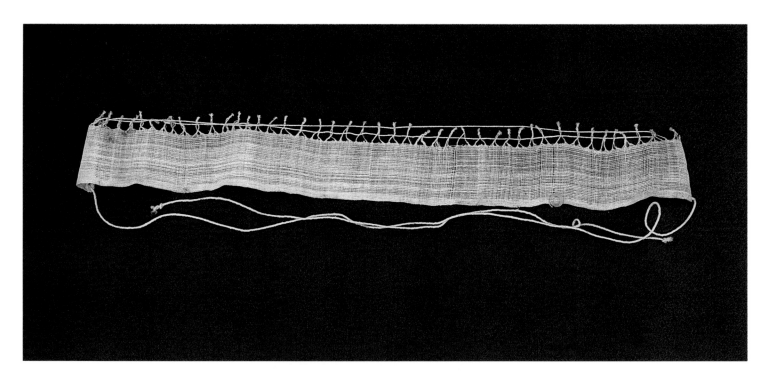

60 MALE MOURNER'S OUTERROBE

(*SIMUI* 深衣)
Choson Period (1392–1910), late 19th century
Hemp
Overall L: 135 cm, W: 180 cm
Sleeves L: 58 cm, W: 48 cm
USNM ECC 77084
Ref.: HKC p. 454; BFN 33

This robe is worn over a man's simple overcoat
(*durumagi* 두루마기) on outings during the
mourning period, probably upon the 1884
enactment of dress-code reform or following the
1894 reformation act known as *gabo gyeongjang*
甲午更張, when old systems were abolished,
including the class system, and replaced with new
codes (for details of the reform, see *GDS*, 1962:
24–25). Worn with *simui* are the *pomang* 포망,
mourner's headband (cat. no. USNM ECC 77091)
and *dugeon* 두건 mourner's cap (cat. no. USNM
ECC 77089), over which a large conical bamboo
hat is worn to hide one's face (cat. no. USNM ECC
77064).

Simui also are made from two separate pieces. The
top section represents *geon* 乾, heaven, the bottom
gon 坤, the earth. The lower section is made of
twelve pieces of cloth sewn together, symbolic of
the four seasons (Kim, 1988b: 324–325). Hough
endorses Bernadou's opinion that the hemp cloth
used for this robe is finer than the inner mourning
robe (cat. no. USNM ECC 77083). *Simui* originally was a white robe with collar and hem edged in
black. During the Koryo Dynasty (918–1392) and
early part of the Choson Period, the robe was worn
by Confucian scholars, together with a black headdress called *bokgeon* 복건.

BFN 33 "...of better quality than the hemp cloth
for tjoung-ton [*jungdan*], but nearly the same shape.
The left side of the garment laps over the right, the
strings fastening in front on the right side."

Collected in Seoul

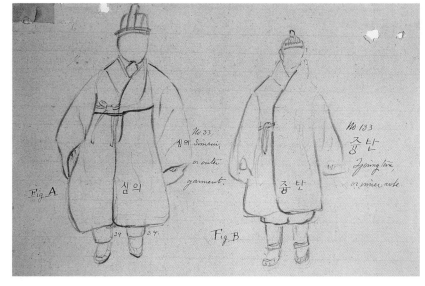

61 MALE MOURNER'S INNERROBE

(*JUNGDAN* D중단 中單)
Choson Period (1392–1910), late 19th century
Hemp
Overall L: 129 cm, W: 183 cm
Sleeves L: 68.5 cm, W: 45 cm
USNM ECC 77083
Ref.: HKC p. 454; BFN 133

This inner mourning robe has a back made of one
straight piece of cloth with two gores extending from
the armpits down. The straight front piece has only
one gore. Two tying strings are attached to the front.
Hough describes the fabric as being like "sackcloth."
He adds that the *jungdan* is worn under the *simui*
深衣 (cat. No. USNM ECC 77084), and that a
mourning costume is "made after a fixed ceremonial
pattern and worn by a son for two years after the

decease of a male parent." Actually, the mourning
period for a son after the decease of a male parent is
three years. In the second year, he changes his
mourning costume and gradually returns to normal
attire (for the three stages of mourning, see Pak,
1990: 163). *Jungdan* also refers to two other
distinctive robe patterns worn between the
undergarment and outerrobe. One, ceremonial, has
wide square sleeves of either white or light green
figured silk or plain weave raw silk. The sleeve ends,
part of the front panels and hemline, are edged in a
darker color. The other type is an innerrobe for a
young dancer. The sleeves taper toward the ends,
and the right side of the front panel and hemline are
edged in black. The fabrics for this type are white
linen for summer and white pongee for winter. The
collar is of colorful silk such as yellow, green or pink
(Kim, 1988b: 448–449).

Collected in Seoul

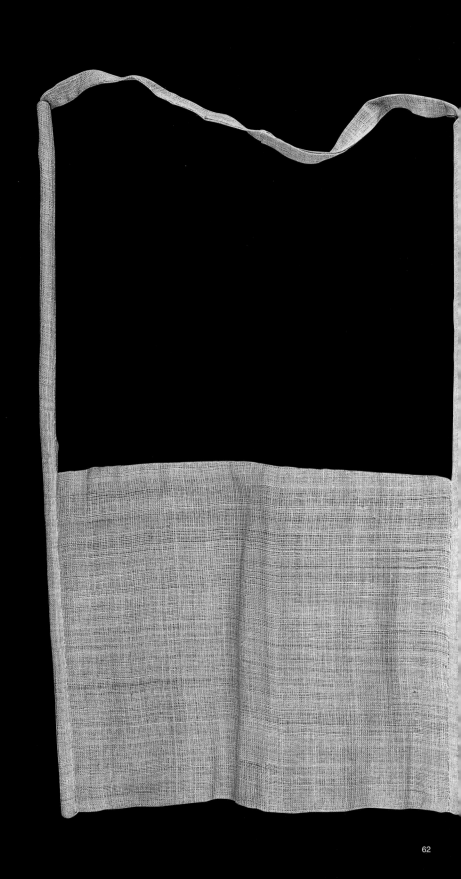

62 FEMALE MOURNER'S SASH
(*SAMTTI* 삼띠; *YOJIL* 요질)
Choson Period (1392–1910), late 19th century
Hemp
L: 181.1 cm
USNM ECC 77090
Ref.: HKC p. 455; BFN 32

Bernadou writes: "... theui [*tti*] or girdle of hemp.
Worn upon the occasion of the death of father.
After the death of his mother, the Korean wears a
strip of hemp cloth as a girdle instead" (BFN 32).
According to Seok, *yojil* is worn by the chief
mourner's wife with a white headdress called
huin-jokduri 흰족두리 (Seok, 1992a: 143).

Collected in Seoul

63 MOURNER'S RECTANGULAR FAN
(*POSEON* 포선 布扇)
Choson Period (1392–1–10), late 19th century
Hemp mounted on bamboo frame
L: 55.3 cm, W: 34.3 cm
USNM ECC 77087
Ref.: HKC p. 455; BFN 35

This fan is constructed of lined hemp cloth fastened
to two bamboo rods, also covered with hemp cloth.
A thin strip connects the two rods at the lower end.
It conceals the mourner's face outdoors.

BFN 35 "... hand screen held in front of the face
when walking in the street and roads. This is worn
with: [mourning hat]" (cat. no. USNM ECC
77066).

Collected in Seoul

62

65

64 MOURNER'S LEGGINGS

(*BE-HAENGJEON* 베행전)
Choson Period (1392–1910), late 19th century
Hemp
L: 24.8 cm, W: 20 cm
USNM ECC 77086
Ref. HKC p. 455; BFN 34

The hemp cloth used for a mourning costume is of the coarsest unbleached fabric, and tends to be darker than the usual hemp cloth for a variety of other clothing. The strings are tied around the calf to cover the junction of the trousers and socks.

Hough describes these leggings as "brown hemp cloth." Bernadou writes "... Haing-tyen [*haengjeon*] or leggings. Of hemp cloth and worn with the mourning dress. The strings are at the tops of the leggings. They are wound around the legs and tied. See large Fig. A." [Figure A on p. 63 refers to his pencil sketch of a standing figure in full mourning costume. The numeral 34, field note number for hemp cloth leggings, is written next to the leggings] (BFN 34).

Collected in Seoul

65 MOURNER'S SANDALS

(*EOM-JIPSIN* 엄짚신)
Choson Period (1392–1910), late 19th century
Twisted rice straw with white paper wound around drawstring and heel
L: 25.5 cm, W: 8.5 cm
USNM ECC 77012
Ref.: HKC pl. XX, fig. 3; BFN 134

The heel yokes and drawstrings of these sandals are covered with white paper. Hough explains that "they differ from common sandals by the paired arrangement of the straw cords which go over sides of the foot."

Bernadou writes "...Om-sin. Mourning sandals. Made from ordinary straw sandals by cutting out alternate parts of the straw braiding on the sides" (BFN 134). The term *"om-sin,"* is a variant of *eom-jipsin* (Martin, Yi, and Jang, 1967: 1148).

An unnumbered Bernadou field note continues: "In dressing model in mourning clothes then, the tjoung-ton [*jungdan* 中單] is first put on, the strings tied in a bow knot on the left side. The p'omang [포망] or mourning band is then secured around the head. Then the haing-tyon [*haengjeon* 행전] or leggings are tied around the legs, after which the white cotton hpo-syon [*beoseon* 버선] or padded

stockings are placed on the feet, and the haing-tyon [*haengjeon*] or leggings are drawn down over the tops of them. Then the om-sin [엄신] or sandals are put on, and lastly the pang-rip [*bangnip* 方笠] or large hat; over the tjoung-tan [*jungdan*] then comes the sim-eui [*simui* 深衣], or outer coat; the strings are tied on the left side and over this is passed the tteui [*tti* 띠] or hemp girdle, one end being allowed to hang down as per sketch. Finally the hands are brought up in front of the center of the body to hold the po-son [*poseon* 布扇] or hand screen." Illustrations in (BFN 29, 30 and 152) shows mourning headdress (cat no. 55), headring (cat. no. 57) and mourning cap (cat. no. 59) which are worn either together or separately; on certain fixed occasions.

Collected in Seoul

67

66 HAT FOR CIVIL OFFICIAL

(*SAMO* 사모 紗帽)

Choson Period (1392–1910), late 19th century
Lacquered paper and woven bamboo covered
with sateen
H: 14 cm, W: 16.7–19.7 cm (oval)
USNM ECC 77063
Ref.: HKC pl. XIX, upper fig. 1; BFN 89

This two-tiered, high-crown hat is made of woven
silk, black-lacquered with a bamboo frame, which
shapes its high, terraced crown. Attached to either
side of the back are rounded rectangular wings
projecting horizontally. These are also bamboo
covered with raw silk gauze. Jenings, citing a
Chinese poet's description, says they are "like the
locust singing in the tree with love and peace
toward all men. And as the locust is the emblem of
peace, the royalty and men of noble rank wear the
locust-wing emblem on their headdress" (Jenings,
1904: 154).

Introduced from Ming China to Korea at the end
of the Koryo Dynasty (918–1392) (Kim, 1988b:
266–68), *samo* was worn with official dress by the
high-ranking officials in the Choson period. The
height of the crown and length of the wings
changed periodically (Kim, 1988b: 266–268; 267
for illustration of five varieties). The hat is either

black or white. The latter was worn by court nobles
with their mourning dress. Commoners also wore
the black *samo* at marriage ceremonies. The custom
continues to this day. Hough points out the similarity of Korean official hats to Japanese official hats,
and also notes that Korean civil officers wore this
winged hat "at an audience, on New Year's day, on
the King's birthday, or on a formal visit of congratu-
lation." The wings at the side of the hat are said to
be for attaching flowers at a particular banquet
given by the royal family, according to Hough, who
must have obtained the information from one of his
Korean consultants. *Samo* being an official hat, the
term *samo gwandae* 紗帽冠帶, or the court official
ensemble, is self-explanatory.

BFN 89 "... Court hat. Worn by nobles when at the
palace and by all officers and eunuchs before the
King. Also worn by men of the upper and middle
classes at the time of the marriage ceremony. The
samo worn by the king differs from that worn by
others in that the wings are vertical instead of horizontal."

Collected in Seoul

67 BLACK HAT

(*GAT* 갓; *HEUNGNIP* 흑립 黑笠)

Choson Period (1392–1910), late 19th century
Bamboo, silk and horsehair
H: 11.4 cm (crown), D: 45.9 cm (brim)
USNM ECC 77060
Ref.: HKC pl. XIX, upper fig. 2; BFN 13

Bernadou explains "The Kat or national hat of the
Coreans and worn by all, from the King, down
except—people in mourning, and men of certain
low callings as the Koreans would say; – butchers,
tanners and executioners. The rim is made of split
bamboo and is neatly covered with fur or grass
cloth. In the better made ones the bamboo is
covered with silk or horsehair, and the crown is
made of horsehair instead as ordinarily of grass
cloth" (BFN 13).

Hough calls the *gat* Korea's national hat after
Bernado's field note and adds that it is "worn by all
classes [only after 1894]...in-doors and out." Regarding the manner of wearing, Hough observes: "It
does not fit over the head, but is placed on the
crown and held in position by the tying strings."
Height of the crown and width of the rim vary
according to rank of the wearer. Following the 1894
reformation, commoners were allowed to wear *gat*,
and its brim reduced dramatically (Kim, 1988b:
18).

Collected in Seoul

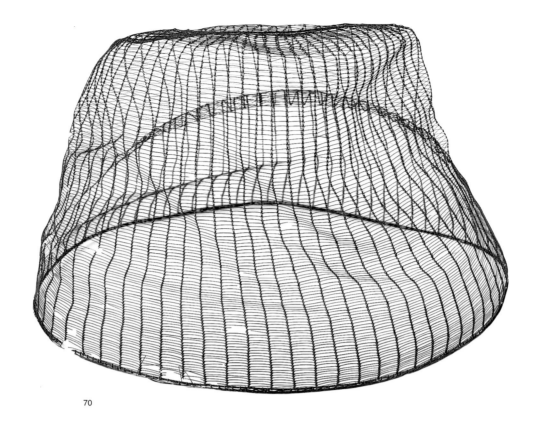

70

68 NOBLEMAN'S HAT

(*GEON* 건; *BANGGEON* 방건 方巾)
Choson Period (1392–1910), late 19th century
Horsehair
H: 19.0 cm, W: 27 cm
USNM ECC 77115
Ref.: HKC pl. XIX, upper fig. 3; BFN 9

This open-top square black cap, which tapers slightly toward the bottom, is made of woven black horsehair mesh. It was worn indoors by men of the aristocratic class (Kim, 1988b: 216).This hat is now missing from the collection.

BFN 9 "... worn by those of the literary class who have not yet passed examinations or held office; also allowed to any one who passes the second grade in merit at literary or military examinations before holding office. The lower class of merchants and laborers, unless after such examination, cannot wear it."

Collected in Seoul

69 HAT FOR STUDENT AT CIVIL EXAMINATIONS

(*YUGEON* 유건 儒巾)
Choson Period (1392–1910), late 19th century
Black cotton
USNM ECC 77057
H: 22.9 cm, D: 17.8 cm
Bernadou, Seoul, 1884–1885
Ref.: HKC pl. XIX, middle fig. 2; BFN 48

This hat has a rectangular centerpiece and triangular side flaps. It was worn by students at the state examinations held to recruit eligible court officials and also during Confucian rituals (Kim, 1988b: 383).

BFN 48 "... examination cap. Of stiffened cotton, and is black in color. Worn only at literary examinations and there by all students."

Collected in Seoul

70 CAP FOR CIVIL OR MILITARY OFFICIAL

(*TANGGEON* 탕건 宕巾)
Choson Period (1392–1910), late 19th century
Horsehair
H: 13 cm, D: 18.5 cm
USNM ECC 77056
Ref.: HKC pl. XIX, middle sfig. 3; BFN 8

The shape of this double-tier cap is similar to that of the official hat with a high dome, *samo* 紗帽 (cat. no. 66), but the gauze-like loose weaving of the cap is distinctive. It is an informal cap worn indoors by aristocrats. It is worn over a headband (*manggeon* 網巾, cat. no. 53) or under a black horsehair hat (*gat* 갓 cat. no. 67) (Kim, 1988b: 492).

As Jenings observes (1904: 162), "The Korean is never hatless, when in the house his head is covered with a gauze skull-cap (ibid: 160, figure 18), which is considered en déshabillé, only intimate friends seeing it worn, and to appear with it on the street would be the height of impropriety."

BFN 8 "... Worn by all officers in the government service, and by those who have been in service. Also allowed as a distinction to those who have passed the first grade in the literary and military examinations. This cap is worn when at home or in-doors by all officers, a few of the lower grades of attendants at the 'ya-ma's' [*yamen's; amun's*] or official homes, such as upper policemen, being alone excepted."

Collected in Seoul

72

71 HAT FOR A ROYAL CEREMONY
(*GEUMGWAN* 금관)
Choson Period (1392–1910), late 19th century
Bamboo wire, gilded papier-mâché, sateen
H: 25.5 cm
USNM ECC 77062
Ref.: HKC pl. XIX, middle fig. 4; BFN 90

At the back of this hat, not located in recent
inventories, was a shield-like construction using
thin woven bamboo strips encrusted with gold
papier-mâché dragons and scrolls. From the gilded
front panel, a black sateen-covered, thin wooden
band projects backward to five rows of gilded wires
placed vertically. A long wooden pin, with tasseled
blue cords thrust through the sides of the back,
adjusts the hat's head rim to fit the wearer.

BFN 90 "...Worn upon the occasion of the King's
offering sacrifices by those officers who assist him in
the ceremony. A similar hat—though not gilt—is
worn by those officiating at the semi-annual sacrifices to Confucius. These are officials throughout
Korea in all districts governed by magistrates."

Collected in Seoul

72 HAT FOR MILITARY OFFICER
(*JEOLLIP* 전립 戰笠)
Choson Period (1392–1910), late 19th century
Black felt and horsehair with red-dyed horsehair
plume
H: 12.8 cm, D: 38.4 cm
USNM ECC 77058
Ref.: HKC pl. XIX, middle fig.5; BFN 11

This hat is of thick felt stiffened to achieve a matte
finish. Attached to the crown are a red cord with
tassels and two carved buttons, one on each side of
the band. A long plume of red-dyed horsehair
known as *sangmo* 象毛 is fastened on top of the
crown by a swivel button, which is called a *jeongja*
頂子 or *jeungja* 증자.

These ornamental buttons vary according to the
wearer's rank (Jang, 1999: 77–79, illustration numbers 82–85). A high-ranking officer would use jade
ornamental buttons and real pheasant or peacock
plumes (Jang, 1999: 76; Bae and Yu, 1988: 34–35,
illustration numbers 78–82 for various types of
soldiers' hats).

BFN 11 "... Syang-mo [*sangmo*]. Distinctive badge
of soldiers. The Koreans say that this ornament, as
well as the red sleeves of the cavalry soldiers are thus
colored in order to accustom the horses to the sight
of blood. Of horsehair, dyed red, and fastened to the
top of the hat by the small leaden slug at the end."

Collected in Seoul

73

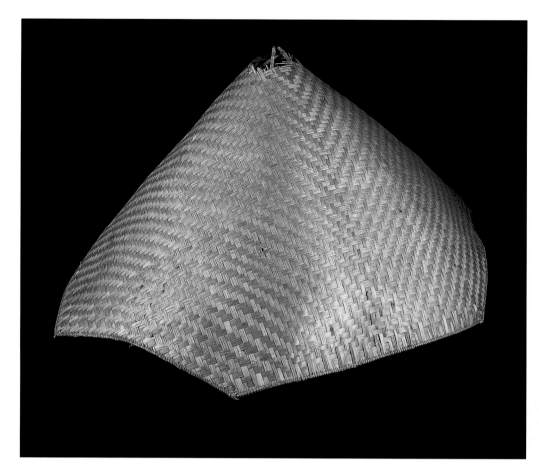

73 Hat for Porter

(*BEONGGEOJI* 벙거지)
Choson Period (1392–1910), late 19th century
Black felt
H: 10.2 cm, D: 38.3 cm
USNM ECC 77061
Ref.: HKC pl. XIX, middle fig. 6; BFN 10

The felt used for this type of hat is usually mixed with pig hair (Seok, 1992a: 217–219). Stiffening of the felt creates a smooth surface. The hat's shape is similar to a soldier's hat (cat. no. 72), without elaborate and colorful ornamentation.

Hough writes that this type of unadorned black felt hat is "worn by chair coolies, hostelers, and road runners who accompany noblemen when on a journey."

Bernadou comments, "... Pang-ko-tji [*beonggeoji*] or hat, as worn by soldiers in attendance at the Yamuns [*yamen* 衙門; *amun* 아문]; and by some of the lowest grades of military officers. The white ornaments are cut in the form of the device in the centre of the Korean flag." (BFN 10)

Collected in Seoul

74 Large Straw Hat

(*SATGAT* 삿갓)
Choson Period (1392–1910), late 19th century
Woven straw with inner frame of bamboo hoops and ribs
H: 40.9 cm, D: 76.5 cm
USNM ECC 77065
Ref.: HKC pl. XVIII, lower figure 2; BFN 107

This large straw hat has a hexagonal edge. It is woven with split stalks of straw, and its geometrical pattern is achieved by using different sides of the stalks. Inside the top of the hat is a built-in bamboo frame. Hough describes the weaving and the construction of the frame as follows: "The weaving is closed at the apex of the hat without showing a break. Braced inside with hoops of bamboo and ribs running from apex to points on the edge."

Originally, this type of hat was designed for use by Buddhist nuns to shield their faces on outings. Over time, it was worn by lower-class women for the same purpose (Seok, 1992a: 249, 703; Kim, 1988b: 252).

BFN 107 "... Coolies' hat. Serves as a protection from sun and rain and as an umbrella in wet weather. Some of these are of great size, nearly large enough to cover the wearer while asleep on the ground."

Collected in Seoul

76

75 RAIN HAT COVER

(*GALMO* 갈모)
Choson Period (1392–1910), late 19th century
Oiled paper
L: 33.5 cm
USNM ECC 77019
Ref.: HKC p. 458; BFN 16

This rain hat cover is made of folded oiled paper.
The cover is worn either on top of another hat or by
itself as a rain hat over a supporting frame, *galmote*
갈모테, of bamboo sticks. Chinstraps of twisted
white paper are joined under the chin. When not in
use, the hat cover can be stored like a folded fan.

Hough calls this hat cover "an interesting form of
the umbrella."

BFN 16 "... Worn in rainy weather over the kat, or
stiff black hat. Of oiled paper and is held in place by
the strings which join under the chin and are held
in the hand. Manufactured at Songdo [now
Kaesong], whence come goods of oiled paper in
great quantity. This cover is sometimes worn over a
light framing of bamboo sticks, which serve as a
support instead of the hat."

Collected in Songdo (modern Kaesong, Kyeonggi
province)

76 RAINCOAT

(*YUSAM* 유삼 油衫; *YUJI BIOT* 유지비옷)
Choson Period (1392–1910), late 19th century
Oiled Paper
Overall, L: 162 cm, W: 72 cm
Sleeves, L: 38 cm, W: 38 cm
USNM ECC 77017
Ref.: HKC p. 458; BFN 109

Sesame oil makes this paper garment waterproof.
The coat resembles a man's outerrobe, except the
front closure is by means of a cotton loop and the
button is in the shape of a lotus flower bud.

Hough mentions that the straw raincoat is used by
the Chinese and the Japanese as well as the Koreans,
adding that men of the serving class wear the straw
coat.

BFN 109 "... Of oiled paper. You-Sam [*yusam*] or
rain coat. Made at Song-do. Such are in common
use in Seoul; in the country they are often replaced
by the rough garments of straw of which there is a
specimen in the Japanese collection [referring probably to the straw rain coat, *mino* 蓑, made of layers
of wide strands of straw, brought by Commodore
Perry from Japan (Houchins, 1995: 105)] in the
U.S. National Museum."

Collected in Songdo (modern Kaesong, Kyeonggi
province)

77 RAIN CLOGS

(*NAMAK-SIN* 나막신)
Choson Period (1392–1910), late 19th century
Wood
L: 28 cm
USNM ECC 77015
Ref.: HKC pl. XX, upper fig. 1; BFN 108

This is a pair of boat-shaped clogs carved from solid
blocks of wood.

Hough calls the clogs "short supports," which "raise
the foot about four inches from the ground." He
compares the Korean *namak-sin* with Japanese footwear called *geta*, which are not used as rain clogs.

BFN 108 "... Mok-sin, or wooden shoes. Worn by
the common people in rainy or wet weather."

Collected in Seoul

77

78 MAN'S UNDERSHIRT
(*DEUNG-DEUNGGEORI* 등등거리)
Choson Period (1392–1910), late 19th century
Rattan
L: 43.4 cm, W: 33.1 cm
USNM ECC 77028
Ref.: HKC p. 458; BFN 151

This sleeveless undershirt is made of openwork-coiled rattan in three panels. The largest panel covers the back, and two split pieces cover the chest (*HMM*, 1975: illustration number 177). The vest is worn under the usual summer cloth to give a cooling effect and, at the same time, to protect fabrics from perspiration.

This example is now missing from the collection.

Collected in Seoul

79 MAN'S WRIST CUFFS
(*DEUNG-TOSI* 등토시)
Choson Period (1392–1910), late 19th century
Rattan
L: 9.6 cm, W: 5.8 cm
USNM ECC 77004
Ref.: HKC p. 458; BFN 132

Rattan cuffs are worn under a jacket with wide sleeves which taper toward the wrist. The diameter of the back end is larger than that of the front (*HMM*, 1975: illustration number 178). The cuffs are worn as a shield from perspiration and to cool. This pair collected by Bernadou has not been located.

Rattan sweat cuffs are worn exclusively by men of the upper class.

Collected in Seoul

80 PAIR OF MAN'S SANDALS
(*METURI* 메투리)
Choson Period (1392–1910), late 19th century
Woven hemp
L: 25.5 cm, W: 8 cm
USNM ECC 77011
Ref.: HKC pl. XX, middle fig. 2; BFN 92

These are woven hemp-cord sandals. Woven hemp-cords are used for the sole, the open toe uppers, covering only the sides of the foot in the front. A single strand of the woven cord forms the heel yoke, which fits over the back of the heel.

Hough's entry for these sandals reads: "Travelers' Sandals." They probably look sturdier than those made of rice straw (cat. no. 81). His rendering of the Korean term, "chip-seki [*jipsegi*]" also is curious. *Jipsegi* 짚세기 is the vulgate of *jipsin* 짚신 (rice straw sandals). Hough considers these hemp-cord sandals as farmers' sandals. In addition to hemp-cord and rice straw, other materials are used for sandals. For instance, *wanggol* 왕골, a type of plant belonging to the sedge (*Cyperaceae*) family, sandals are worn by upper-class men as summer footwear.

BFN 92 "Mei-t'ouri [*meturi*] A better grade, such as are worn by house servants of nobles and the middle classes in the country."

Collected in Seoul

81 MAN'S SANDAL
(*JIPSIN* 짚신)
Choson Period (1392–1910), late 19th century
Twisted rice straw
L: 26.8 cm
USNM ECC 77013
Ref.: HKC pl. XX, middle fig. 4; BFN 91

As Hough notes, footwear of rice straw are "between a shoe and sandal." Twisted strands cover the sides of the foot in the front. A single twisted strand fits over the heel. These coarsely made rice-straw sandals are worn by lower-class commoners such as farmers and laborers. Unfortunately, this pair in the Bernadou Collection is missing.

Bernadou describes, "... Straw shoes. Worn by coolies and people of the lower class. No attempt is made at repairing them; they can be bought for a few cash and as fast as one pair is worn out, another is bought. Coreans say that in average good weather, they will last about thirty English miles" (BFN 91).

Collected in Seoul

80

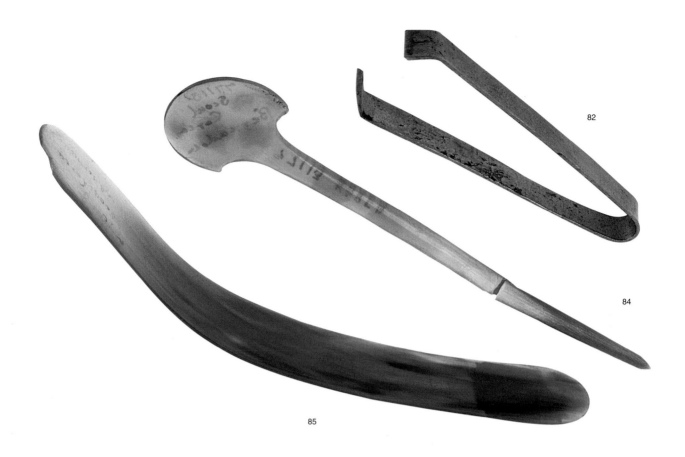

82
84
85

82 Tweezers
(*JJOKJIPGAE* 쪽집개)
Choson Period (1392–1910), late 19th century
Brass
L: 10.2 cm
USNM ECC 77051
Ref.: HKC p. 459; BFN 98

Hough describes these tweezers as a rudely bent brass strip and adds that they are carried in an accessory bag. Men wore the pouch on the trouser belt (Kim, 1988b: 443). It held valuables, tobacco and other items. Women also used accessory bags for toiletries and small personal items.

Collected in Seoul

83 Pocket Mirror
(*JUMEONI GEOUL* 주머니거울)
Choson Period (1392–1910), late 19th century
Glass in red-stained wood frame
L: 6.4 cm, W: 6.4 cm
USNM ECC 77049
Ref.: HKC p. 459; BFN 97

This mirror was set in a square, red-stained wood frame with a pivot lid (Seok, 1992a: 262; Jang, 1999: 157, 180).
It is now missing from the collection.

BFN 97 "Kyol [*geoul*] Small looking-glass, one of the toilet articles usually carried by every Korean man and boy."

Collected in Seoul

84 Comb Cleaner and Hair Parter
(*BITCHIGAE* 빗치개)
Choson Period (1392–1910), late 19th century
Horn
L: 10.2 cm
USNM ECC 77115
Ref. HKC p. 459; BFN 102

This thin strip of horn has a shield-shaped end and pointed tip.

The pointed end may be used to clean the teeth of a comb; it may be used by a woman to part the hair in a straight line down the center of the head; or the flat shield-like end can apply oil to the head.

Collected in Seoul

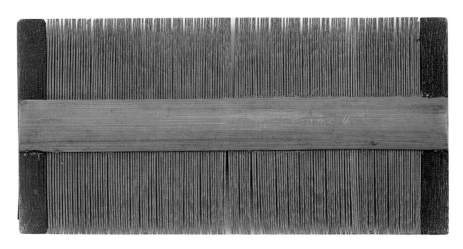

85 MAN'S HAIR TUCKER
(*SALJJEOK-MIRI* 살쩍미리)
Choson Period (1392–1910), late 19th century
Horn
L: 11.1 cm, W: 3.8 cm
USNM ECC 77048
Ref.: HKC p. 459; BFN 111

This instrument pushes hair on a man's forehead or temple up and under the horsehair cap known as *manggeon* 網巾 (cat. no. 85).

BFN 111 "...Kou-mirikei [*saljjeok-miri*] for pushing the hair back under the manggon or horsehair headband. Of horn."

Collected in Seoul

86 MAN'S COARSE COMB
(*EOLLEBIT* 얼레빗)
Choson Period (1392–1910), late 19th century
Wood
L: 9.6 cm, W: 5.8 cm
USNM ECC 77044
Ref.: HKC p. 459; BFN 23

This coarse wooden comb has thick teeth for untangling hair.

BFN 23 "... O-om-pit or coarse comb. Made from wood coming from the island of tjei-tjou [*Jeju* (formerly *Cheju*)] or Quelpart. The manufacture of combs from this wood is carried on in many southern provinces."

Collected in Seoul

87 MAN'S FINE-TOOTH COMB
(*CHAMBIT* 참빗)
Choson Period (1392–1910), late 19th century
Bamboo
L: 9.6 cm, W: 5.2 cm
USNM ECC 77045
Ref.: HKC p. 460; BFN 24

Here a series of thin bamboo slivers are fastened between bamboo cleats to form a double-tooth comb. Hough remarks that all classes of Koreans give "great attention to the care of the hair."

BFN 24 "... Fine comb, of bamboo. The best come from the province of Cholla-do in the south. There is a great trade in these combs in Korea and every man and boy carries both a coarse and a fine one in a small bag secured at the waist by a cord, and which serves as a pocket."

Collected in Seoul

88

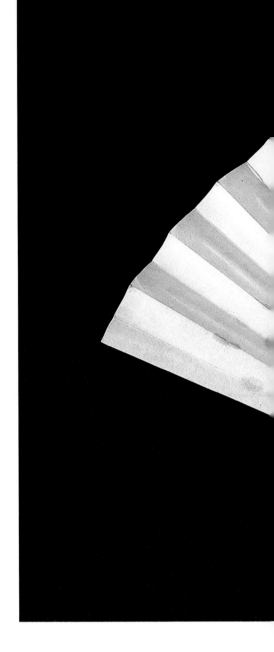

89

88 Bead for Hair Ribbon

(*DAECHU SEOGUNGHWANG* 대추석웅황;
DAENGI KKOTCHI 댕기꽃이)
Choson Period (1392–1910), late 19th century
Red clay
L: 7 cm, W: 4.1 cm
USNM ECC 77050
Ref.: HKC p. 461; BFN 65

This hair ornament is shaped in the form of a date and painted red. It was worn on a black silk ribbon for the queue worn by Korean boys before coming of age. It could adorn women's hair ribbons as well.

The queue was worn until the initiation ceremony took place or until one was betrothed. Therefore, the age range for wearing the queue was roughly until 15–20 years of age (Yang and Im, 1974: 204).

BFN 65 "Red-stone ornament. The Coreans admire these greatly, and small ones such as the specimen are worn in the hair as ornaments by the women; or rather on the black ribbons hanging at the back of the winter cap."

Collected in Seoul

89 Pocket Knife

(*JUMEONI KAL* 주머니칼)
Choson Period (1392–1910), late 19th century
Iron blade with wood handle and with engraved brass end clips
L: 15.3 cm (when opened)
USNM ECC 77043
Ref.: HKC p. 461; BFN 110

The knife here has a wood handle and one soft iron blade. The handle has brass clips ornamented with an engraved dragonhead. The knife has no spring. The curved blade end has a nail depression. It is a multipurpose knife, which a man might carry in his pouch or pocket.

Collected in Seoul

90 FOLDING FAN
(*SEONJA* 선자 扇子; *BUCHAE* 부채)
Choson Period (1392–1910), late 19th century
Bamboo sticks covered with oiled mulberry paper
L: 25.5 cm, W: 43.5 cm (when unfolded)
USNM ECC 77020
Ref.: HKC p. 462; BFN 55

White, oiled mulberry paper is pasted to the front sides of twenty-seven flat bamboo ribs (*sal* 살), which are fastened with a steel rivet at the bases. The number of sections or bamboo ribs used for fans vary; in China, folding fans for men have sixteen or twenty sections or at most twenty-four, while women's fans never have less than thirty (Eberhard, 1986: 99). Eberhard claims that "the folding fan appears to have been invented in Korea, does not appear in China till the tenth century AD" (ibid.).

BFN 55 "Large fan, such as used by servants in fanning a nobleman. Of oiled paper and with sticks of bamboo. Made in the southern provinces of Cholla-do and Kyong-sang-do."

Collected in Seoul

91 ROUND FAN WITH YIN-YANG SYMBOLS
(*TAEGEUK-SEON* 태극선 太極扇)
Choson Period (1392–1910), late 19th century
Bamboo frame covered with oiled and varnished paper and with black-lacquered wood handle.
L: 33.1 cm
USNM ECC 77021
Ref.: HKC p. 462; BFN 53

This round, rigid fan is of varnished and oiled paper which covers both the front and back of a frame. The frame is of fine splinters of bamboo linked with fine thread and fits into a black lacquered wood handle. Both front and back of this fan face are decorated with a pair of black (*yin*) and red (*yang*) symbols coiled in a circle.

Taegeuk, or the so-called yin-yang design, represent the essence of the positive and negative, and appear exclusively on fans for women (Ha and Cheon, 1994: 138–140, illustration numbers 214 and 220). Hough remarks that the *taegeuk* fan is "carried by the better class of Korean women." Unfortunately, this example was not located in a recent inventory.

BFN 53 "Fan of the kind called ter-eul-son [*taegeuk-seon*]. Made at Kyong-sang-do, at the town of Tai-Kou [*Daegu* (formerly *Taegu*)], also in parts of Chollado. Frame of bamboo covered with dyed and varnished oiled paper. Design is that of the centre of the Korean flag. Of a kind in common use among Korean women of the better class."

Collected in Seoul

92 Comb Wrapper

(*BITJEOP* 빗접)
Choson Period (1392–1910), late 19th century
Oiled and stencil-decorated paper
L: 117.5 cm, W: 136.5 cm (when opened)
USNM ECC 153612
Ref.: HKC p. 462

This is a folded, square piece of oiled paper used by women for storing combs and other implements and for use while combing hair. Here the top fold is decorated with four white stenciled ideographs, one in each of the four corners, and each one within a circle. Read together the message says:

subok gangnyeong 壽福康寧 [May you be blessed with peace, health, and long life]. An ideographic design

known as *ssang-hui* 囍 or double-joy, is stenciled within a roundel in the center. The reverse also is decorated with a pair of white stenciled cranes facing each other in flight, within a large circle in the center, on a geometric ground. When unfolded, this becomes a rectangular mat. Several pocket-like folds are designed to hold combs and *bitchige* 빗치게 [hair parting implement] (Seok, 1992a: 73; for illustration, ibid., p. 262). When laid flat, it can also serve to catch falling strands as a woman combs her hair.

Hough's entry for this item says, "Woman's mat," and "the purpose of the mat is to catch the hair."

Collected in Seoul

93 Pair of Rank Badges for Civil Official

(*HYUNGBAE* 흉배 胸背)
Choson Period (1392–1910), late 19th century
Embroidered blue silk
L: 25 cm, W: 24 cm
USNM ECC 77030
Ref.: HKC pp. 482–483; BFN 18

The square patches here are embroidered in yellow-green and reddish-brown on dark blue silk. They are called *hyungbae*, literally "chest and back." The design is a typical single-crane insignia, *danhak hyungbae* 單鶴胸背 (for illustrations, see Seok, 1979: 59–76), of a white crane flying with its wings spread wide. It holds *pulloch'o* 不老草, immortal fungus, in its beak. Believed to be a mythical creature that lives for 1,600 years, the crane is an important motif in Korean art. The scene shows other auspicious symbols: clouds, water, waves, rocks, and a *svastika*. The *svastika* is a Hindu symbol (from *svasti*, "welfare" in Sanskrit), but here it symbolizes secular happiness, especially the

yellow *svastika*, as here, meaning unending prosperity (Yun, 1997: 318). These rank patches were sewn onto the formal robe of government officials, one on the chest and one on the back. The formal uniforms of court officials, worn at work, consist of *samo* 紗帽, official hat (cat. no. 66), *dannyeong* 團領, official robe, *hyungbae* insignia, *dae* 帶, belt, and *mokhwa* 木靴, boot-like black shoes (Kim, 1988b: 57; 198, for types of *mokhwa*).

Hough finds the embroidery well done. "The stitch is mainly plain embroidery, or plumage stitch, but some Kensington and stem stitch is used." He finds the overlapping circles at the base of the square, representing waves, are "often seen at the bases of Japanese and Korean vases and on money typical of circulation." During the Choson period, almost every element of one's official attire represented his status. Imported from Ming Dynasty China (Seok, 1979: 134), *hyungbae* were embroidered on high quality silk called *sara neungdan* 紗羅綾緞, which was often criticized as being too luxurious. The royal family wore circular insignia called *bo* 補. The emblems accorded with rank: cranes, pheasants, wild geese, or egrets for civil officials; tigers or mythical beasts for military officials (for illustrations of a variety of insignia and assigned terminology, see Seok, 1979: 23–98). After the dress-code reform in

1871, until its abolition in 1899, only cranes were used for civil officials and tigers for military officials. Double-crane insignia, *sanghak hyungbae* 雙鶴胸背, or double-tiger insignia, *ssangho hyungbae* 雙虎胸背, designated officials of first through third ranks; single-crane insignia, *danhak hyungbae* 單鶴胸背, or single tiger insignia, *danho hyungbae* 單虎胸背, for officials of lower rank (Kim, 1988b: 563–564).

BFN 18 "Worn by nobles in court dress; one in front over the stomach, the other on the back. Officers of the literary class wear hyonug pai [*hyungbae*] embroidered in silk, the device being the white Manchurian crane. These are worn also by the nam-haing [*namhaeng* 南行], or men selected for office by the king and who enter without examination. Military officers wear instead of the crane the tiger. When the officer is of certain higher grades, those entitling him to wear a button of gold or jade on the headband, behind each ear, there are two cranes or tigers on the hyonug pai [*hyungbae*]; otherwise there is but one. There is no series of devices as with the Chinese."

Collected in Seoul

94 HAT ORNAMENT FOR MILITARY OFFICER OR ROYAL GUARD

(*GONGJAK-U* 공작우 孔雀羽)
Choson Period (1392–1910), late 19th century
Peacock feather
L: 27.8 cm
USNM ECC 77036
Ref.: HKC p. 483; BFN 112

Here peacock plumes are arranged in the shape of a fan and inserted into a lead swivel button. The plumes are meant to be attached to the top of a *jeollip* 戰笠, military hat (cat. no. 72).

The peacock feather is a sign of official rank or promotion in Korea and China, as it symbolizes dignity and beauty (Eberhard, 1986: 229).

BFN 112 "...Peacock's feather ornament. Worn by military officers and by soldiers of certain guards near the King."

Collected in Seoul

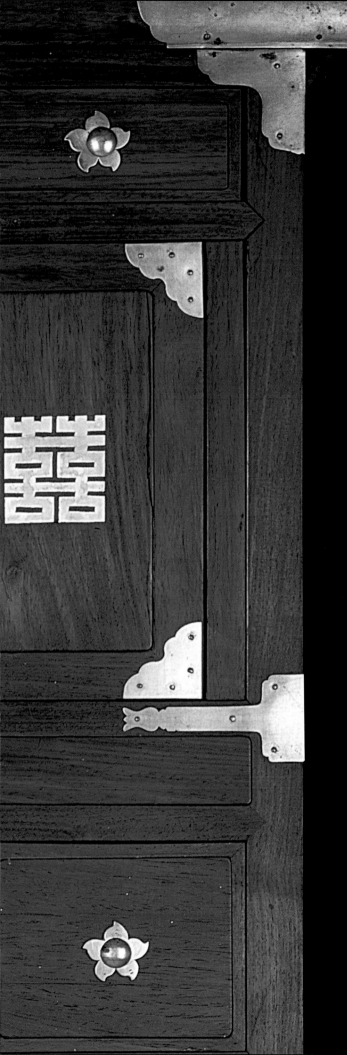

96 (top section, interior view)

95 STATIONERY CHEST
(*MUNGAP* 문갑)
Choson Period (1392–1910), late 19th century
Persimmon and pine wood with engraved brass
fittings
H: 58.6 cm, L: 86 cm, W: 34.3 cm
USNM ECC 77009
Ref.: HKC pl. XIV; BFN 116

Hough and Bernadou catalogue this as a chest with
drawers and one double-door front panel. It also has
open shelves. The chest's metal fittings are in bat,
prunus, and lozenge designs. A stationery chest,
such as this one, is used for storing paper, brushes,
ink sticks, inkstones, and other writing-related
materials. Regrettably, additional details cannot be
provided as the chest was "condemned. Trans[ferred]
to Procurement Division. Treasury Dept. 5/23/41,"
according to a handwritten note on the original
catalog card.

Mungap were used by the Choson period literati,
but by women as well. Women's stationery chests
are usually smaller and made in pairs. Choices of
wood and decorations for them differ from the ones
used in men's studies (Kim, 1996: 29).

BFN 116 "... The conventional bat, common in
Korean design, is here shown. A fair specimen of
Korean cabinet work."

Collected in Seoul

96 THREE-TIERED STORAGE CHEST
(*SAMCHEUNG-JANG* 삼층장)
Choson Period (1392–1910), late 19th century
Chinese juniper wood with white-brass fittings
and Chinese-character appliqués
H: 112 cm, L: 61.2 cm, W: 76.5 cm
USNM ECC 77008
Ref.: HKC pl. XV; BFN 115

This three-tiered chest is for storing cloth. It is of
Chinese juniper and the metal fittings are in white
brass known in Korean as *baekdong* 白銅. The center
of each front panel is decorated with a Chinese
character commonly known as *ssang-hui* 囍 (double
joy) of silver inlaid in copper. Fitted behind the
front panels are either drawers or open shelves.

Hough identifies this piece as a cabinet and gives
the Korean term, *meoritjang* 머릿장, which literally
means, bedside chest, placed near the head of the
bed, which is smaller in size and is not tiered.
Hough and Bernadou call the border design on the
locks Grecian, but it is the meander design called
hoe-munui 회무늬 or *hoemun* 回紋. This pattern
bears a strong resemblance to the Chinese ideograph
hoe 回, meaning "to return," therefore, the meander
design symbolizes "rebirth" or "eternity" (Im, 1986:
57; Eberhard, 1986: 183).

BFN 115 "... Of Chinese wood (Chinese juniper),
but made in Korea and is of Korean workmanship
and design. The cover ornaments and hinges are of
Chinese white metal; those in the centre of the front
panels are of silver inlaid in copper. The design of
the latter is a Chinese character signifying long life.
This is the best specimen of Korean work that I
have seen or heard of. The locks are curious, the
Grecian pattern as shown around their edges is a
common ornamental device in Korea."

Collected in Seoul

99

97 Tobacco Pipe

(*DAMBAETTAE* 담뱃대; *JANGJUK* 장죽 長竹)
Choson Period (1392–1910), late 19th century
Bamboo shaft and white metal bowl and
mouthpiece
L: 30 cm
USNM ECC 77041
Ref.: HKC p. 463; BFN 100

This is a long, straight bamboo tobacco pipe with a
white metal pipe bowl and mouthpiece.
Tobacco was introduced to Korea from Japan in the
early 17th century (Yi, 1962, vol. 1: 373). The
smoking pipe with gold, jade, agate or another
gemstone mouthpiece was fashionable among
upper-class men (Kim 1992: 215). Hough makes
reference to an interesting comment by the collector
William Woodville Rockhill that "time is even
reckoned by them [the Koreans] by the number of
pipes smoked. Thus you will hear them say 'han tae
man moku torawatta;' he only stopped long enough
to smoke one pipe" (Rockhill, 1891: 183).

BFN 100 "Pipe and mouthpiece of Chinese white
metal. There is a considerable trade in this alloy
with China, as it is not made in Korea and as most
Korean pipes are made of it. The shape of this specimen is characteristic; as there is very little difference
in this respect in any Korean pipes." The alloy to
which Bernadou refers is a mixture of copper, zinc
and nickel.

Collected in Seoul

98 Pipe Bowl

(*DAMBAETONG* 담배통)
Choson Period (1392–1910), late 19th century
White brass
D: 2.8 cm, H: 2 cm (pipe bowl)
USNM ECC 77040
Ref.: HKC, page 463

This is a pipe bowl of white metal, an alloy of
copper, zinc and nickel, known in Korean as
baekdong 白銅

Collected in Seoul

100

99 Tobacco Box

(*YEONCHO-HAP* 연초함; *DAMBAE-GWAK* 담배곽)
Choson Period (1392–1910), late 19th century
Iron inlaid with silver
L: 10.2 cm, W: 6.7 cm, H: 7 cm
USNM ECC 77038
Ref.: HKC pl. XXI, fig. 3; BFN 81

The four sides of this box are hollowed out, and into one side is inserted a sliding compartment. A pull handle is fitted on the sliding front panel. The side panels are decorated with longevity symbols such as a stork, tortoise, deer, and the plant called *pulloch'o* 不老草, a legendary plant believed to be an elixir of life. The top ornamentation is an ideograph known as *ssang-hui* 囍 or double-joy. Meander inlay covers the sides and top of the box.

Hough provides a description of the technique of iron inlay used here. "[It] is to hack the surface of the iron, lay on the wire design and fasten with pressure and hammering." He adds, "The Korean silver inlaying [*eunipsa* 銀入絲 or *eunsanggam* 銀象嵌] is excellent and well known art work."

BFN 81 "Silver inlaid box for tobacco Tampai-ho-rap [*dambae seorap* 담배서랍]. Ornamental work of this kind is made in the N.W. province of Pyong-an-do, whence come decorated pipes firebowls and boxes. There is quite a trade in these articles. The work varies greatly in quality. Similar but very much better done work is now to be found in Japan. The ancestors of the present Japanese artisans were brought by the Japanese from Korea, after the invasion, about three hundred years ago [invasions of 1592 and 1597, see also cat. no. 144]."

Collected in Seoul

100 Tobacco box

(*YEONCHO-HAP* 연초함; *DAMBAE-GWAK* 담배곽)
Choson Period (1392–1910), late 19th century
Iron inlaid with copper
H: 7.7 cm, D: 10.2 cm
USNM ECC 77039
Ref.: HKC pl. XXI, fig. 5; BFN 82

This is a lidded circular iron tobacco box with copper inlay.

Hough explains the inlay technique: "The iron is first made rough by filing or hacking and the wire [filature] design laid on and burnished down." The surface is burnished and polished. The lid here is decorated with a Chinese character that reads *su* 壽 (long life). The sides are inlaid with felicitous chrysanthemums, birds, and insects.

Metal tobacco boxes decorated with silver or copper filature inlay design are customarily "used by a government official or upper class scholar to store cut tobacco" (Adams, 1987: 27). Tobacco boxes are rectangular, circular or hexagonal.

Collected in Seoul

101 BLIND

(*MUNBAL* 문발)
Choson Period (1392–1910), late 19th century
Bamboo and green cotton with black-lacquered rollers
L: 120.1 cm, W: 142.8 cm
USNM ECC 77053
Ref.: HKC p. 443; BFN 50

Although the shade has not been located, Hough and Bernadou describe plain and colored bamboo splints joined closely at intervals with a warp of green cotton twine. Black lacquered bamboo rods secure the top, middle, and bottom so that one can roll the shade up and down. The shade has geometric ornamentation surrounded by a meander design called *hoe-munui* 회무늬 (for symbolism, see cat. no. 96).

Hough finds this article of particularly superior quality. According to him, the bamboo splints are first boiled to make them soft prior to weaving. Bernadou thought the shade was for a window; it is more likely to be a door screen or shade.

BFN 50 "Window screen paal of split bamboo. The Coreans are very skilful in the manufacture of articles of bamboo, as is shown in their hats and such screens as this specimen. Made in the southern province of Chollado [Jeollado] where bamboo is abundant. The "Grecian pattern" on the border is noticeable as a departure from the usual conventional decoration designs of far eastern countries."

Collected in Jeolla province

102 SUMMER FLOOR MAT

(*WANGGOL DOTJARI* 왕골돗자리
WANCHOSEOK 완초석 莞草席)
Choson Period (1392–1910), late 19th century
Woven arrowroot-rush and hemp
L: 183.2 cm, W: 61.2 cm
USNM ECC 77010
Ref.: HKC p. 443

This mat is decorated with green, purple, and red stripes, and the side of the mat is fringed. The sedge mat is used for covering floors in summer.

Hough's entry reads: "Rush Mat. Made by hand on a weighted loom" with hemp warp and rush woof, which form the fringe at the side of the mat. *Wanggol* is a type of material woven from sedge and string, which is made of the dried inner bark of arrowroot (Ha and Cheon, 1994: 135).

Collected in Seoul

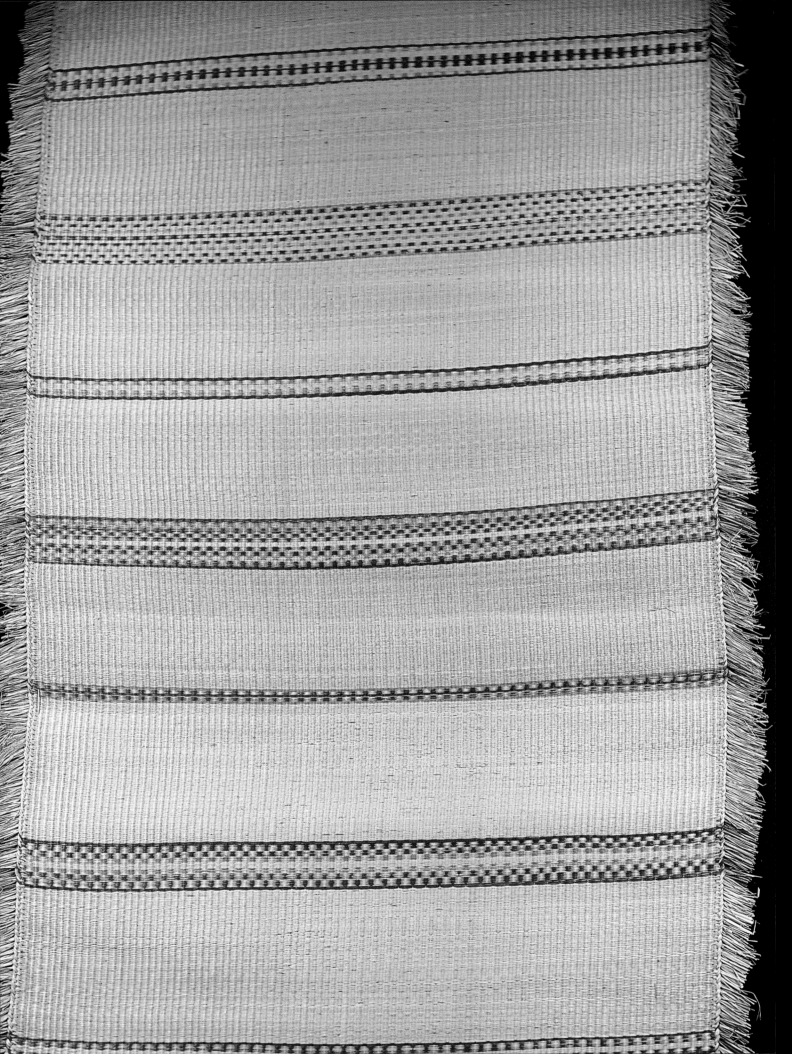

**103 COOKING POT AND BRAZIER
ON STAND**
(*GOPDOL SINSEOLLO* 곱돌신선로)
Choson Period (1392–1910), late 19th century
Polished and blackened green soapstone
H: 19.0 cm, D: 22.5 cm
USNM ECC 77054
Ref.: HKC pl. XVI, fig. 2; BFN 86

This cooking vessel has a detachable base. The
cooking bowl surrounds the conical furnace and a
lugged cover fits tightly around the furnace chim-
ney. The base or firebox is open to maintain draft.

Sinseollo literally means a cooking pot for Taoist
immortals, and is used as a chafing dish in which
meat, poultry, fish, and fancy varieties of vegetables
are cooked in seasoned broth. Hough states that the
vessel "is commonly used for frying meat when
several friends assemble and cook this portion of
their food according to a Korean custom."

Sinseollo is not just for cooking meat, and it is not
always communal cookware. Hough points out a
Chinese prototype used for brewing herb drinks,
cooking soup or stew, and finds the Korean version
primitive.

BFN 86 "... Pot of a certain stone called 곱돌, a soft
material found in many parts of Korea; in Cho-la-do,
in Kang-ouen-do, and in Ham-kyong-do. The stone
is worked up into many shapes, such as pots for
boiling rice which are esteemed as they do not dis-
color or affect the rice in any way; into dishes, and
into more complicated pieces such as this specimen.
Here the food is heated in the ring shaped dish by
hot coals placed in the furnace in the center. Such a
vessel is commonly used for frying meat when several
friends assemble and cook this portion of their food
according to a Korean custom. Such vessels of stone
are quite common, though valued very much more
than similar ones of clay or pottery."

Collected in Seoul

104 PAIR OF SQUARE CHOPSTICKS AND SPOON
(*JEOTGARAK GWA SUTGARAK* 젓가락과 숫가락)
Choson Period (1392–1910), late 19th century
White brass
Chopsticks L: 20.4 cm, Spoon L: 22.9 cm
USNM ECC 77042
Ref.: HKC p. 444; BFN 20

One uses chopsticks to pick up dry food and spoons for rice, stew-like dishes and soup. The Korean spoon has an oval and shallow receptacle with a long narrow handle, unlike that of Chinese or western versions. The size and material of chopsticks and spoons vary according to the user's sex, status and age.

Hough's description adds that the spoon and chopsticks are made of white brass, *baekdong* 白銅, and used by the poor. His Korean consultants must have informed him that the wealthy use silver spoons and chopsticks. Another term, considered more refined, for spoon and chopsticks is *sujeo* 수저.

BFN 20 "Spoon and chopsticks of brass. These are of the pattern in common use. The spoon is used only for rice [also for soup and dishes with broth]; the other food being picked up with chopsticks and prepared in such a manner as not to necessitate the use of a knife. In the use of the spoon the Koreans differ from the Chinese."

Collected in Seoul

105 BOWL AND COVER
(*JUBAL* 주발 周鉢)
Choson Period (1392–1910), late 19th century
White brass
H: 11.2 cm, D: 13.8 cm
USNM ECC 77037
Ref.: HKC p. 444; BFN 7

Jubal means rice bowl for serving rice to men. Its size is larger than *bari* 바리 for women. This bowl is made of white brass, *baekdong* 白銅, and is for use in winter.

Hough and Bernadou remark that the white metal alloy comes from China but that the products are native to Korea.

BFN 7 "Sapal [*jubal*] a rice bowl of brass. These bowls are in common use, and are made in quantities at and around Soul [Seoul]; also at many other places. They are made both by hammering and casting the former being the most esteemed. The white metal [*baekdong*] used in making the alloy comes from China; the copper is generally Korean."

Collected in Seoul

106 SEAM IRON FOR CLOTHING
(*INDU* 인두)
Choson Period (1392–1910), late 19th
century
Iron and wood
L: 32.5 cm
USNM ECC 77026
Ref.: HKC pl. XVII, fig. 1; BFN 95

This flatiron has a boat-shaped head and angular
iron bar set into a wooden handle. The head has a
smooth underside. A rude chiseled ornamentation
is on the bar.

There are two kinds of seam irons: one is used for
everyday sewing to press down seams and the other
is used for quilting fabrics for winter clothing. The
seam iron is used to help line up separate pieces of
fabric (Kim, 1988b: 399). Hough states that one
kind of seam iron is capable of the two different
functions and likens the Korean seam iron to a
soldering iron.

BFN 95 "In-to [*indu*] Iron used for ironing seams
after sewing. Pieces of clothing are commonly taken
apart upon washing and resewed afterwards."

Collected in Seoul

107 PAIR OF STICKS FOR FULLING CLOTH
(*BANGMANGI* 방망이; *BANGMAENGI* 방맹이)
Choson Period (1392–1910), late 19th century
Wood
L: 41.7 cm, D: 2.6 cm
USNM ECC 77027
Ref.: HKC pl. XVII, fig. 2; BFN 96

This pair of hardwood sticks has rounded middle
sections and squared front and back ends. The
diameter of the back end of the stick is smaller in
size, functioning as a handle.

Hough closely follows Bernadou's description and
use of the specimen. However, he adds that the
winter garments are ripped apart before washing
and the "parts are sewed together and the seams
ironed down with the seam iron." His additional
information regarding winter garments is presumably from one of his Korean consultants. The caption for plate number XVII, illustrating the seam
iron and fulling sticks, reads: "Korean Domestic
Appliances."

BFN 96 "... Used in ironing. Korean clothes-wash-
ing is done by first boiling the articles in a weak lye
obtained by lixiviating wood ashes. They are then
thoroughly washed in fresh running water, and
pounded with a wooden club [*ppallae bangmangi*
빨래방망이] to remove the dirt. Finally they are
wrung out, dipped in a starch prepared from rice
and roughdried. They are then folded carefully into
small square piles, laid upon a heavy wooden roller
[*hongdukkae* 홍두깨 or upon a fulling stone called
dadeumitdol 다듬잇돌] and beaten for a long time
with two short wooden sticks, like the specimen.
This softens the pile and gives the fabric a remarkable gloss. The noise made by this work is to be heard
at all times when walking in the streets of Soul
[Seoul] and is one of the first subjects of remark of
strangers."

Collected in Seoul

108 BASKET
(*CHAERONG* 채롱; *CHAENONG* 채농)
Choson Period (1392–1910), late 19th century
Wicker
H: 22.9 cm, L: 57.7 cm, W: 28 cm
Ref.: HKC p. 447

The oblong-lidded wicker basket here is of oiled
paper in two sections. The larger is used as a lid. It
has not been located but Hough writes it was "used
for holding the laundry, etc."

The term *chaerong* or a variant pronunciation,
chaenong, means box-shaped wicker basket (Martin,
Yi, and Jang, 1967: 1578; Nam, 1987: 64).

Collected in Seoul

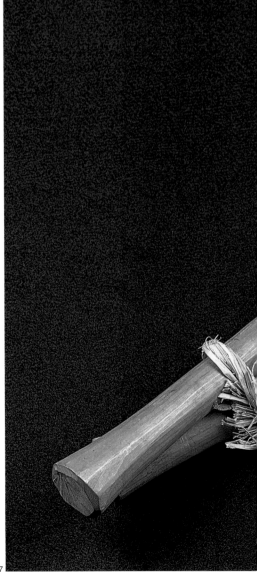

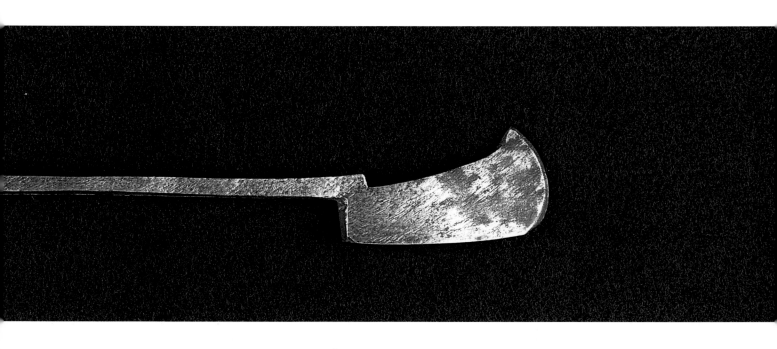

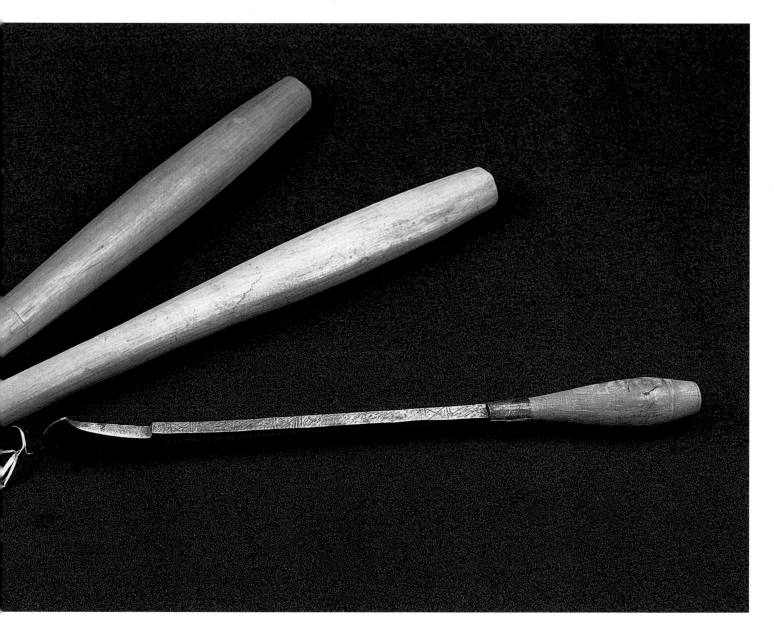

109

110

109 Pillow End-Plaque

(*BEGAENMO* 베갯모)
Choson Period (1392–1910), late 19th century
Reverse-painted oxhorn roundel mounted on wood
D: 15.3 cm
USNM ECC 77035
Ref.: HKC pl. XXII, fig. 1; Published (*MBM*, 1989: 142)

The Korean pillow is made of a cylindrical case stuffed with buckwheat husks or millet, which requires plaques to be fastened to both ends of the pillow. Wooden pillow-ends have holes bored around the edges so that they can be sewn to the pillow. Elaborate design motifs used for pillow end plaques are based on "three main themes, which are long life, good luck, and protection against misfortune" (Strom, 1973: 29). The evergreen pine here symbolizes long life, while the tiger represents amuletic power to guard against misfortune. The materials used for pillow-ends, size and method of decoration vary.

Collected in Seoul

110 Pillow End-Plaque

(*BEGAENMO* 베갯모)
Choson Period (1392–1910), late 19th century
Black-lacquered wood inlaid with mother-of-pearl
D: 20.4 cm
USNM ECC 77032
Ref.: HKC pl. XXII, fig. 3; Exhibited "Korean Heritage at the Smithsonian," 16 April–31 May 1988

This circular pillow plaque is of black-lacquered wood inlaid with a dragon in mother-of-pearl. The scattered dots below the figure of the dragon represent the sea and the rows of horizontal bars the sky. Hough describes "the great dragon rising from the sea into the sky." Another way of interpreting the dotted space below the dragon is that it is the earth, and it is therefore a scene of the great dragon rising into the sky representing spring (Eberhard,1986: 83). Hough also views the scene as suggestive of spring and adds, "In pure art the whole body of the dragon is not shown, but partly shrouded in clouds."

Collected in Seoul

111 Pillow End-Plaque

(*BEGAENMO* 베갯모)
Choson Period (1392–1910), late 19th century
Black-lacquered wood inlaid with mother-of-pearl
D: 17.8 cm
USNM ECC 77033
Ref.: HKC pl. XXII fig. 4; BFN 3

Another black-lacquered wood pillow plaque is inlaid in mother-of-pearl with a stylized ideograph reading: *su* 壽, "long life." Numerous graphic as well as ideographic stylizations are used as design motifs and decorative patterns (Im 1986: 77–85 for illustrations).

BFN 3 "Disk at end of Korean pillow. Device a Chinese character inlaid, in mother o'pearl. These disks form the ends of cylindrical hair stuffed pillows in common use. The inlaid work is from the southern province of Kyong-sangdo and Cholla-do, where are situated the pearl fisheries."

Collected in Seoul

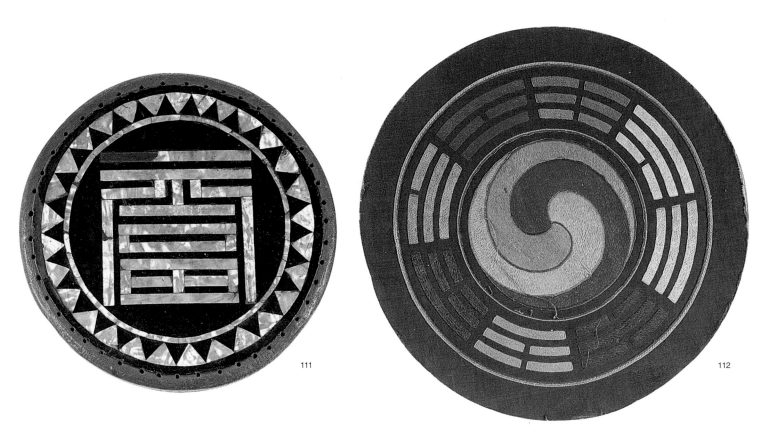

111

112

112 PILLOW END-PLAQUE

(*BEGAENMO* 베갯모)

Choson Period (1392–1910), late 19th century
Embroidered blue silk backed with paper
D: 11.3 cm
USNM ECC 77034
Ref.: HKC pl. XXII, fig. 5; BFN 4

Unlike the three wooden pillow end-plaques decorated with painted ox horn and mother-of-pearl inlay (cat. nos. 109, 110, 111), this fabric plaque is backed with paper. It is embroidered with the *taegeuk* 太極 or yin-yang (the ultimate, the universe, origin of all things). *Taegeuk* is customarily two comma-shaped patterns coiled in a circle, but here, three instead of two, are arranged in a circle. An eighth-century example found in the *Gameunsa* 感恩寺 temple also uses three (Im, 1986: 68). The Japanese call this pattern *mitsu-tomoe* 三つ巴繪, a dynamic design pattern used as a heraldic device, or for various other decorative and talismanic purposes (Dower 1971: 145–146).

Embroidered pillow-end sizes and shapes vary greatly, though they are predominantly round. The diameters of the round shape range from 11.3 cm to 6.3 cm; the smallest is known as child size. The octagonal pillow end is called *palgak-chim* 팔각침, square *gubong-chim* 구봉침, and rectangular *toe-chim* 퇴침 (Yi 1973: 112). Embroidery patterns for pillow-ends from North Jeolla province are well known and widely copied. Thirty-six patterns are illustrated in an article titled "*Sunchang byeogae subon* 淳昌벼개繡本" (see ibid: 110–113 for woodblock print illustrations). Hough calls the yin-yang symbol "Chinese tai-ki [*tai-ji*], three." His description includes *palgwae*, the eight trigrams for divination grouped around the circle, "the eight geometric signs."

BFN 4 "Pillow end. Embroidered pattern."

Collected in Seoul

WRITING PAPER and ENVELOPE.— Roll of mulberry paper in sheets; pasted at edges. Fiber, long and silky.

Sheets, 15½ inches long; 9 inches wide.

SEOUL, KOREA, 1885.   77,031.

Collected by Ensign J. B Bernadou, U. S. Navy.

Used in writing to a distant place.

Paper is made in Korea from the bark of the *tak* tree, or paper mulberry. The shoots of this tree are cut early in the fall; they are at once steamed, stripped, and the dark outer coating (used in making inferior paper) is scraped off and the strips are dried. When ready to make the paper, these strips are sprinkled with water and pounded with stones to separate the fiber. They are then boiled in weak lye and the mass afterwards steamed and washed clean in fresh water. The stems of a plant called *tak poul*, which is cultivated for the purpose, are macerated and boiled. The strained liquor is then mixed with the fiber already prepared and water added until it is of the proper consistency. From this paste paper is made by catching a film on the surface of a bamboo screen by a quick passage of this through the pulp. The successive sheets are piled up and separated at one end by straws.

113 Mulberry Bark Sheet of Paper
(*HANJI* 한지)
Choson Period (1392–1910), late 19th century
L: 111.2 cm, W: 75 cm
USNM ECC 77069
Ref.: HKC p. 440; BFN 88

This thick, unglazed sheet of paper is made from mulberry bark, customary throughout Asia. Hough characterizes it as "very tough, even with the grain tearing with great difficulty and running in wide shells." He also comments, "Korean paper is even tougher than the Japanese, and is one of the few Korean things that had made a reputation in the world before its home had become truly a part of the community of nations. [Citing Percival Lowell, 1886: 314–15] It is used in several thicknesses to make armor and was exported to Japan for that purpose, also to China, where it is now used for garment linings. Used in civil service examinations. Taken in payment of tribute by the Government and generally used as currency by the people." Both Hough and Bernadou devote detailed paragraphs to the techniques of Korean paper making. "Myŏng tch'i [possibly meaning *myeongji* 明紙, Ming-Dynasty paper, or *myeongji* 名紙 "famous" paper]. Paper from the bark of the tak-namou [*dak namu*], the tak tree or paper mulberry. The shoots of this are cut early in the fall; they are at once steamed so as to facilitate the removal of the bark. The bark is then taken off in strips, the outer coating (used for making paper of inferior quality)

is scraped off, and the strips are dried. When ready to make the paper, these strips are sprinkled with water, and pounded with stones so as to separate the fibre. They are then boiled in weak lye, and the mass is afterward strained and washed clean in fresh water." (BFN 88)

Collected in Seoul

114 Roll of Writing Paper
FOLDED LETTER PAPER AND ENVELOPE
(*GANJI* 간지; *GANJANGJI WA* 간장지 簡狀紙와 *BONGTU* 봉투)
Choson Period (1392–1910), late 19th century
Mulberry bark
L: 23.7 cm, W: 33.7 cm (paper within the envelope)
L: 23.7 cm, W: 5.4 cm (envelope)
L: 23.7 cm (roll)
USNM ECC 77031
Ref.: HKC p. 440; BFN 153; Exhibited (USNM, Smithsonian Institution [1886])

This roll of white mulberry bark paper holds a folded letter paper inside an envelope.
Ganji or *ganjangji* refers particularly to the type of paper made for use as "letter paper." Korean paper is classified by differences in: the base material used; production process; use; size and thickness; and the locality of production. For a list of paper terminology, see (Pak, 1982: 601). Jeonju in South Jeolla

Province is known for producing the best-quality letter paper (Ye, 1969: 296). Hough describes the fiber of the paper here as "long and silky," and makes the interesting statement that it is "used in writing to a distant place."
BFN 153 "Writing materials. Paper in a roll of the usual form. Torn off in lengths according to the size of the letter. Envelope of thick paper of common form for unofficial communications."

Collected in Seoul

115 Sheet of Oiled Paper
(*YUJI* 유지 油紙)
Mulberry bark applied with sesame-seed oil
L: 56 cm, W: 91.5 cm
USNM ECC 77068
Ref.: HKC p. 441; BFN 87

Korean oiled paper is made by steeping sheets of mulberry-bark paper in the oil prepared from sesame seeds.

Use of oiled paper is varied. It is mainly found as floor covering of the *ondol* 온돌, heated room. *Ondol* refers to the Korean under-floor heating system. Other uses are for making hats and coats as rain gear, including umbrellas. It also is used for fan construction.

BFN 87 "... Rain clothes are made of it; the earthen floors of a heated room are covered with it ... Made at many places, but principally at Songdo (now Kaesong, Kyeonggi province), the old capital, about forty miles from Seoul. Prepared by steeping in the oil prepared from the seeds of sesamum."

Collected in Seoul

116 OCTAGONAL BRUSH HOLDER

(*PILTONG* 필통)
Choson Period (1392–1910), late 19th century
Serpentine
H: 13.7 cm, D: 12.1 cm
USNM ECC 38329
Ref.: HKC p. 475; BFN 80

Both Bernadou and Hough have entries for this
item as "pencil jar," which is easily understandable
as average Westerners were then unfamiliar with a
writing implement such as a writing brush. Hough
calls the item an "octagonal vase of precious
serpentine" and lists inkstones and tobacco boxes
made of the prized stone. Bernadou's packing list
describes the stone as "yellow and green marble."
BFN 80 "P'il-t'ong or pencil jar. Of a green marble
called tch^ng-kang-s^k [*cheonggangseok*], found in
Ham-gy^ng-do, the NE province. This stone is
prized highly by the Koreans, who make of it a
variety of articles such as tobacco boxes, ink-stones
and pencil-jars." Unfortunately, this brush holder is
now missing from the collection.

Collected in Seoul

117 WOODBLOCK OF KOREAN SYLLABARY, ANIMALS AND ASTROLOGICAL CHARTS

(*BANJEOL-PAN* 반절판 半切版)
Choson Period (1392–1910), cyclically dated in
accordance with 1819 or 1879
Wood
H: 31 cm, W: 19.5 cm
USNM ECC 77018
Ref.: HKC pl. XXIII; BFN 5

Both ends of this printing block are wedge-shaped,
designed to fit into a holder and used for hand
printing. The major section of the block contains a
table of the Korean alphabet or, more accurately, the
Hangul syllabary 한글 carved in relief. Above this
section is a group of animal figures. Each figure
corresponds to a syllable: for instance, *gae* 개 (dog)
for the syllable *ga* 가, *nabi* 나비 (butterfly) for *na* 나,
and so on. Added to the main section are astrological charts based on a sexagesimal cycle predicting
the fate of human beings. There also is a marriage
horoscope, the so-called *gunghap* 宮合, drawn up in
accordance with astrological data to predict the
compatibility of a male and female. Another chart

117

deals with the fates of individuals born under different planetary influences. A multiplication table is
also appended. A date on the block reads: *gimyo
singan banjeol* 己卯新刊半切 (the new edition of
printing block in the year of the hare [1819 or
1879]). Hough's commentary focuses on printed
material from this printing block's use as an educational tool. He says the printed alphabet sheet is to
teach children *eonmun* 언문, meaning Hangul, non-
Chinese Korean native script. Considering a variety
of subject matter added to the printing block, more
likely it was designed to informally teach women at
home. Learning Hangul was available to those who
were denied the study of ideographs, such as women
and persons of the lower class, in order to become
literate and thus be considered learned. During the
Choson period, Hangul was used exclusively for
writing popular novels and by women for compos-
ing informal letters. Another use was for instructive
materials to be read by people less educated in the
classics. The Japanese usage of *banjeol*, written with
identical characters 半切 or *hankiri*, refers to letter
paper, which is also known as *hankiri-gami* 半切紙

(literally, paper for letter writing) (*NKDJ*, vol. 16,
1976: 508). Hough's comment on various astrological charts and other subject matter included in the
printing block is perfunctory, but his added statement quotes a passage from writings by an English
Orientalist, Sir Ernest Mason Satow (1843–1929):
"There are some Korean books dating back to 1317
and 1324, printed with movable type." Ink residue
is still visible on the block.

BFN 5 "Printing block of wood. Although movable
type are in use, yet blocks are largely used. This
specimen is of a very common block, the one used
for printing the alphabetic sheet, from which the
children learn the on-moun [*eonmun*] or native
Korean characters. The characters are arranged in
vertical columns, and above each is a rough pictorial
representation of something containing the initial
consonant sound of the characters in the column.
The writing on the left is of astrological import
containing characters corresponding to the year of
birth of which a superstitious use is made."

Collected in Seoul

VI

PAINTINGS,
WOODCUT
PRINTS, AND
DRAWINGS

118 TEN SYMBOLS OF LONG LIFE
(*SIPJANGSAENG-DO* 십장생도 十長生圖)
Choson Period (1392–1910), late 19th century
Color on paper
H: 93 cm, W: 52 cm
USNM ECC 77052: 1
Ref.: HKC p. 468; Published (Houchins, 1982:
58–60); (*MBM*, 1989: 150)

The ten longevity symbols painted here are: the sun, moon, mountain, water, turtle, deer, crane, bamboo, pine tree and an imaginary plant called *pulloch'o* 不老草. "*Pulloch'o*" means immortal grass, known to the Chinese as *lingchi* 靈芝, the sacred fungus, a symbol of immortality and longevity. This painting was popular in non-aristocratic households. Hough notes that such a painting is used for house decoration by "the lower-class Koreans." Founder of the Emille Museum in Seoul, and pioneer folk-art enthusiast Jo Ja-yong 趙子庸 (1926–1999) produced, in the early 1970s, a number of publications dealing with Korean

minhwa 民畫 (folk painting). His *The Humor of Korean Tiger, Korean Art Series, vol. 1* (1970), and *Spirit of the Korean Tiger, Korean Art Series, vol. 2* (1972), received much attention. They were followed by other publications dealing with folk paintings. Folk paintings were produced by anonymous artists of low social class, but their paintings were used by people of all social strata including the royal household. Hough mentions the "ten long lives," illustrated in the painting, are "those things in nature existing longer than human beings."

Collected in Seoul

119 PHOENIXES, PAULOWNIA, ROCK
AND SUN
(*BONGHWANG JANGSAENG-DO*
봉황장생도 鳳凰長生圖)
Choson Period (1392–1910), late 19th century
Color on paper
H: 93 cm, W: 52 cm
USNM ECC 77052: 3
Ref.: HKC p. 469; Published (Houchins 1982:
58–60); (*MBM*, 1989: 150)

The painting depicts a Korean legend about an
imaginary bird, the phoenix, and its association
with the birth of a sage or the era of peace brought
by a wise ruler (Yun, 1997: 105–111). Male and
female phoenixes are shown with their offspring
inside a rock under a paulownia tree. These
legendary birds are also symbols of immortality
(bulsajo 不死鳥, "the bird who does not die"). Other
longevity symbols represented here are: the sun,
moon, mountain, water, bamboo, rock, pine tree
and the immortal sacred fungus known as
pulloch'o 不老草.

The style of painting and placement of objects are
identical to the other painting of ten longevity
symbols (cat. no. 118).

Collected in Seoul

120 PHEASANTS AND BIRDS, PLUM AND MOON
(*SSANGCHI HWAJO-DO* 쌍치화조도 雙雉花鳥圖)
Choson Period (1392–1910), late 19th century
Color on paper
H: 92 cm, W: 52 cm
USNM ECC 77052: 4
Ref.: HKC, page 469; Published (Houchins, 1982: 60–61); (*MBM*, 1989: 150)

In addition to birds and flower blossoms, the painting includes traditional auspicious symbols such as bamboo, rocks and streams. The pair of small swallows perched on top of the plum tree is placed within the sun disk. Flowers and birds are often paired with the sun, water, and rocks.

Hwajo-do (bird-and-flower painting) were usually attached to small folding screens of eight panels in the rooms of newlyweds or women (Eom, 1994: 87).

The pheasant is a common emblem of beauty and good fortune and also of love (Williams, 1976: 322–323).

Collected in Seoul

121 FLOWERS AND AUSPICIOUS SYMBOLS
(*HWAHWE-DO* 화훼도 花卉圖)
Choson Period (1392–1910), late 19th century
Color on paper
H: 67 cm, W: 52 cm
USNM ECC 77052: 5
Ref.: HKC p. 469; (*MBM*, 1989: 150)

The vase on a stand is filled with a stylized bouquet of oversized wild roses, chrysanthemums, lotuses and two peaches. The vase is decorated with Taoist devices of change, movement, and energy (Legeza, 1987: 21–24). On the flower at the right side of the vase, there is a citron (*Citrus decumana*) or *yuja* 柚子 with numerous seeds. *Yuja*, the Korean word for this citron, is a fertility symbol due to its homonym, *yuja* 有子, having children. To the left of the vase is *pulloch'o* 不老草, fungus symbolic of eternity. This genre of painting is hung in women's quarters.

Collected in Seoul

122 Scholar's Articles
(*CH'AEKKORI* 책거리)
Choson Period (1392–1910), late 19th century
Color woodcut
H: 34.5 cm, W: 30 cm
USNM ECC 77052: 7
Ref.: HKC p. 469; Published (Houchins, 1982: 61–63); (*MBM*, 1989: 148)

A painting of books, such as this one, includes not only those objects commonly considered scholar's paraphernalia, but others imagined to be associated with scholars. Some of these items are unrelated. Here a dish of peaches (symbolic of longevity) is placed on top of the pile of books. Objects, in "bookpile" paintings, can include: teakettle, game table, fan, clock, vase, even a woman's skirt, shoes, crown of flowers worn at weddings, and a variety of plants and animals. Variants of bookpile paintings are *munbangsau-do* 文房四友圖 (paintings of scholars' four friends, namely paper, brush, inkstick, and inkstone) and *munbangu-do* 文房具圖 (painting of

stationery) (Kim, 1979b: 219; plates 160–167 for illustrations). Also pictured in this print are: coral and peacock feathers in a vase, several empty jars, and a stand for rolled stationery or *durumari* 두루마리. A bowknot, wavy lines and spirals used in amulets (*bujeok* 符籍) decorate the main objects. This small single-sheet print, unlike a painting for a screen, was used to decorate a stationery chest door, usually affixed to the inside of the door panel, or to decorate the door leading to a *darak* 다락, a loft over the kitchen used as a storage area. The door of the *darak* led into the adjoining main room.

Collected in Seoul

123 SCHOLAR'S ARTICLES

(*CH'AEKKORI* 책거리)
Choson Period (1392–1910), late 19th century
Color woodcut
H: 34.5 cm, W: 30 cm
USNM ECC 77052: 10
Ref.: HKC p. 469; Published (Houchins, 1982: 61–63)

This is one of two prints of scholars' objects (*ch'aekkori*) in the Bernadou Collection (see also cat. no. 122). Hough remarks on the inclusion of a dish of persimmons, "Korean fruit." The word *kam [gam]*, meaning persimmon, is written on the top center of the print. Hough states again that this print was to be hung on a closet door, without realizing such a print as this also decorates a stationary chest. It was not used only by common people.

Collected in Seoul

124 COCKEREL

(*MUNBAE-DO* 문배도 門排圖)
Choson Period (1392–1910), late 19th century
Color woodcut
H: 34.5 cm, W: 29 cm
USNM ECC 77052:6
Ref.: HKC p. 46 ; Exhibited, Brooklyn Museum,
"From the Land of Morning Calm: Korean Art at
the Brooklyn Museum," October 16, 1987–
January 8, 1988. Published (Jo, 1974a: 51);
(Moes, 1983: 87 and 116); (*MBM*, 1989: 148)

This rainbow-tailed rooster, standing on one leg
hung on a gate or door to safeguard a home. The
cockerel's pose suggests watchfulness to drive away
evil spirits when he crows at dawn. Stylized bamboo
leaves and pine branches serve as minor design
elements. Use of five primary colors, blue or green,
red, black, white and yellow, is the Korean
adaptation of the Chinese concept of five elements
or primary substances (water, fire, wood, metal and
earth). The numeral five is felicitous (Williams,

1976:186 and 295 for symbolism; Kim, 1979a:197
for shamanistic association), and use of the quantity
of five is common throughout East Asia. Hough
refers to this painting as one of four in the collection
of "watchful animals." He adds: "One of the four
pictures such as are found hanging on the outside of
the storeroom in the dwellings of the common
people." According to twentieth-century scholarship
on Korean folk painting, the four Bernadou
munbae-do were first introduced by the Emille
Museum in "*Geonchuk gwa hoehwa* 建築과 繪畵"
(Jo, 1974a: 49–51).

Collected in Seoul

125 Dog with Collar of Bells
(*MUNBAE-DO* 문배도 門排圖)
Choson Period (1392–1910), late 19th century
Color woodcut
H: 34.5 cm, W: 29 cm
USNM ECC 77052:9
Ref.: HKC p. 469; Published (Jo, 1974a: 51);
(*MBM*, 1989:145)

Munbae-do are talismanic paintings or prints hung on gates or doors to safeguard the home or warehouse by repulsing evil spirits or actual intruders. The bells suspended from the dog's collar, and the decorations on the bells are amuletic patterns of circles and wavy trails. (Huhm, 1980:55–59, and 64). Dog paintings have even been used in shamanistic rituals (Kim, 1979a:187). The dog here shows his watchfulness with large round eyes and a penetrating backward stare. Hough points out that this is one of a set of four *munbae-do* in the Bernadou collection (cat. nos. 1214–127).

Collected in Seoul

126 Chinese Lion
(*MUNBAE-DO* 문배도 門排圖)
Choson Period (1392–1910), late 19th century
Color woodcut
H: 34.5 cm, W: 29 cm
USNM ECC 77052:11
Ref.: HKC p. 469; Published (*MBM*, 1989:149)

The mythological Chinese lion, or *haetae* 해태, represents energy and power. This print safeguards against fire. The flames issuing from the lion's head and paws allude to the principle of sympathetic magic. The collar with bells resembles the print of a dog (cat. no. 125). In Korean shamanistic tradition, the bells are to communicate with spirits. The pattern of spirals utilized here is talismanic as well as part of the decoration. Below the lion's right foot are coral branches. Coral is a symbol of longevity in Chinese tradition (Hawley, 1971: illustration number 140 in the section under the title *The Hundred Antiques*). Hough notes this print is one of a set of four *munbae-do* in the Bernadou collection.

Collected in Seoul

127 TIGER, MAGPIE, PINE, AND
SACRED FUNGUS (*SONGHO-DO* 송호도 松虎圖)
Choson Period (1392–1910), late 19th century
Color on paper
H: 100 cm, W: 62.5 cm
USNM ECC 77052:8
Ref.: HKC p. 469; Published (Houchins, 1982:
61–63)

A large, white tiger with a long tail curling upward
to a pine branch, has fur rendered in geometric
stripes, dots and roundels. A small magpie sits on a
pine branch. Three *pulloch'o*, sacred fungus, are in
front of the tiger's mouth as if he were about to
consume them in order to attain immortality
himself. A certain element of humor can be
detected in the tiger's expression in the presence of
his adversary, the magpie. The magpie announces
the tiger's whereabouts to villagers. This is the
reason for the appearance of "tiger and magpie
painting" (Jo, 1970:8–15; ibid., 1974b:20).
Hough, in his customary manner, dismisses the
painting as a "Gaudy picture bought by the
common people." The statement reflects the
attitudes of the nineteenth-century Korean experts
upon whom Hough relied for information. *Kkachi
horangi* 까치호랑이 is the Korean term for tiger and

magpie painting. Interpretations of this combination have invited several conflicting theories. Some
scholars view the tiger as a representation of the
male, and the magpie as the female. Others believe
the tiger represents the ruler, the strong, the
powerful, and the bird the masses, the ruled, the
weak. The magpie is considered a good omen in
Chinese legend and female (Eberhard, 1986:174–
175). The inclusion of three funguses, indeed the
trio of tiger, magpie and pine, suggests the *samjae
sasang* 三才思想, the basic trinity of heaven, earth,
and man.
Collected in Seoul

128 STANDING BEAUTY

(*MIIN-DO* 미인도 美人圖)
Choson Period (1392–1910), late 19th century
Color on paper
H: 122 cm, W: 53.4 cm
USNM ECC 77071
Ref.: HKC p. 468

The woman's costume is the standard ensemble consisting of a long, floor-length blue skirt or *chima* 치마 and a short jacket called *jeogori* 저고리. Unlike the usual color combination of a blue skirt with either yellow, light jade or white top, the jacket is dark green. Red ribbons hang from the jacket, while the white tie strips hanging from the skirt waist are partly hidden. The woman's left hand held under the chin shows a gold double ring. The coiffure is a chignon, known as *nangja-meori* 낭자머리, worn exclusively by married women. *Binyeo* 비녀 a long crossbar hairpin with a curved head, is used to secure the chignon. A variety of materials are used for this kind of hairpin, and the sizes vary as well (see cat. no. 38 for detailed descriptions of various types, their methods of decoration and associated symbolism). Hough's entry reads: "Scroll Picture of a Korean Lady" and "This picture gives an idea of the mode of wearing the hair and the house costume of the Korean ladies." The cloth and the hairstyle is not necessarily the house costume; he must have meant that a Korean lady would wear cape-like apparel, *jangot* 장옷 or outerwear in the street. His additional comment reflects the collector Bernadou's observation (Appendix III, Bernadou letter of 2 September 1884, Seoul, to Baird in

USNM Registrar's Office accession number 16970) and his own observation of Japanese pictorials for the common people. He says: "The pictures used in the decoration of the inner or living rooms of the common people are gaudily colored and stiffly drawn. The subjects of Korean common pictorial art are flowers, fruits, animals, etc., in contrast with the dramatic and blood-curdling common prints of the Japanese."

A prominent Korean art historian points out: "portraits of women are the least conspicuous category of Korean portrait paintings" (Jo, 1994:80). Although several well-known portraits of women exist, the subjects invariably are courtesans, not ladies in a strict sense.

A letter of 2 September 1884, Seoul, to Baird from Bernadou (Appendix III), reads in part: "I will try to briefly summarize what work I have accomplished under the heads given below, commencing with such articles as would come under the general head of art.... Painting. There appears to be no living artist of note in Corea; one whose works have any renown. Coarse portrait of Chinese and Corean heroes...and pictures of officials in their robes are common, and are made by the hundreds. The people buy them to decorate the interiors of their houses."

Collected in Seoul

129 FLOWERS AND AUSPICIOUS SYMBOLS

(*HWAHWE-DO* 화훼도 花卉圖)
Choson Period (1392–1910), late 19th century
Color on paper
H: 67.5 cm, W: 52 cm
USNM ECC 77052:2
Ref.: HKC p. 469; Published (Houchins, 1982:60–61); (*MBM*, 1989:150).

The vase on a stand is filled with hibiscus, chrysanthemum, lotus, bellflower, ornamental grasses and grapes. Alongside is a fish bowl with two fish. A vase decorated with yin-yang symbols alone holds wild roses. The vase below contains peonies, emblematic of feminine beauty and wealth. Another object on the floor is a citron (*Citrus decumana*) or *yuja* 柚子 in Korean, a fertility symbol due to its homonym, *yuja* 有子, meaning having sons or children.

Hough states that " These paintings would be usually seen in living rooms of the common people." More specifically, paintings of a flower vase combined with fertility symbols decorate women's quarters.

Collected in Seoul

130 TIGER, PINE, AND SACRED FUNGUS

(*MUNBAE-DO* 문배도 門排圖)
Choson Period (1392–1910), late 19th century
Color woodcut
This is one of a set of four color woodcut *mundaedo*. (See cat. nos. 124, 125 and 126)
H: 34.5 cm, W: 29 cm
USNM ECC 77052:12
Ref.: HKC p. 469; Published (Jo, 1974b: 51); (*MBM*, 1989: 149)

A tiger stands under a pine tree, viewing *pulloch'o* 不老草, sacred fungus. The tiger's yellow-orange fur is accented with black geometric stripes and roundels, and its tail touches the pine branch. The tiger's eyes are white circles with black pupils in an expression of watchfulness. The fungus portends longevity for the tiger, and owner of the print. It is painted in red, the color believed to repel evil spirits. The print is hung on the outside of the storeroom or on the house gate to prevent intruders.

Collected in Seoul

131 TRIBUTE MISSION TO THE CHINESE COURT

(*BYEONGPUNG* 병풍)
Choson Period (1392–1910), mid 19th century
Eight panels of an eight-panel screen; color on silk
H: 140 cm, W: 216.5 cm
USNM ECC 77116
Ref.: HKC pp. 469–470; Published (McCune, 1983:14–15, 17–19)

This screen illustrates an imaginary scene of the Chinese Emperor receiving tribute from the areas bordering China. The eight panels "illustrate the final stage in the three days of ceremony that tribute missions took part in before being allowed to trade" (McCune, 1983:14–15, 17–19 for illustration). The first panel depicts their arrivals at the imperial court, while the fifth to seventh panels show ceremonial courses of presenting gifts to the Chinese Emperor. The scenes are elaborately drawn, probably by a Korean court painter, a *Dohwaseo* 圖畫署 (Office of Paintings) specialist (ibid.). Hough gives the classic interpretation of the scenes as Ming-Dynasty (1368–1628) court, and notes that eight-panel silk screens such as this one are old and rare. According to Evelyn B. McCune, "The architecture is of that of the Forbidden City in Peking perhaps of Yuan (1206–1341) times as the costumes appear to be." Hough further comments, "This screen is worthy of close study for the number of nationalities depicted ... [and] the scene is of about four hundred years ago; the Koreans with pardonable pride have placed themselves in the front rank." Though originally an eight panel screen, the panels are now separate.

Collected in Seoul

132 LANDSCAPES AND ANIMALS WITH FLOWERS

(*GEURIM* 그림; *HOEHWA* 회화 繪畫)
Choson Period (1392–1910), late 19th century
Color or ink on paper
Varied sizes
USNM ECC 77117:1-26
Ref.: HKC pp. 470–471

Bernadou collected a number of watercolors on paper and ink drawings of various subjects. Though these have not been located, Hough catalogues about twenty paintings of animals, four landscapes and several scenes thought to be from the life of the famous calligrapher, Han Seok-bong 韓石峯 (1542–1605).

In the Hough catalog, 77117:21 is omitted, and 77117:1-22 were not found in the collection according to an inventory conducted on 21 June 1973. In March 1884, 77117:23-26 were transferred to NAA where they are currently stored.

Though several of the paintings originally collected cannot be located at this time, the titles of all of the paintings, together with commentaries provided by Hough, are listed below:

77117:1 Mandarin duck.

77117:2 White cock, hen, chicks by the bamboo brake.

77117:3 Hawk on cliff overhanging the sea, with captured duck. This picture is well drawn; the spray under the seaweed-covered rock and the fierce mien and pose of the hawk are well executed.

77117:4 Hawk about to attack a monkey, which hides itself under the trunk of a pine tree. The monkey is not found in Korea.

77117:5 Eagle perched in a plum tree.

77117:6 White eagle with quarry; a pheasant.

77117:7 Swans among the reeds. Poetical.

77117:8 Korean hunting falcon in pursuit of a white hare.

77117:9 Flock of cranes on a pine tree. Poetical and mythological illustration.

77117:10 Crane and fragrant plum tree. Poetical and metaphorical, the crane signifying the child and the plum tree the mother.

77117:11 Lion under pine tree. Very poor representation.

77117:12 Tiger crouching under a pine tree.

77117:13 Gray squirrel on branch of pine tree.

77117:14 Pair of musk deer. Probably an illustration of some poem.

77117:15 Pair of antelope.

77117:16 Well-groomed horse tied to a willow tree. Spring scene; often painted by Korean artists.

77117:17 Horses at play, leaping and rolling. Spring scene; illustration of a poem.

77117:18 Pair of dogs under trees. Mythological dogs, illustrating a folk story.

77117:19 Sea monster (whale) swallowing a junk.

77117:20 Manchurian crane.

77117:21 Description missing.

77117:22 Sepia drawing [of] landscape, winter scene; mountains partly covered with snow. Shows a pagoda and the roof of a temple.

77117:23 Landscape, summer scene; shown by thick foliage and people sitting in the open pavilions.

77117:24 Landscape, spring scene; village at sunset, men reading by the window, and fishers [fishermen] returning across a quaint bridge.

77117:25 Landscape, autumn; maple trees, water flowing under a stone bridge, a man on a two-wheeled sedan of the kind probably used in Korea in old times.

77117:26 Illustrates the story of a man who was famous for his good handwriting. No one has attained to his excellence since his death.

132:1 MALLARD AND MANDARIN DUCKS IN MOONLIGHT

(*EOHAE-DO* 어해도 魚蟹圖)

Black and white photograph of a painting (non-located) mounted as a hanging scroll; original painting probably Choson Period (1392–1910), late 19th century.

H: 25.5 cm W: 20.2 cm (8 x 10 in)

USNM ECC 77117:1 NAA 047567.00

Ref.: HKC p. 470

The size of the original painting is unknown, but, as the photograph shows, the painting depicts groups of ducks in the water among the reeds; some are perched on a reed branch. The inclusion of a crescent moon suggests that it is a scene captured at dusk.

132:2 HAWK ON PLUM BRANCHES
(*HWAJO-DO* 화조도 花鳥圖)
Black and white photograph of a painting (non-located) mounted as a hanging scroll; original painting probably Choson Period (1392–1910), late 19th century
H: 25.5 cm W: 20.2 cm (i.e.8 X 10 inch print)
USNM ECC 77117:5   NAA 047567.00
Ref.: HKC p. 470

132:3 Geese and Reeds
(*NOAN-DO* 노안도 蘆雁圖;
BAEGAN-DO 백안도 百雁圖)
By an anonymous artist
Black and white photograph of a painting (non-
located) mounted as a hanging scroll; original
painting probably Choson Period (1392–1910),
late 19th century
H: 13 cm W: 15.4 cm (i.e.8 X 10 inch print)
USNM ECC 77117:7   NAA 047567.00
Ref.: HKC p. 470

Collected in Seoul

133 AUTUMN LANDSCAPE IN MOONLIGHT

(*CHUGYEONG SANSU-DO* 추경산수도 秋景山水圖)
Choson Period (1392–1910), late 19th century
Color on paper
H: 27 cm, W: 31.5 cm
USNM ECC 77118:1   NAA MS 7165:1
Ref.: HKC p. 470

Mostly bare trees, some with fall colored leaves, and a few green pine trees, surround a man looking at the moon. He wears a red robe, indicative of aristocratic status. Partly shown is the interior of a structure, probably a study, with a desk and a lamp. An unidentifiable seal mark is in the upper right-hand corner.

Hough describes the painting as "autumn moonlight scene" and adds, "the maple and bamboo surround the student's house."

Collected in Seoul

134 SNOW LANDSCAPE
(*SEOLGYEONG SANSU-DO* 설경산수도 雪景山水圖)
Choson Period (1392–1910), late 19th century
Color on paper
H: 27 cm, W: 31.5 cm
USNM ECC 77118:2   NAA MS 7165:2
Ref.: HKC p. 471

This snowscape after a storm is predominantly white, with blue-green, wind-blown trees. On the upper left stands a snow-covered structure sheltering two snowbound people. An unidentified artist's seal is in the bottom left. The description is based on Hough's, as the painting has dark brown stains which now cover nearly two-thirds of the surface.

Collected in Seoul

135 BUTTERFLIES AND FLOWERS
(*HWACHEOP-DO* 화첩도 花蝶圖)
Choson Period (1392–1910), late 19th century
Artist's seal: Han Jin-u
Color on paper
H: 27 cm, W: 31.5 cm
USNM ECC 77118:3   NAA MS 7165:3
Ref.: HKC p. 471

Brown and black butterflies perch on an orange day lily in full bloom, on a large pink peony blossom and on lavender cornflowers with sprays of green leaves. A white butterfly is in the far upper left and a gray one in the upper right. This genre of Korean folk painting decorates women's quarters. Hough writes that the painting was made by an artist Han, although the reading of the seal in the lower left has not been confirmed.

Collected in Seoul

136 FISH AND SHELLFISH IN SEA
(*EOUHAE-DO* 어해도 魚蟹圖)
Choson Period (1392–1910), late 19th century
Color on paper
H: 27 cm, W: 31.5 cm
USNM ECC 77118:4   NAA MS 7165:4
Ref.: HKC p. 471

Against a predominantly blue-green background,
black and gray crabs are in motion while on the far
left several varicolored clams are still. Fish and
shrimp in the upper portion of the painting seem to
swim upstream. Hough describes this watercolor as
"submarine view, crabs, shrimps, mollusks, and
seaweed," and adds, "the picture bears marks of
having been drawn by a literary man rather than a
regular artist." The seal in the lower left, however,
has not been identified.

Collected in Seoul

137: 1-4 SCENES OF DAILY LIFE
(*PUNGSOK-DO* 풍속도)

Choson Period (1392–1910), late 19th century
Artist: Han-jin-o
Four of eight published engravings on tear sheets;
original images from album of drawings; India
ink on paper
Sizes unknown
USNM ECC 77119:1-28
Ref.: HKC pp. 472–474; Published (Houchins,
1981:58–61)

According to the museum record, i.e. the ledger,
ACB and ECC entries, Hough's commentary and
published sources, such as *Science* (Mason,
1886:115–118) and *Scientific American* (Mason,
1888:20–21), Bernadou collected a "picture book"
containing these twenty-eight drawings, which are
not currently included in the Bernadou collection.
The quote under remarks in the ECC reads:
"Bought for 200 cash [200 *ryang* 량, pre-1910
Korean coinage unit] for my little boy." Hough has
examined the complete set of twenty-eight drawings
and compiled a list with accompanying commentaries such as those describing the following four
scenes, which have been rearranged with arbitrary
sub-numbers given by Mason. Hough writes:

"By far the better pictures in the collection are the
following outline sketches in India ink, which may
be entitled 'Scenes from the Social Life of Korea.'
They are a revelation in Korean art, since they show
bold drawing, free treatment, and humorous carica-
ture like that found in the realistic school of Japan.

These pictures illustrate the social customs and
industrial arts of the people. They were originally
bound together to form a boy's picture book. They
are supposed to be nearly three hundred years old."

137:1 "Instruction in archery
Teacher showing lad how to draw the bow. The
awkward pose of the beginner is well caught. Others
are stringing the bow and straightening the arrow."

137:2 "Begging bonzes on the road side
On a large sheet of paper are a number of strips
upon which are written sums of money or grain as
paid for certain efficacious prayers. The woman in
front is about to throw down a few coins, for which
the prayers will be said. The bonzes carry small
boat-shaped drums, and sing the sacred songs in-
voking blessings on the contributors. The lady's
attendant carries a smoking outfit on her head and
fan in her hand. These priests are not regular beggars but perform this office according to the rules of
a certain sect."

137:3 "Marriage procession of the groom visiting
his intended bride
Men in advance carry lanterns for the occasion,
followed by the bearer of a wild duck or model of
one, the symbol of domestic felicity. Then comes
the bridegroom in court dress, always worn on such
occasions by all except coolies. As a rule the young
man's former nurse follows."

137:4 "Country peddlers
Man carries large basket of vegetables or salt fish on
his head; woman carries child and cradle-shaped
basket containing crabs. The child is carried as in
Japan, seated inside the loose upper garment."

What remain of these twenty-eight India ink drawings are eight published engravings on tearsheets
from *Science* (6 August 1886: 115–118) and from

Scientific American (14 July 1888: 20–21) under the
title, "Corea By Native Artists." Author Otis T.
Mason assigns numbers one through eight to the
engraved figures.

Mason assesses these drawings as "a small but wisely
chosen collection of art products to illustrate social
and industrial life in Corea" (Mason, 1886: 115).
These drawings by Han-jin-o (Hough, 1892: 472)
are copies of the artwork by Kim Hong-do, the
Choson-period court painter (1745–1818), or
Danwon. They are selected extracts from Danwon's
album of genre paintings titled, *Danwon Kim Hong-do
pungsok Hwacheop* 檀園 金弘道 風俗畵帖, which now
is in the collection of the National Museum of Korea
and has been designated as Korea's National Trea-
sure, no. 527 (Jeong, 1993:66, plate number 82).
According to Jeong, "His [Danwon's] faithful renderings of day to day life included all strata of society, high and low. ... He adapted the traditional
Chinese genre of depicting farming and weaving to
Korean style" (ibid., p. 68). Contrary to Jeong's
observations, Danwon's genre scenes are noted as the
result of the artist's direct contact with the life of the
common people, thus limited subject matter depicting typical common folk's day-to-day life (An,
1986:39).

In his caption for figure 1, "A Lesson in Archery,"
Mason points out the importance of archery to the
Koreans as amusement, and to their soldiers' highly
prized skills in archery. He also comments on the
great care the Koreans give to both bows and arrows.
Gungsul 弓術, art of archery, is the original Korean
title given.

Figure 2 titled "Bonzes Selling Charms" in Danwon's
album poses an interesting contrast to Hough's title,
"Bonzes Begging." The Korean title is *Siju* 施主,
meaning a benefactor, the one who supports
Buddhism by acts of charity or giving to the priest or
temple. Another Korean title, *Bosi* 布施, was given
to the scene by anthropologist Kim Dong-uk in his
study of Danwon's genre paintings published in
Japan (Kim, 1976:13). *Bosi* means Buddhist alms, a
temple offering. Both of these Korean titles fit the
scene; more appropriate than the interpretation
given by Mason. In the Buddhist tradition, the scene
is unrelated to "selling" or "buying." Whatever is

displayed in front of the bonzes is not considered
merchandise. When money is paid, it is a means of
charity or "giving." When the monks reciprocate
with charms, it is "receiving." What Mason terms
charms are likely to be *bujeok* 符籍, paper amulets
on which are printed prayer-like inscriptions
expressing one's wishes and fears. Mason relays
Lowell's characterization of Korean society by
stating that there is no religion in Korea except
Confucianism for the upper class and superstition
for the lower class. At the upper left corner, there is
an added drawing of a wooden clog worn by
Koreans in rainy weather. It is an illustration of the
Bernadou collection specimen, *namak-sin* 나막신
(cat. no. 77).

Figure 3 depicts "A Wedding Procession." Mason's
statement contradicts that of Hough's (cf. Hough's
list of titles with comments above). The bride is not
in the scene; the woman on a donkey trailing behind the groom is not the bride but the groom's
former wet nurse. Another drawing at the upper left
corner is a court official's hat called *samo* 紗帽 (cat.
no. 66). Since the groom is allowed to wear official
garb on his wedding day, an introduction of the
type of hat Bernadou collected in this context is
rather effective. The Korean title, *Jeonan* 전안 refers
to the ceremony of carrying a live duck or a model
of a duck to the bride's home by the groom's party.

For figure 4, Mason provides the title as "Peddlers
on the Road," saying such a common scene is found
throughout Korea. Mason notes that the scene
shows the lower class Koreans' costumes and their
methods of carrying loads and children. Some of the
Bernadou collection specimens are pictured in the
lower left corner, a straw sandal or *jipsin* 짚신 (cat.
no. 81), while a conical, loosely woven reed or
bamboo hat called *satgat* 삿갓 (cat. no. 74), worn by
farmers and laborers, is shown in the upper right
corner. The Korean title is *Haengsang* 행상, which
in translation means itinerant traders, peddlers.

Collected in Seoul

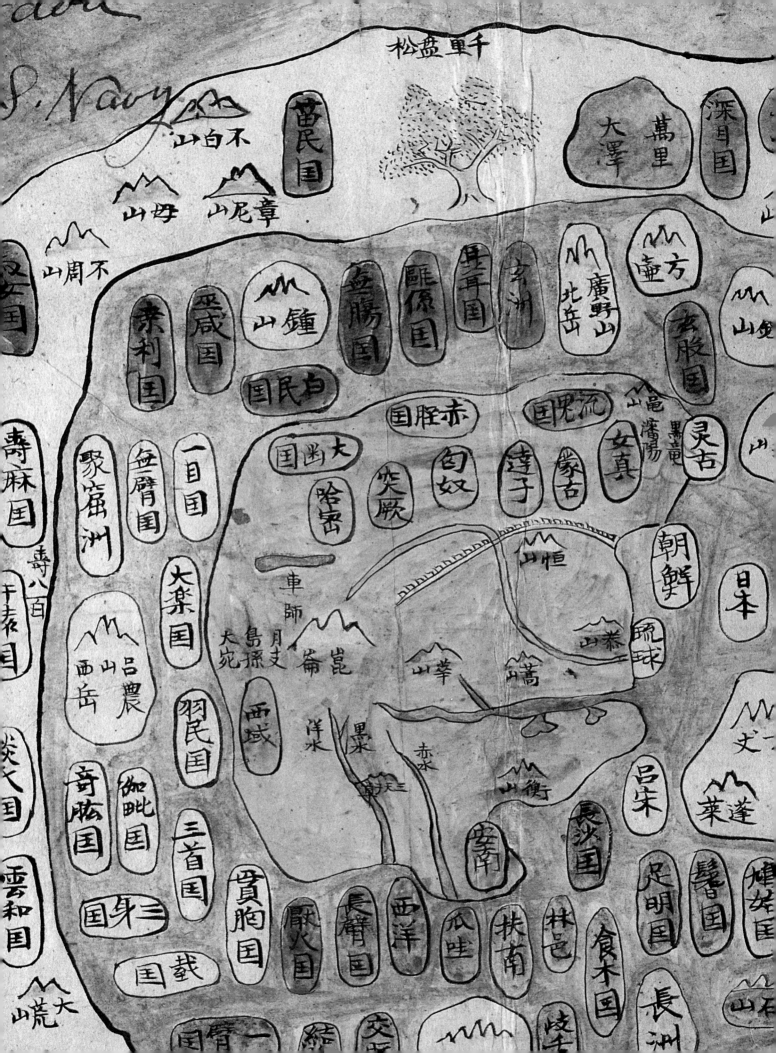

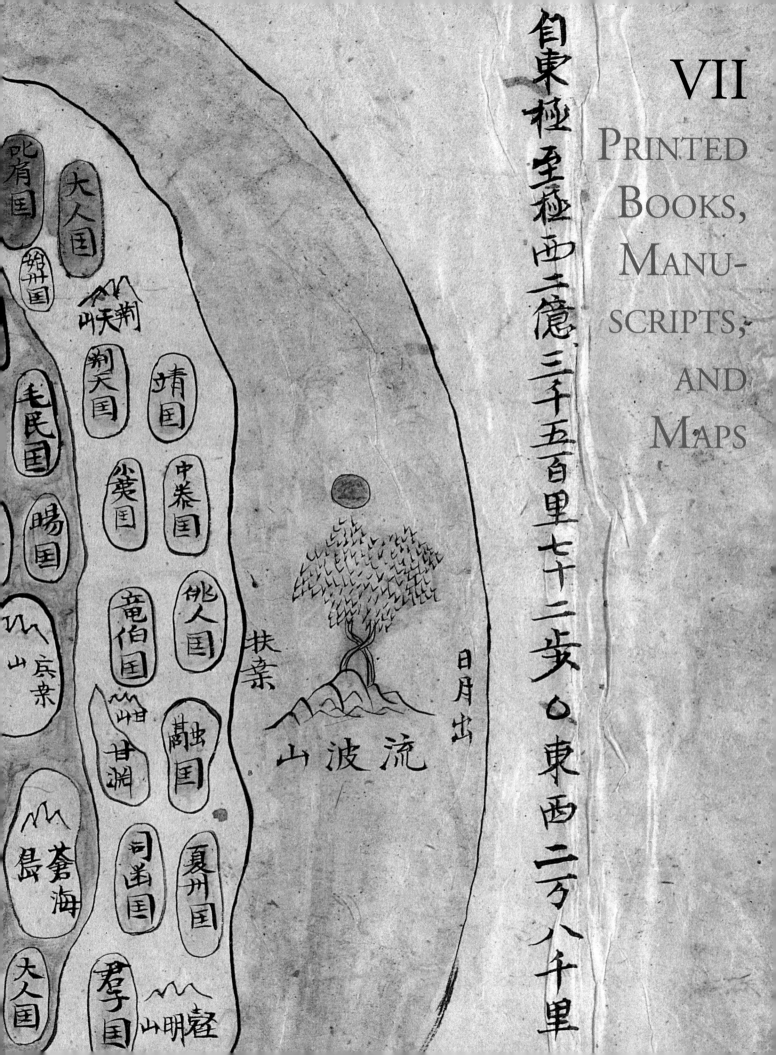

VII

PRINTED
BOOKS,
MANU-
SCRIPTS,
AND
MAPS

139

138 THE THOUSAND CHINESE CHARACTERS

(*CHEONJAMUN* 천자문 千字文)
Choson Period (1392–1910), late 19th century
Book of 41 leaves, woodblock-printed paper
USNM ECC 77122
Ref.: HKC p. 486; BFN 22

This is said to be a rectangular thread-bound, unpaginated book of forty-one leaves containing one thousand basic Chinese characters, arranged in groups of four for easy memorization (Deuchler, 1977:5). It has not been located in a recent inventory.

Cheonjamun is the traditional introductory text to Chinese characters and calligraphy.

There are diverse theories about its origin, and some claim that it was first compiled during the Three Kingdoms Period (220–265) of China. It has been widely distributed among the literati and many editions of different calligraphers have emerged since the Tang Dynasty (618–907) (GDS, 1963:1524). Although the date *Cheonjamun* was imported to Korea is not clear, it must have been quite early. It became a compulsory textbook of elementary education for young children.

BFN 22 "Book for teaching the Chinese language through use of the Corean on-moun [*eonmun* 언문], with an attempt at representing the Chinese sound of the Chinese character by use of the on-moun. It commences with the "Thousand Character Classic" giving the Chinese sounds."

Bernadou's letter to Baird, 2 September 1884 (Appendix III), reads in part: "There is one common school-book, in which about fourteen hundred Chinese characters are given with the sound and meaning in the ern [*sic*]-moun [*eonmun*]. Here the

native writing supplies a difficulty felt by the Chinese, there being nothing definite in a Chinese character to indicate to a beginner the sound or meaning."
Collected n Seoul

139 QUESTIONS AND ANSWERS ON THE IMPORTANT DOCTRINE OF HOLY RELIGION

(*SYEONGGYO YORI MUNDAP*
성교요리문답)[JESUIT CATECHISM]
Choson Period (1392–1910), 1883
Book of 55 leaves, woodblock-printed paper; 2nd edition
L: 17.5 cm, W: 11 cm
USNM ECC 77120
Ref.: HKC p.486

This book is double-leaf and thread-bound. It has a total of fifty-five unpaginated leaves. The title in Korean script on the first page reads: *Syeonggyo yori mundap*, literally "Questions and Answers on the Important Doctrine of the Holy Religion." This book is a second edition, printed in 1883. Bernadou attached a note to the back of the cover sheet, adding corresponding Chinese characters and English translation. It reads: "聖妙要理問答, Sicuo Myo Yo Ri Mun Tap [*Seongmyo yori mundap*] Holy Excellent or Admirable Important Doctrine, Ask Questions & Reply Answers. Catechism," in which he apparently mistook *gyo* 教, meaning religion, for *myo* 妙, meaning excellent or admirable. This book explains the basic doctrine of Catholic practice, in question and answer form. Written in Hangul script, presumably it was published for commoners or women of higher classes unable to read Sino-Korean. The contents are questions and answers on baptism, and the fundamental doctrine of the Catholic Church; rules and procedures of baptism; procedures of confession; rules for the sacrament of

Holy Communion; how to become a disciple of Jesus.

Hough claims this book is a "holy, excellent, important doctrine," issued by the Jesuits. The history of the Korean Catholic Church is unique in that Catholicism was introduced into Korea, not by the missionaries, but by the Korean scholars who visited China in the seventeenth century. First called *seohak* 西學, meaning Western studies, it appealed to progressive scholars, not as religion, but as an alternative philosophy which might reform unyielding Confucianism. Later, as Catholic influence grew and spawned many converts, Catholics were caught in the middle of a heated battle between the conservatives and the progressives. Numerous converts were martyred during the bloody persecutions in the eighteenth and nineteenth centuries, and international tensions developed between Korea and France, who supported their missionaries (GDS, 1963:1524–1525). This book was collected just a few years after Christianity was allowed, following the opening of Korea in 1882. How it was obtained is not known. Considering the signature next to the title on the first page, apparently not Bernadou's, it may have belonged to a missionary who presented it to him.

Collected in Seoul

140 TANTRIC DIAGRAMS AND TEXTS

(*BIMILGYO* 비밀교 秘密敎)
Choson Period (1392–1910), cyclically dated in accordance with 1784
Book of 93 leaves, woodblock-printed paper; second edition; text in Sanskrit with annotations in Chinese characters and Hangul syllabary
L: 25.9 cm, W: 18.7 cm
USNM ECC 77121 NAA Inv. 09006800
Ref: HKC pp. 486–487; BFN 56

This book is double-leaf and thread-bound, printed on mulberry paper. Without title page or colophon, it has a total of ninety-three leaves, each part paginated separately. The title, handwritten on the cover, reads: *Bimilgyo* 秘密教 [Tantrism], meaning "Secret Religion" (Mun, 1981: 32). There are two prefaces: one is written under the name of "an old hermit of Mount Ha" and the other by a Buddhist monk of Mount Bulleong 佛靈山. The locations of the mountains are not clear and the names may be symbolic. These prefaces, describing the date, the purpose, and how the book was published are followed by a table of contents, written by a Kim Deok-yun 金德潤 of Mount Bunseong 盆城. Hough presumed the cyclical date of each preface to correspond to 1644 and 1652, but that is not likely. The two prefaces and the table of contents all give the same date of the 6th month and a cyclical year, *gapjin* 甲辰. More clues as to dating are given in the second preface. It reads: "*sungjeong giwon hu sam-gapjin* 崇禎紀元後三甲辰*,*" which means the third *gapjin* [eleventh year in the Chinese sexagesimal cycle] after the reign of Emperor Chongzhen 崇禎 (r. 1628–44) of the Ming Dynasty, indicating that this book probably was published in 1784. This book is largely devoted to prayers, but an introduction gives textual instruction. How to read the Sanskrit text by use of Hangul are presented in Chinese characters. Also presented is the essence of Tantrism, along with its overall cosmography, which includes symbolized diagrams of the universe. The prayers consist of magical formulas, called *darani* 陀羅尼, *jineon* 眞言, or *ju* 呪. Along with brief translations, explanations of how the ritual was practiced, or the occasions when these prayers were chanted, are given in Chinese. However, the meanings generally are not presented, probably because the ritual of repeating mantra was considered more important than studying meaning.

Hough entered the title as "Pimil Kiao [*Bimilgyo*]" or "Secret Religion" and explained the book as "Made up of magical formula or *dharani*, written in a kind of Sanskrit resembling Nepalese, which to the uninitiated is secret or hidden." He shows great interest in the languages used in this book. He points out that it "begins with the on-moon [*eonmun*], or Korean alphabet," and continues, "The sounds of this [Hangul] are defined by Chinese characters, for which the student is directed to substitute the sound of the corresponding word in the Korean colloquial language." Hough also writes, "The bulk of the book is taken up with prayers, (dharani) addressed to Avalokitshwara, and begin with ôm or ôm-mani padmé-hûm." According to Bernadou in a letter to Baird and his fieldnote below, this book was obtained after an extensive effort to find Sanskrit books, the language of Mahayana Buddhism and Tantrism. Many of these Sanskrit originals are no longer extant, but before they were lost they were translated into Chinese and Tibetan and are now preserved in those languages (Crim, 1989: 134). Citing Dr. D.[Divie] B.[Bethune] McCartie (1820–1900), Hough stated: "The "secret" or "mysterious" characters are a modification of the Sanskrit alphabet ascribed to Brahma, and seem to be identical with those used in the Sanskrit books, said to have been brought to Japan by Kôbô Daishi弘法大師 , better known as Kûkai 空海 (774–835) (Papinot, 1972: 321), early in the ninth century."

Tantrism or esoteric Buddhism is one of the three Buddhist vehicles: Theravada Buddhism [*sangjwabu* 上座部], Mahayana Buddhism [*daeseung bulgyo* 大乘佛教], and Tantrism [*milgyo* 密教]. While Tantrism prevailed in Tibet, in Korea it existed only as a subdivision of the Textual School [*Gyojong* 教宗] of the predominant Mahayana Buddhism. However, many tantric elements were incorporated into mainstream Buddhism and Shamanism.

BFN 56 "Sanscrit Chinese on-mooun [*eonmun*] book. Printed in Korea. Is remarkable for giving the sound of the Sanscrit characters by use of the On-mooun or native Korean alphabet. But no translation of the Sanscrit is given. Only a number of Sanscrit syllables with the Korean sounds; the use of the prayer and its approximate meaning are told in Chinese. Obtained in a Buddhist temple of Pang-Yong, where it was said to have come from Kim-kang-san in Kang-suen-do [*sic*], where there is a great number of Buddhist temples."

Bernadou's letter to Baird, 2 September 1884 (Appendix III) reads in part: "I have given some little time to endeavors to find Sanscrit books. That a knowledge of Sanscrit once existed here is well known. Five hundred years ago, Buddhism was the court religion. It has been replaced by Confucianism. I have succeeded in obtaining one book in Chinese and Sanscrit; giving the pronunciation of the Sanscrit characters in the ern-mun [*eonmun*]. It contains a number of prayers, and the meaning of the characters is described in Chinese. I was unable to find a trace of either a Sanscrit dictionary or a grammatical work. A German, who examined mines for Coreans, had permission to go to a certain well-known Buddhist monastery to enquire for Sanscrit manuscripts. He found none, although armed with considerable power, and after searching through a library of a thousand volumes, returned with a copy of the book now in my possession and one other, a similar one."

Collected in Seoul

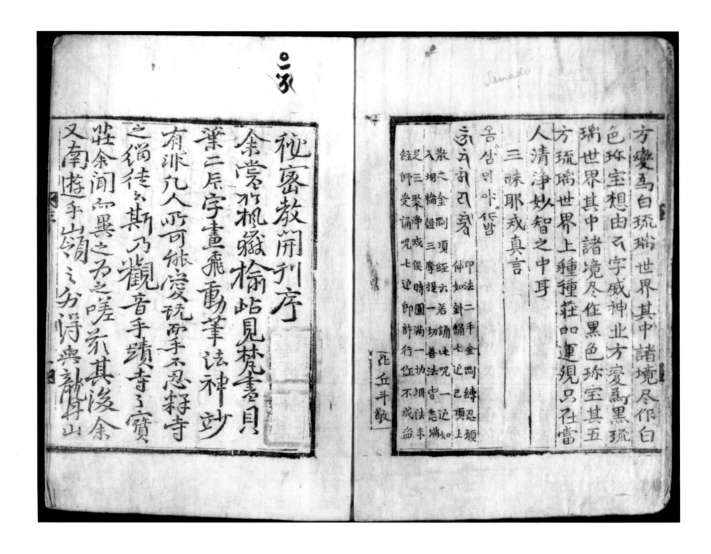

Samadi

141 CANON OF FILIAL PIETY
(*DAEBO BUMO EUNJUNG-GYEONG*
대보부모은중경 大報父母恩重經)
Choson Period (1392–1910), late 19th century
Manuscript of 76 double leaves
L: 36 cm, W: 24 cm
USNM ECC 77123
Ref.: HKC p. 487; BFN 154

This is a Korean text about the great obligations one owes to one's parents. Now missing from the collection, the canon reputedly originated in India and was edited in China. As a counterpart of *hyogyeong* 孝經, an essential Confucian teaching about filial piety, it became one of the most popular texts of the Choson Period (Mun, 1981: 113).

Hough documents the title of this book as *Taipo-pumo-eun-tchyang-kying* and translates it as "Parents' very precious evening-bell prayer book," which "contains tales of the life of Buddha for popular instruction in Buddhism; 74 pages." He also mentions it as "good paper and excellent writing; most probably that of a lady."

BFN 154

Collected in Seoul

142 MANUAL OF THE FOUR RITES
(*SARYE PYEOLLAM* 사례편람 四禮便覽)
Choson Period (1392–1910), postscript to vol. 1 dated 1844
Book, 4 vols.; woodblock-printed paper
L: 30.8 cm, W: 21 cm
USNM ECC 77124
Ref.: HKC p. 487; BFN 21

This is a complete opus in Chinese divided into four double-page, thread-bound volumes. These volumes contain unpaginated subsections dealing with *sarye* or "four rites": coming of age, wedding, funeral and ancestor worship. A table of contents and introductory remarks appear at the beginning of the first volume and the 1844 postscript by Jo In-yeong 趙寅永 (1782–1850) appears at the end of the last volume.

Hough believed this compendium to be a Korean version of a Chinese work, "the great Chinese handbook of etiquette."Actually, *Sarye pyeollam* was compiled by a Korean Confucian scholar, Yi Jae 李縡 (1680–1746) in the early eighteenth century (Deuchler, 1977: 5). It was published in 1844 by Yi Jae's descendant, Yi Gwang-jeong 李光正 (also known as Yi Hwi-jeong 李輝正, 1760–?), and has

served as the main text for most Korean families for these rites (*GDS*, 1962: 647).

BFN 21 "Manual of the Four Rites or sa-ryei-pyel-lam [*Sarye pyeollam*]. Description of the ceremonies of (1) assuming the "Koun" or cap, indicating entrance into the state of manhood; (2) marriage, Also giving (3) the order and method of procedure at death and burial; and (4) the same at the offering of sacrifices to the dead."

Collected in Seoul

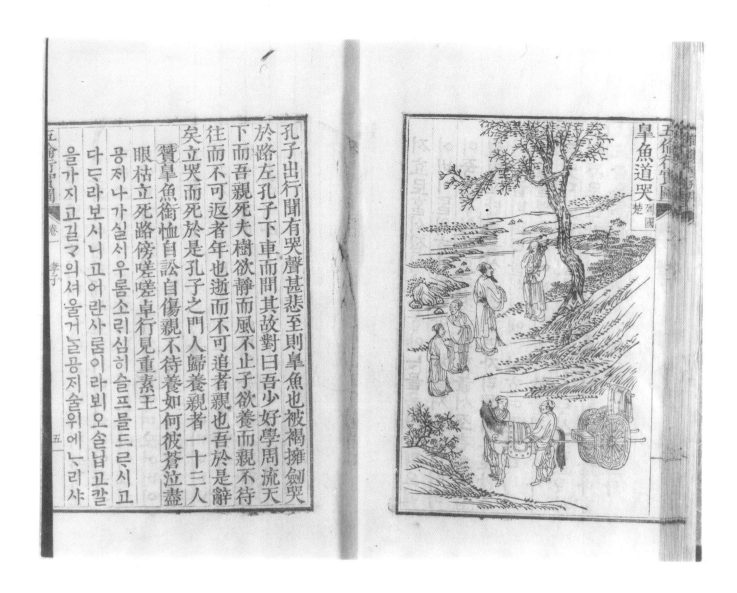

143 THE FIVE MORAL IMPERATIVES
(*ORYUN HAENGSIL-DO*)
오륜행실도 五倫行實圖)
Choson Period (1392–1910), 1859
Book, vol. 1 of 4; woodblock-printed paper,
text in Chinese and Korean
L: 21 cm, W: 31.5 cm
USNM ECC 130585 NAA Inv. 08994400
Ref.: HKC p. 487

This is an illustrated book of stories relating to
the five moral imperatives, thread-bound and
double-leaf. The text is in Chinese followed by
Korean. Each story is accompanied by a
captioned illustration on the opposite page.
Oryun haengsil-do is an illustrated collection of
stories about proper application of the five
Confucian virtues. This book is the first of
four volumes, altogether containing 150
stories, 33 of which are about sons' filial
imperatives. This first volume has a total of
eighty-three leaves containing stories arranged
chronologically of personalities mostly from
Chinese classics.

Oryun haengsil-do was first published in 1797

under the royal order of King Jeongjo 正祖 (r. 1752–
1800), who led a cultural renaissance. This
woodblock-printed volume is from the second
edition published in 1859. *Oryun* 五倫, the five
Confucian moral imperatives, are: *Gunsin-yuui*
君臣有義, the relationship between sovereign and
subject governed by righteousness; *Buja-yuchin*
父子有親, the relationship between father and son
governed by parental authority; *Bubu-yubyeol*
夫婦有別, the relationship between husband and
wife governed by their separate duties; *Jangyu-yuseo*
長幼有序, the relationship between elder and
younger brothers; and *Bungu-yusin* 朋友有信, the
relationship between senior and junior guided by
faithfulness (Deuchler, 1977: 2). All five rules aim
to maintain social equilibrium.

Collected in Seoul

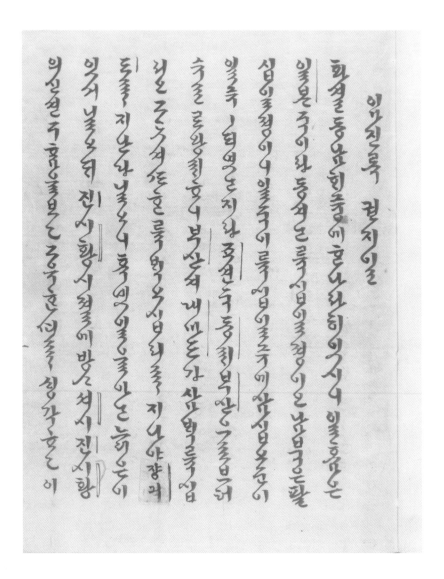

144 RECORD OF THE JAPANESE INVASION OF KOREA

(*IMJIN-NOK*임진록)

Choson Period(1392–1910)

Manuscript of 178 leaves; ink on paper

L: 17.8 cm, W: 24.3 cm

USNM ECC 130583   NAA Inv. 09006900

Ref.: HKC p. 487

This handwritten book in Korean is thread-bound and has a total of 178 leaves with three chapters paginated separately. The collector's signature appears on the front cover. The title on the first page reads: *Imjin-nok* [Records of Japanese Invasion of Korea in 1592]. Proper names are marked as follows: single lines for place names; double lines for personal names; and double dots for individuals.

Hough remarks that this book "is an abridgment of an official history of the war between Korea and Japan, near the close of the seventeenth century," and states, "The account is incorrect."

Imjin-nok is historical fiction, based on the invasions of Korea in 1592 and 1597 by Japan's great commander, Toyotomi Hideyshi 豊臣秀吉, (1538–

1598). Hideyshi's campaigns were unsuccessful except for his capture of many Korean craftsmen who greatly influenced the production of art, particularly ceramics, in Japan. Neither the author nor the date of the account is known, but presumably it was written shortly after the war. There are many different accounts or versions, both in Chinese and Korean. Influenced by the renowned Chinese war novel *Samgukjiyeonui* 三國志演義 [Romance of the Three Kingdoms], *Imjin-nok* recreated legends of patriotic soldiers who defeated the Japanese in enthralling derring-do (*GDS*, 1963: 1281).

Collected in Seoul

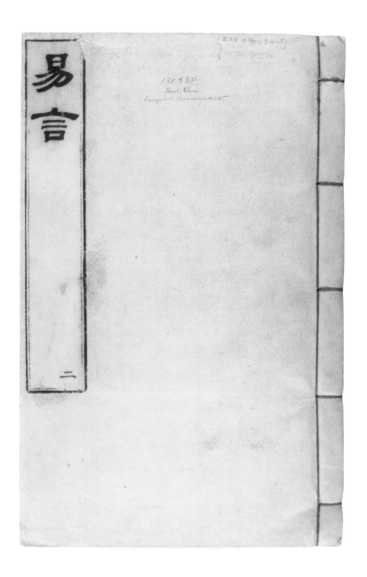

145 *YIYAN* (KOR. *IEON*) [DISCOURSE ON SOCIAL REFORM], 1871

(*IEON*이언 易言)
Chen Kuan-ying (1841–1923)
1 vol.; woodblock-printed paper
L: 20.4 cm, W: 32.3 cm
USNM ECC 130584   NAA Inv. 09007000
Ref.: HKC p. 487

This Korean translation of volume two of the Chinese *Yiyan* 易言, a social reform prospectus, is a thread-bound with fifty-eight leaves, inclusive of a table of contents. The book consists of nine chapters dealing with respective areas of reform policy: adopting Western technologies; naval and shipbuilding; minting; postal service and communications; salt production management; intelligence sources establishing a parliamentary system; educational and examination systems; and local government administration. The title, *Ieon*, in Chinese ideographs written on a paper label, is affixed to the front cover. On the back of the front cover, Bernadou has inscribed: 美國兵 船士官 藩於道 *Miguk byeongseon sagwan Beon Eo-do* (United States Naval Officer Bernadou). The original Chinese work was written by Chen Kuan-ying 鄭觀應 (1841–1923) in 1871 and advocates social reform by adopting Western technologies (Yi, 1982b: 20–21). It was brought back to Korea in 1880 by Kim Hong-jip 金弘集 (1842–1896), a special envoy to Japan. The book drew great interest from Korean intellectuals, and a facsimile of it was published in 1883 in Korea by royal order (ibid., p. 26). This book is a special edition in Hangul. Hough states that it was written in the 1880s to encourage favor of western civilization. Another edition is held in the library of the Seogang University in Seoul (ibid., p. 27).

Collected in Seoul

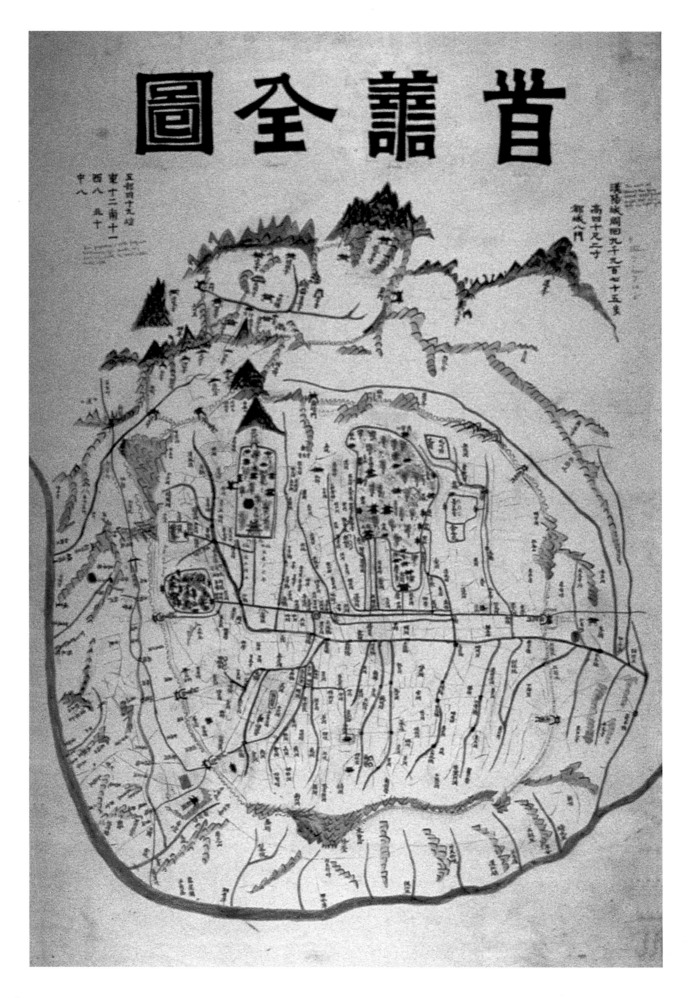

146 MAP OF SEOUL

(*SUSEON JEONDO* 수선전도 首善全圖)
Choson Period (1392–1910), late 19th century
Hand drawn and hand colored paper
H: 101 cm, W: 67 cm
USNM ECC 77067
Ref.: HKC p. 488; BFN 25

This map of old Seoul and its environs encompasses the areas surrounded by Mount Bukhan 북한산and the Han River 한강. *Jeondo* means complete map or whole view. Information about the Seoul city wall and the administrative districts is inscribed in Chinese on each side under the title. The inscription reads: the city wall is 9,975 *bo* 步 [approximately 17 kilometers] in circumference, 40 *cheok* 尺 2 *chon* 寸 [approximately 12 meters] high, and has eight gates; Seoul is divided into five districts under the administrative division called *bu* 部 and the districts are subdivided into forty-nine smaller sections known as *bang* 坊. Bernadou has inscribed a note on pronunciation and translation in English in the margin. This map includes pictorial features of mountain ranges, palace structures, temples, and city gates, all of which face the center of the city. Color codes are: green for mountains; blue for rivers; red and black for roads; and yellow for the

palace boundary. Locations of city walls, gates, palaces, temples, government offices, villages, schools, graves, roads, bridges, storage facilities, mountains, etc. are also given in Chinese.

Neither the identity of the cartographer nor the date of manufacture is known. There is no scale nor legend. Hough criticizes the map as "very poor cartography, not drawn to scale, and having no profile hatchings." The map may be reconsidered as an example of folk painting (Yun, 1997: 35; for illustrations 273–277) with archival value.

BFN 25 "Korean map of Soul [Seoul]. Showing Nam-san or South Mountain where the signal fires are lighted nightly. Also, the Pouk-kan or north fortress, and the walls and gates of the city. The two principal streets are also shown and streams of water indicated as running through the town are in reality wide ditches in which refuse matter of all kinds is thrown and which are only thoroughly cleansed at the time of the heavy summer rains."

Collected in Seoul

147 MAP OF THE WORLD AND NINE REGIONAL MAPS OF KOREA

(HAEDONG JEONDO 해동전도 海東全圖)
Choson Period (1392–1910), 19th century
World map hand drawn and hand colored paper;
regional maps of Korea photo-lithographs
Various sizes. The world map is: 28.1 cm (H)
33.3 cm (W). The heights of the other maps range from 55.3 cm to 71.1 cm, and the width from 39.8 cm to 43.3 cm.
USNM ECC 167553
No entry in HKC; Published (*Map of the World*, 1860s, cover, Department of State Bulletin, June 1982)

Here is a series of Korean regional maps:

(1) Korea, titled *Haedong jeondo* 海東全圖 (2) southern Hamgyeong 함경 Province; (3) northern Hamgyeong Province; (4) Gangwon 강원Province; (5) Gyeongsang 경상 Province; (6) Jeolla 전라 and Jeju 제주 Provinces; (7) Gyeonggi 경기 and Chungcheong 충청 Provinces; (8) Hwanghae 황해 Province; (9) Pyeongan 평안 Province; (10) and a map of the world. Bernadou's signature is inscribed on each side of the ten maps. The cartographer and

the date are unknown, but the 1828 census records on the back of the map of Korea suggest that they were made sometime between 1828 and 1884, when Bernadou purchased them. Proper names and legends are in Chinese, with transliterations in Hangul, seemingly added later. The map of the world is actually an iconography rather than a map. The earth is presented as circular, with a dimension of about 200,000 *li* 里, that is, 488,000 miles. At the extreme east and the extreme west are two mountains where the sun rises and sets. China is at the center of the world with Korea, Japan, India and Mongolia clustered around. This section is surrounded by imaginary nations with curious names such as the nation of giants, of little people, of women, of one-eyed people. The maps of Korea and its eight provinces are quite accurate and thorough. Census records on the back of the map of Korea provide an overall understanding of Korea in the nineteenth century, including statistics on population, households, farmland, warehouses, reservoirs, temples, ships, stations and markets. On the margin of the map of North Hamgyeong province is a cartographer's statement about the purpose and methodology of making maps. Bernadou has pinned on the map of North Hamgyeong province a roughly hand-drawn map of Korea, indicating each province in order to help viewers see its relative location. The cartographer also wrote that he focused on the harsh landscape and the distance between cities so that these maps could be of practical use to travelers. He used *Baengni-cheok* 百里尺, the reduced scale of one *cheok* 尺 to 100 *li* 里, equivalent to the scale of 1 to 12,900 (*KLPC*, 1960: 714). He used color specifications for instant reading: green for mountains, blue for water, red lines for roads, yellow lines for borders, and towns of each province colored differently. Also indicated are geographical features such as mountains, rivers, and islands, local government and military posts; roads, both land routes and waterways; distances between the capital and major geographical points; descriptive statements of major points of interest. Accompanying the maps is a folder containing twenty-six pages of field notes in Bernadou's hand, which include: 145 nations represented in the Korean map of the world in Chinese characters, their pronunciations in English, and occasionally literal English translations; notes on other individual maps; notes on the method of making Korean ink; notes on various colors of silk used for jewelry wrappings.

Collected in Seoul

USNM ECC 167553
The map of the world is labeled:
1. 赤脛國 or Juckkyöng nation.
2. 流鬼國 or Yukei nation.
[3.] 女眞 These are the ancient 肅愼 They inhabited the country to the East of the river 混同江 or Sounggair at the foot of the mountains 長白山 in the North of the Corea at the sources of the 鴨綠江. They had the 室韋 on the North and they were bounded by the 渤海 on the West (eighth century). The family name of the Princes was 王姓拏氏. They belonged originally to the black river 黑水靺鞨 tribe. In 1170, the following hordes were living in their neighbourhood: 鐵勒, 噴訥, 怕忽, □沒
4. 蒙古 or Mongolia.
5. 達子 Darlja.
6. 匈奴. The name generally given to the Turkish tribe since 600 B.C. An ancient people of Mongolia. Under the Tsin and Han, they were formerly called 獫狁.

7. 突厥 or Turks properly so called. Bands of the 匈奴, who retreated into the Altai mountains. The family name of their princes was Assena. They became powerful towards the middle of the sixth century.
8. 大齒國 or Daikei [Daechi] nation.
9. 哈密 or Harp-mil.
10. 車師 or Uigurs. They were divided into anterior and ulterior Uigurs and occupied the country around Khamil and Toufun. Fifteen hundred families (200 B.C.).
11. 崑崙 or 崑屯 Chinese name of the Island of Puloconder in China sea. [Khunlun Shan]
12. 華山 or Hwasan or Bright mountain. [Hua Shan]
13. 嵩山 or Gosan [Hansan] or Fern mountain. [Hao Shan]
14. 西域 or West bound. [India]
15. 恒山 or Hwarngsan [Hangsan] or Continuous mountain. [Heng Shan]
16. 泰山 or Taisan or Great mountain. [Thai Shan]
17. 長城 or Jarng-seung or Great wall.
18. 衡山 or Heungsarn or Balanced mountain. [Heng Shan]
19. 三天子章 or Sam-c'hun-jac'harng.
20. 琉球 or Loochoo Islands. [Ryukyu Islands]
21. 朝鮮 or The ancient name of Korea.
22. 日本 or Japan.
23. 灵古 or Young-go.
24. 姑射山 or Go-sa mountain.
25. 毛民國 or Nation of hairy people.
26. 明祖國 or Meung-cho nation.
27. 暘國 or Tang [Yang] nation.
28. □□山, 東岳 or Dong-ark or Eastern (mountain) peak.
29. 方丈 or Great square.
30. 蓬萊 or Pong-nai or a fabulous mountain where angels frequent. [In Taoist thoughts, it is the home of divine spirits and apotheosized immortals who had discovered the secret of immortality and become perfect in their earthly lives. (Aero, 1980: 143)]
31. 瀛洲 or Yeung-chu.
32. 呂宋 or Philophine [Philippine] Islands.
33. 長沙國 or Nation of long sands.
34. 安南, The Empire of Annan [Annam] comprising Tonquin, Cochin China, and the kingdom of Tsiampa on the Southeast of China. The capital is called 交州. [Vietnam].
35. 蒼海島 or Charng-hai-do or Green-sea island.
36. 小人國 or Nation of small people.
37. 鳩始國 or Goo-chi nation.
38. □國 or No [Gi] nation.
39. 足明國 or Chok meung nation.
40. 食木國 or Seek-mok nation.
41. 林邑 or Wooded town or Forest.
42. 扶南 or Poo-nam or Belong to South.
43. 爪哇 The Island of Java.
44. 西洋 or West water.
45. 長臂國 or Nation of long armed people.
46. 厭火國 or Hun-hwa. [Yeom-hwa nation]
47. 結胸國 or Nation of tied or fastened breasted people.
48. 交脛國 or Koi-kyöng nation.
49. 長離山 or Nam-ark or South (mountain) peak.
50. 歧舌國 or Ji-sul [Gi-seol] nation.
51. 長洲 or Charng-chu or Long water.
52. 蓮石山 or Continuous rocky mountain.
53. 大人國 or Nation of large people.
54. 貫胸國 or Kwan-heung nation, where the people were supposed to have hole in the middle of breast.
55. 一臂國 or Nation of one armed people.
56. 三首國 or Nation of three headed people.
57. 國 or Jai-nation [Jil nation].

58. 三身國 or Nation of three bodied people.
59. 伽毗國 or Ka-pi nation.
60. 奇肱國 or Kei-hwang [Gi-goeng] nation.
61. 驪山, 酤 or West (mountain) peak.
62. 羽民國 or Nation of feathered people.
63. 大樂國 or Great musical nation.
64. 一目國 or Nation of one eyed people.
65. 無臂國 or Nation of armless people.
66. 聚窟洲 or Watery cave.
67. 桑利國 or Sang-ye [Sang-ni] nation.
68. 巫咸國 or Moo-ham or perfect nation.
69. 鍾山 or Bell mountain.
70. 白民國 or Nation of white people.
71. 無腸國 or Nation of stomachless people.
72. 甌係國 or Hwarng-kei [Gu-gye] nation.
73. 長耳國 or Sap-ye [Jang-i] nation.
74. 玄洲 or Black water.
75. 廣野山 or Northern (mountain) peak.
76. 方壺 or Square bottle.
77. 玄股國 or Heun-yeuk [Hyeon-go] nation.
78. 鍾山 or Bell mountain.
79. 芳民國 or Parng-min nation.
80. 千里盤松 or A pine tree can be seen at a distance of a thousand miles.
81. 萬里大澤 or A pool of ten thousand miles circumference.
82. 深目國 or Nation of deep eyed people.
83. 封淵 or Sealed pool.
84. 叱肩國 or Ta-mi [Jil-gyeon] nation.
85. 北極山 or Extreme north mountain.
86. 大人國 or Nation of large people.
87. 始州國 or Si-chu nation.
88. 荊天山 or Thorny heaven mountain.
89. 荊天國 or Thorny heaven nation.
90. 靖國 or C'hung nation.
91. 小弟國 or So-ri nation.
92. 中泰國 or Choong-tai nation or Central great nation.
93. 龍伯國 or Yong-pack nation.
94. 佻人國 or Cho-en [Jo-in] nation.
95. 甘山 or Sweet mountain.
96. 甘淵 or Sweet pool.
97. 融國 or Yeung nation.
98. 司齒國 or Sa-yu [Sa-chi] nation.
99. 夏州國 or Ha-chu nation.
100. 君子國 or Nation of wise and humble people.
101. 堅明山 or Kei-meung [Hak-myeong] mountain.
102. 明星山 or Bright star mountain.
103. 中容國 or Choong-yong nation.
104. 塤民國 or Kei-min [Hun-min] nation.
105. 蘇門山 or So-mun mountain.
106. 倚天山 or Kui-chun mountain.
107. 晨姓國 or Hwang-seung nation.
108. 白洲 or White pool.
109. 盈民山 or Yeung-min mountain.
110. □山 or Kai mountain.
111. 國 or Kei-yeu [Jeon-ok] nation.
112. 不死國 or Nation where the people have ever lasting life.
113. □里国 or A-ri nation.
114. 重京山 or Choong-kyöng mountain.
115. 季万國 or Kai-man nation.
116. 驦頭國 or Yur-do nation.
117. 義和國 or Eui-hwa nation.
118. 天□山 or Chun-chung mountain.
119. 金山 or Golden mountain.
120. 互人國 or Ho-in nation.
121. 融天山 or Lofty heavenly mountain.
122. 火山國 or Fire mountain nation.
123. 火炎山 or Firy [fiery] hot mountain.
124. 靈鰲山 or No-soo [O-o] mountain.
125. 大荒山 or Greatly dry mountain.
126. 月母國 or Moon mother nation.

128

126. 月母國 or Moon mother nation.
127. 雲和國 or Bright cloudy nation.
128. 女子國 or Nation of women.
129. 氏國 or Yeum-si nation.
130. 金門山 or Golden gate mountain.
131. 軒轅國 or Heun-hwan [Heon-won] nation.
132. 丈夫國 or Nation of stout and strong people.
133. 壽麻國 or Soo-ma nation.
134. 淑女國 or Sook-yeur nation.
135. 不周山 or Not arounded mountain.
136. 母山 or Mother mountain.
137. 不白山 or Not white mountain.
138. 章尼山 or Jarng-ye [Jang-ni] mountain.
139. 苗民山 or Moi-min nation.
140. 日月出 or where sun and moon rise.
141. 扶桑 or Double mulberry tree.
142. 日月入 or where sun and moon set.
143. 盤松 or flat pine tree.
144. 洋水 or Great water.
145. 黑水 or Black river.

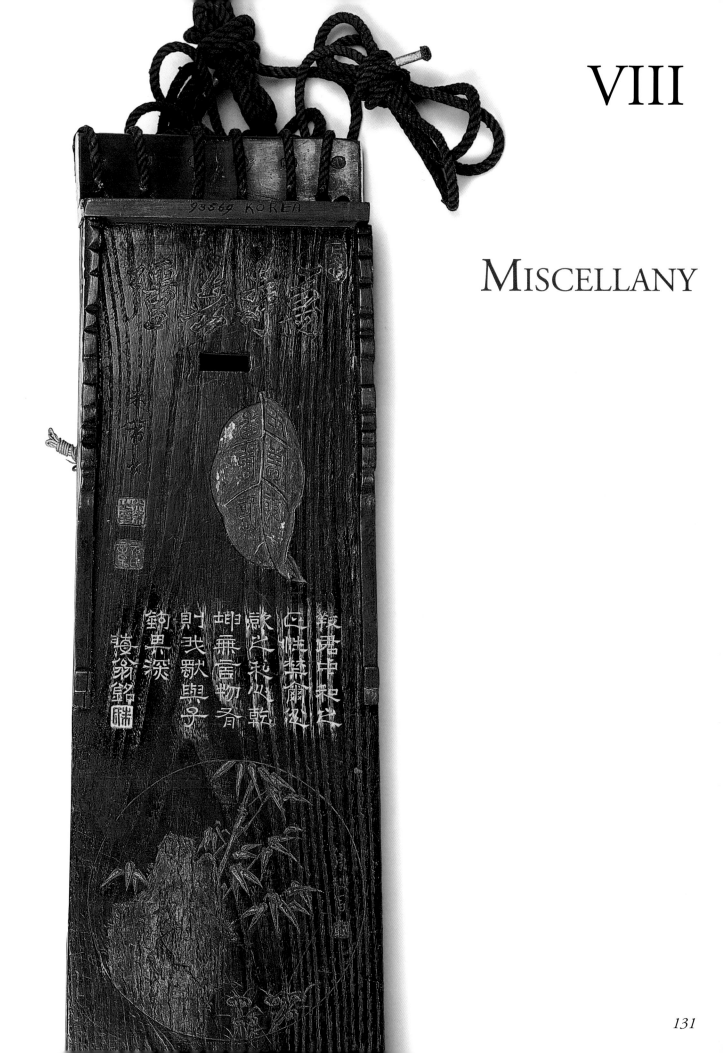

VIII

MISCELLANY

148 WRAPPING CLOTH

(*BOJAGI* 보자기)
Choson Period (1392–1910), late 19th century
Printed cotton
L: 122 cm, W: 138 cm
USNM ECC 153613
Ref.: HKC p. 476; BFN 44

This large wrapping cloth made of coarse cotton has tying ribbons sewn on to each of its four corners. The ribbons are folded cotton bands. The cloth is printed in black with the ideographs *su* 壽 (long life) and *bok* 福 (blessings) and a dragon and butterfly roundels. Large wrappers, like this one, accommodate bulky items either for storage or for carrying. *Bojagi* refers to a small wrapping cloth, often a patchwork type, which is also used for covering food on a tray or table. Both of these, either large or small, are square or rectangular. The materials and colors vary. Cotton, silk, and ramie pieces are decorated with embroidery, block printing, appliqué, painting and patchwork in geometric and floral designs. Korean wrapping cloths have similar functions to those of Japanese *furoshiki* ふろしき or Okinawan *uchikui* うちくい (Hauge, 1978: 253, and 165 for illustrations). Both Korean and Japanese wrappers are for everyday use as well as for special occasions such as wedding and ceremonial gift-giving. The traditional Korean home had sparse furnishing. Flexible wrapping cloths for storing and carrying articles are convenient. Decorative wrappers also covered special food for weddings and ancestor-worship ceremonies and prayer-food offerings to Shamanist spirits as well as to the Buddha (Heo, 1987: 128; Heo, 1988: 144–149, especially for historical references and recommended classificatory system).

Collected in Seoul

149 PLAYING CARDS

(*TUJEON* 투전 鬪箋)
Choson Period (1392–1910), late 19th century
Ink on varnished paper
L: 20.4 cm, W: 3.2 cm
USNM ECC 77047
Ref.: HKC pl. XXIV, fig. 1; BFN 17

The set consists of eighty-one cards with suit signs marked in black on all but one blank card. The blank one is probably used to replace a lost card. There are eight suit signs, known as the eight general cards, each with its own value: 1) The man (*injang* 人將); 2) fish (*eojang* 魚將); 3) hawk (*jojang* 鳥將); 4) pheasant (*chijang* 雉將); 5) deer (*jangjang* 獐將); 6) star (*seongjang* 星將); 7) horse (*majang* 馬將); 8) hare (*tojang* 兔將). This game is played by four people (Culin, 1958: 123–126). Each person takes twenty cards (Jo and Prunner, 1984: 58). The numerals, which are placed above the suit marks, run up to nine for each suit, and the tenth card is the general (*jang* 將). Players are from the lower classes, yet men of higher rank used the cards to gamble (Culin, 1958: 123-126).

The term, *tujeon*, might be translated as "fighting tablets" or "fighting arrows," as the suit marks resemble the feathers of arrows. A homonym of *tujeon*, rendered in different ideographs 投錢, means gambling. Originally, the cards were made of bamboo and sixty cards made a set, but only forty cards were used in the game (*DHM*, 1980: 330). The Onyang Museum of Folkcrafts holds a set of cards bearing value signs in a series of ideographs representing literary compounds (for illustration, Ibid.).

BFN 17 "....There are several varieties differing as to the number of suits, and cards in a suit. Some of these are forbidden by law on account of their use in gambling. Those caught using them are fined and beaten. Others however are allowed, such as these, the Koreans saying that games cannot be played fast enough with them for any one to lose any great amount of money. There are eight suits, the man, fish, hawk, pheasant, deer, star, rabbit, and horse; and ten cards in each, the numerals up to nine and a general."

Collected in Seoul

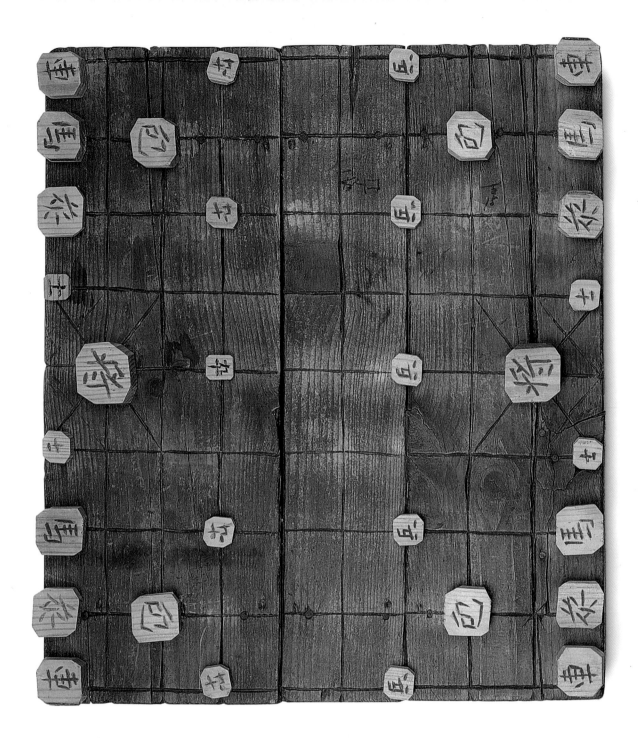

150 KOREAN CHESS

(*JANGGI* 장기)
Choson Period (1392–1910), late 19th century
Canted-square wood tiles incised with
ideographs painted blue or red
Varied sizes
USNM ECC 77025
Ref.: HKC pl. XXIV, fig. 2; BFN 15

The ideographs on these blocks represent
individual values and are painted blue or red. The
game is called "game of war." The king, in this
case the general (*jang* 將), is the largest, while the
chariot (*cha* 車), elephant (*sang* 象), horse (*ma* 馬)

and cannon (*po* 包) are of medium size. The smallest
are the pawns or soldiers. Other small pieces are the
counselors (*sa* 士) (Culin, 1958: 83). Hough's entry
mentions "Chinese chessmen," but notes that
Chinese chessmen are of uniform size and that
Korean chessmen are hexagonal and of various sizes.
W.H. Wilkinson (1894: 30–31) explains, "Korean
chess is admittedly a variant of Chinese, yet, there
are some important differences between the two
games... The men, again, have the same names in
China, and, except that the King is placed in the
center of his 'camp,' and that the 'horse' and
'elephant' are interchangeable, occupy the same
positions at starting. But their powers and privileges
in most cases differ largely" (op. cit. Culin, p. 82).
The Korean government exhibited a set of circular

chessmen at the Columbian Exposition in 1893 in
Chicago. They are now in the Museum of the
University of Pennsylvania.

Collected in Seoul

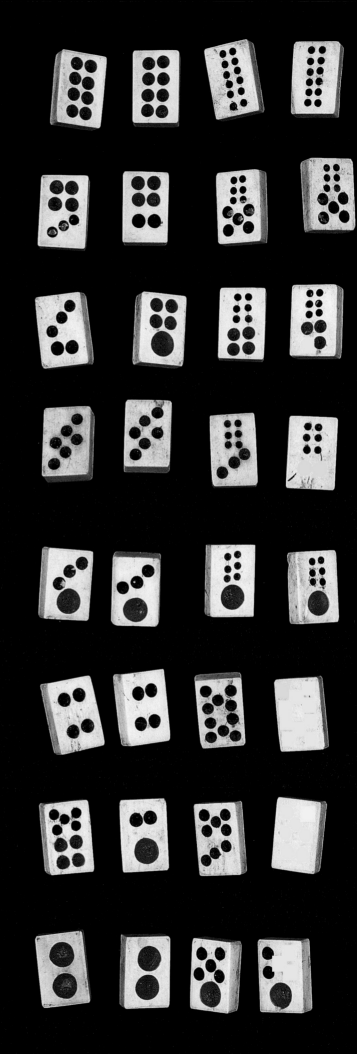

151 DOMINOES

(*GOLPAE* 골패)
Choson Period (1392–1910), late 19th century
Painted ivory
L: 4.1 cm, W: 3.8 cm
USNM ECC 77024
Ref.: HKC pl. XXIV, fig. 3; BFN 104

The oversized "one" spot and the "four" spots on these dominoes are in red; all other spots are in black. The game is played by three or four people. The player who first draws the piece with the highest number of pips becomes the *jangwon* 장원, literally meaning a candidate who won first place in a state examination during the Choson period. The object of the game is to obtain certain combinations of three pieces, which are called perfect tablets. *Golpae* are also known as *hopae* 호패, "foreign tablets" (Culin, 1958: 104) or Chinese tablets. According to Hough, the arrangement of the pips on Korean dominoes is identical to the Chinese. The *golpae* set is used for a variety of games, including gambling and fortune telling (*DHM*, 1980: 331).

BFN 104 "...Korean dominoes. With these are played games similar to our own."

Collected in Seoul

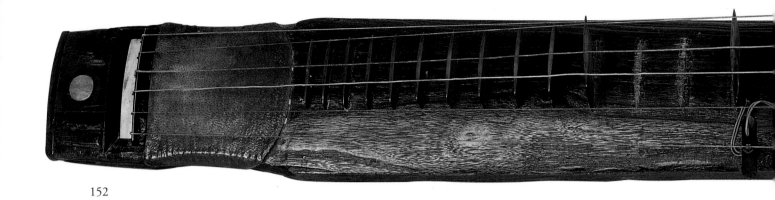

152

152 Instrument with Six Strings
(*GEOMUNGO* 거문고)

Choson Period (1392–1910), late 19th century
Paulownia wood with silk strings
L: 162 cm, W: 17 cm, H: 11.5 cm (center)
USNM ECC 93569
Ref.: HKC pl. XXV; BFN 113

This instrument has six strings of twisted silk; the second, third, and fourth strings are stretched over sixteen fixed frets, which are tuned by round pegs. The other strings are stretched over three movable bridges and are tuned by moving the bridge to the right or left (*SMI*, 1998: 42–43 for Korean terms for different parts of the instrument). When played, the *geomungo* is laid flat and the strings are plucked with a bamboo rod held between the index and middle fingers of the right hand. The left hand presses on the strings to produce microtones. This instrument was featured in a chamber ensemble or as accompaniment to classical lyric songs. *Geomungo* also became popular to play folk tunes. The wood is decorated with a bat and a rebus for blessings, and the longevity symbols: rocks, bamboo, and *pulloch'o* 不老草, fungus of immortality.

Hough compares this Korean harp to the Japanese *koto* "played like it with the plectrum." He adds that "Koreans regard it quite an accomplishment to master this instrument," and offers a lengthy statement about Korean music. "Music is an important institution in Korea. The government educates and maintains musicians and allows bands to furnish music for official receptions and at the palace. There is a system of notation; the notes are circles and their tonal value is indicated by the shaded area. Vocal classes are taught the range through which the voice should rise and fall by the inclination of a rod in the hands of the teacher. This is similar in effect to the Tibetan descriptive score. There are many musical instruments of all classes. The double headed drum *janggu* 장구 *janggo* 장고 produces four

distinct sounds, according to the place struck; by combination these sounds may be increased to seven. The drum has a hollow wooden body of hour-glass shape; the heads are drawn over the ends of the body and extend over two iron rings. The lacing of rope with tighteners runs between these rings. The larger head is of skin and the smaller of membrane. The deepest sound is made by striking the skin head in the center, the rim gives another sound, the membrane head gives a lighter, noisier sound."

BFN 113 "Korean musical instrument. The Koreans consider it an accomplishment to be able to perform upon this. Resembles the Japanese koto or harp. Made of a certain wood only (*Jatropha curcas* [paulownia]); the Koreans say no other will answer."

Collected in Seoul

153 Expiatory Effigy
(*JEUNG* 제웅)

Choson Period (1392–1910), late 19th century
Straw
L: 90 cm
USNM ECC 77055
Ref.: HKC pl. XXXII; BFN 156

This straw man is called *jeung* 제웅, *chuyeong* 芻靈, or *cheoyong* 處容 (Kim, letter, 25 April 1994). Making the *jeung* was a common practice to avoid bad luck during the New Year. It was made in human form, stuffed with coins, rice and a piece of paper on which was written the year, month, day, and time of birth of the one who wished to avoid bad luck. On the night corresponding to January 14, this figure was tossed into the road, and whoever picked it up, most likely wandering beggars, assumed the misfortune in exchange for cash. According to *Dongguk sesi-gi* 東國歲時記 (Korean Almanac), written by Hong Seok-mo 洪錫謨 (act. late 18th–early 19th century), children

asked for the *jeung* at every house and, upon receiving it, they collected the coins and hit the *jeung*, as they roamed along the road (Yang, 1974: 21–22; Kim, 1994: 186; *GDS*, 1963: 1388, Yi, 1984: 304–305).

Hough's caption for the straw man reads: "Korean expiatory offering." He makes an extensive note on making the *jeung* and the folk beliefs underlying this practice, citing Byeon Su 邊燧 (1861–1891), one of his consultants. He also puts considerable effort into describing astrological aspects of this practice with the help of another expert, Seo Gwang-beom 徐光範 (1859–1897). The chart of "Jik Sung" [*jikseong* 直星], the stars that are believed to rule human fate] with their Korean and Chinese terms, translation, and English correspondents is very informative. The practice of the *jeung* is closely related to the belief that human fate is influenced by the astrological system. Its origin is traced to *guyo-jae* 九曜齋, the sacrifice to the nine stars made on the 14th day of the first month during the Koryo Dynasty (918–1392) (Kim, 1994: 186). The nine stars believed to rule human fate are: *nahu* 나후 or *jeung* 제웅 [an imaginary star that causes the solar or lunar eclipse], *to* 土 [Saturn], *su* 水 [Mercury], *geum* 金 [Venus], *il* 日 [Sun], *hwa* 火 [Mars], *gyedo* 計都 [unknown], *wol* 月 [Moon], and *mok* 木 [Jupiter]. When boys reach eleven and girls ten, they come under the influence of the stars in the above order, and they must follow certain procedures at the beginning of the year (*HMD*, vol. 4, 1982: 161–163). The first *nahu* star is considered the most evil and making *jeung* is a way of avoiding the misfortune it causes. One also could throw away a small colored gourd bottle, with blue, red, and yellow tassels. When a girl at fourteen, or a boy at fifteen, comes under the influence of the sun, she or he is supposed to make a paper model of the sun and stick it into the ridge of the tiled roof. Upon reaching the age under the sign of Mercury, the nature of which is water, one wraps rice with paper and throws it into a well during the night to avoid ill

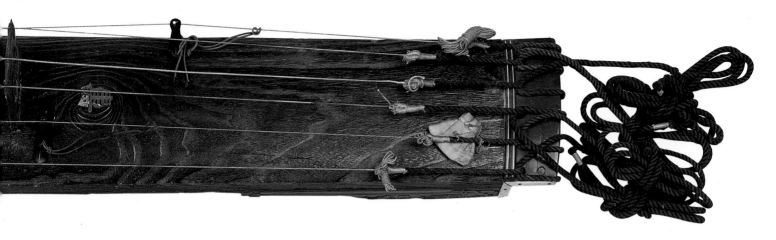

will (Kim, 1994: 186). The alternate name of *jeung*, *cheoyong* 處容, is the spirit believed to have repelled smallpox during the Unified Silla Dynasty (668–935) (*GDS*, 1963: 1388). Since then the people of Silla put representations of *cheoyong* on their doors to repel bad spirits. Pictures of generals, spirits, cocks, or tigers, who correspond to *cheoyong*, are believed to repel evil spirits and are hung on doors at the beginning of a new year. *Cheoyong-bu* 處容符, an amulet with the picture of *cheoyong*, and *cheoyong-mu* 處容舞, a masque dance, also originate from this legend (*GDS*, 1963: 1517; Han, 1975: 23–26). Similar straw figures are found in Japan. When people suffered from *okori* おこり, a fever similar to malaria which was very prevalent in Japan, they reputedly made straw effigies of themselves, rubbed their bodies with them, and after due ceremony threw them into a river (De Garis, 1947: 30). Straw figures also are used by Japanese women to wreak vengeance upon recreant lovers. At the Hour of the Ox (1–3 A.M. in the sexagesimal cycle), they visit a sacred tree at a Buddhist temple of Fudō 不動 and impale upon the tree with nails the straw images of their estranged lovers, nightly until the objects of their incantation sicken and die. This is called *ushi-toki mairi* うしときまいり [ox-hour-visit] (De Garis, 1947: 96): more correctly, *ushi no toki mairi* うしのときまいり or *ushi no toki mōde* うしのときもうで (*KJE*, 1982: 184).

Collected in Seoul

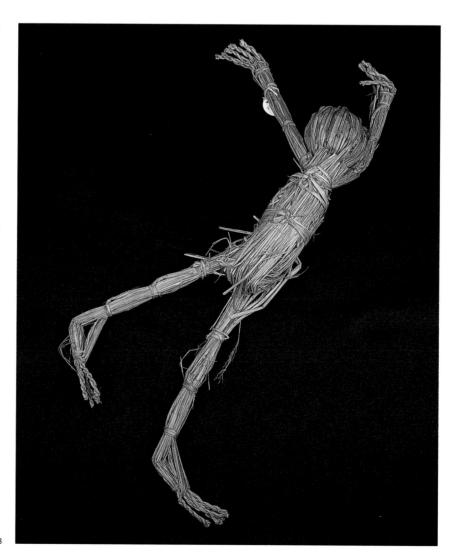

153

Bibliography

Adams, Edward B.
1987. *Korean Folk Art and Craft*. Pages 27, 35. Seoul: Seoul International Publishing House. [First published by Onyang Folk Museum in 1983 as a museum catalog in Korean.]

Aero, Rita
1980. *Things Chinese*. Page 143. New York: Doubleday & Company, Inc.

Allen, Horace N.
1901. *A Chronological Index* (ACI)*: Some of the Chief Events in the Foreign Intercourse of Korea From the Beginning of the Christian Era to the Twentieth Century*. [Seoul], Korea: Press of Methodist Publishing House.

1991. *Horace Newton Allen's Diary*. In *Gu-Han mal gyeokdonggi bisa Allen ui ilgi*
舊韓末 激動期 秘史 알렌의 日記 [A Secret History of the Turbulent End of the Choson Kingdom], Part 4, pages 393–671. Seoul: Dangook University Press–檀國大學校 出版部 [translated to Korean by Kim Won-mo.]

An, Hwi-jun [Ahn, Hwi-joon]
1986. Painting. In *Korean Art Treasures*, pages 31–90. Seoul: Yekyong Publications Co., Ltd.

Bae, Yeong-dong 裵永東 and Yu Yong-hwan 柳龍桓, editor
1988. *Teukbyeol-jeon dorok 2: Choson sidae ui gwanmo* 特別展 圖錄 2: 朝鮮時代의 冠帽 [Special Exhibition Catalog, No. 2: Headgear of the Choson Dynasty]. Pages 22, 29, 34–35. Onyang: Onyang minsok bangmul-gwan 溫陽民俗博物館 [Onyang Folk Museum.]

Bernadou, J. B.
Ms. 1883. Bernadou letter of 2 November 1883, Washington, D.C. to Baird, Director of the U.S. National Museum. Smithsonian Institution Archives Record Unit 29.

1884. Bernadou letter of 10 March 1884, Seoul, Korea to Baird, Director of the U.S. National Museum. Smithsonian Institution Archives Record Unit 29.

1884. Bernadou letter of 2 September 1884, Seoul, Korea to Baird, Director of the U.S. National Museum. National Museum of Natural History, Smithsonian Institution, Registrar's Office accession Number 16970.

1884. Bernadou letter of 4 October 1884, Seoul, Korea to Baird, Director of the U.S. National Museum. Smithsonian Institution Archives Record Unit 29.

1884–1885. Notes on Collections of Korean Articles. Smithsonian Institution Archives Record Unit 305.

1885. Bernadou letter of 20 April 1885, Chemulp'o, Korea, *USS Ossipee* to Baird, Director of the U.S. National Museum. Accompanying Packing List. National Museum of Natural History, Smithsonian Institution, Registrar's Office accession number 16970.

1890. Korea and the Koreans. *The National Geographic Magazine*, vol. 2, No. 4, pages 231–242. Washington, D.C.: National Geographical Society.

Byeon Su 邊燧
1891. Agriculture in Japan. In *U.S. Bureau of Statistics (Department of Agriculture) Report of the Statistician, No. 89*, pages 563–583. Washington, D.C: Department of Agriculture.

Carles, W. R.
1886. Recent Journeys in Korea. In *Proceedings of the Royal Geographical Society and Monthly Record of Geography, No. 5*, (May), pages 289–312. London: Edward Stanford.

Choe, Bong-yeon [Choy, Bong-youn]
1982. The History of Koreans in America, Part 1: Leaving the Land of Morning Calm, *Korean Culture, vol. 3, No. 2*, (July 1982), pages 35–36. Los Angeles: Korean Cultural Service.

Choe, Nam-seon 崔南善
1943. *Gosa-tong* 故事通 [A Survey of Historical Events]. Page 132. Keijo [Seoul]: Samjung-dang 三中堂.

Choe, Seong-ja 최성자
1993. *Hanguk ui mi: seon, saek, hyeong* 韓國의美: 선, 색, 형 (Lines, Colors, and Shapes: The Korean Tradition). Pages 190–191. Seoul: Jisik saneop-sa 한국국제교류재단.

Crim, Keith, editor
1989. *The Perennial Dictionary of World Religions*. Page 134. San Francisco and New York: Harper & Row. [Originally published in 1981 under the title: *Abingdon Dictionary of Living Religions*, by Abingdon Press.]

Culin, Stewart
1958. *Games of the Orient: Korea, China, Japan*. Pages 82–91, 104, 123–128. Rutland, Vermont and Tokyo: Charles E. Tuttle Company. [First published in 1895 under the title: *Korean Games with Notes on the Corresponding Games of China and Japan*, by the University of Pennsylvania.]

De Garis, Frederic
1947. *We Japanese, vol. 1*. Pages 30, 96. Yokohama: Yamagata Press. [Written for Fujiya Hotel, Ltd. In Miyanoshita, Hakone, Japan and first published in 1934.]

De Rosey, Leon
1886. Caractères Physiques et Intellectuals. In *Les Coréens aperçu Ethnographique et Historique, vol. 6*, chapter 3, pages 41–91. Paris: Maisonneuve Frères et Ch. Leclerc, Éditeurs.

Deuchler, Martina
1977. The Tradition: Women during the Yi Dynasty. In *Virtues in Conflict: Tradition and the Korean Woman Today*, Sandra Mattielli ed., pages 1–47. Seoul: Samhwa Publishing Co., Ltd.

Dower, John W.
1971. *The Elements of Japanese Design: A Handbook of Family Crests, Heraldry and Symbolism*. Pages 90–92, 145–146. New York and Tokyo: Walker/Weatherhill.

Eberhard, Wolfram
1986. *A Dictionary of Chinese Symbols: Hidden Symbols in Chinese Life and Thought*. Pages 75–76, 83, 92, 99, 174–175, 177–178, 183, 229, 288–289. London and New York: Routledge. [Translated from German by G. L. Campbell.]

Eom, So Yeon
1994. Minhwa: A Precious Look at Traditional Korean Life. In *Korean Cultural Heritage, vol. 1: Fine Arts (Painting, Handicrafts, Architecture)*, pages 84–91. Seoul: The Korea Foundation.

Gale, J. S.
1892. A Map of the World. *Korean Repository, vol. 1*, (September), pages 336–341. Seoul: The Trilingual Press.

Gilmore, George W., Rev.
1892. *Korea from its Capital: With a Chapter on Missions*. Page 217. Philadelphia: Presbyterian Board of Publication and Sabbath School Work.

Gompertz, G. St. G. M.
1963. *Korean Celadon*. Page 78; plate 23A. London: Faber & Faber, Ltd.

1968. *Korean Pottery & Porcelain of the Yi Period*. Page 44. New York: Praeger.

Goode, G. Brown
1892. The Condition and Progress of the U.S. National Museum During the Year Ending June 30, 1891. In *The U.S. National Museum Annual Report (USNM-AR) for 1891*, pages 3–131. Washington, D.C.: Smithsonian Institution.

Greey, Edward
1888. *Hand-book of A Unique Collection of Ancient and Modern Korean and Chinese Works of Art, Procured in Korea during 1883-1886, by Pierre L. Jouy of Washington, D.C.* [Auction Catalog]. New York: Brower Brothers.

Griffis, W. E.
1882. The Corean Origin of Japanese Art. In *Scribner's Monthly*, (December), pages 224–229.

1885. *Corea, Without and Within*. Philadelphia: Presbyterian Board of Publication.

1894. *Corea the Hermit Nation*. New York: Scribners.

Gungnip jungang bangmul-gwan 國立中央博物館 (The National Museum of Korea)
1975. *Hanguk minye misul* 韓國民藝美術 (HMM) (Folk Art of Korea). Seoul: The National Museum of Korea 國立中央博物館.

1988. *Hanguk ui mi: uisang, jangsingu, bo* 韓國의美: 衣裳, 裝身具, 褓 (HUM) (Beauty of Korea: Traditional Costumes, Ornaments, and Cloth Wrappings) [Exhibition Catalog]. Pages 18, 19, 31, 35, 47, 49, 72, 78, 142. Seoul: Tongcheon munhwa-sa 通川文化社.

Gungnip minsok bangmul-gwan 國立民俗博物館 (The National Folklore Museum) [Currently known as the National Folk Museum]
1980. *Gungnip minsok bangmul-gwan* 國立民俗博物館 (GMB) (The National Folklore Museum) [Illustrated Collection Catalog]. Seoul: Tongcheon munhwa-sa 通川文化社.

1995. *Hanguk ui jongi munhwa* 한국의 종이문화 (HJM) (Traditional Korean Paper Culture) [Exhibition Catalog]. Pages 99, 175. Seoul: Sinyu munhwa-sa 신유문화사.

Ha, Hyo-gil 하효길, and Cheon Jin-gi 천진기, editor
1994. *Miguk Pibadi Essex bangmul-gwan sojang 100 nyeon-jeon Hanguk pungmul: Yu Gil-jun gwa gaehwa ui kkum* 미국 피바디에섹스박물관 소장 100년전 한국풍물: 유길준과 개화의꿈 (Korean Collection from the Peabody Essex Museum) [Exhibition Catalog]. Pages 75, 96–97, 135. Seoul: The National Museum of Korea and the Chosun ilbo-sa 국립중앙박물관, 조선일보사.

Hakwon-sa, editor
1960. *Korea: Its Land, People and Culture of All Ages* (KLPC). Page 714. Seoul: Hakwon-sa, Ltd.

Han, Jeong-seop 韓定燮
1975. *Sinbi ui bujeok* 神秘의 符籍 [Mystics of Talisman]. Pages 23–26. Seoul: Beomnyun-sa 法輪社.

Han, U-geun [Han, Woo-keun]
1971. *The History of Korea*. Honolulu: East-West Center Press. [Originally published in 1970 by the Eul-Yoo [Eulyu] Publishing Co., Ltd. And translated from Korean by K. S. Lee.]

Hanguk inmyeong dae-sajeon pyeonchansil 韓國人名大事典 編纂室, editor
1967. *Hanguk inmyeong dae-sajeon* 韓國人名大事典 (HID) [Dictionary of Korean Biography]. Seoul: Singu munhwa-sa 新丘文化社.

Harrington, Fred Harvey
1944. *God Mammon and the Japanese: Dr. Horace N. Allen and Korean-American Relations, 1884-1905*. Madison: The University of Wisconsin Press.

Hauge, Victor, and Takako Hauge
1978. *Folk Traditions in Japanese Art*. Pages 165, 253. Washington, D.C.: International Exhibitions Foundation.

Hawley, W. M.
1971. *Chinese Folk Designs*. New York: Dover Publications, Inc. [First published in 1949.]

Heo, Dong-hwa [Huh, Dong-hwa] 許東華
1988. *Yet bojagi* 옛보자기 (Pojagi: Cloth Wrappings). In *Hanguk ui mi: uisang, jangsingu, bo* 韓國의美: 衣裳, 裝身具, 褓 (HUM) (Beauty of Korea: Traditional Costumes, Ornaments, and Cloth Wrappings) [Exhibition Catalog], pages 144–149. Seoul: Tongcheon munhwa-sa 通川文化社.

Heo, Dong-hwa [Huh, Dong-hwa] and Pak Yeong-suk [Park, Young-sook]
1987. *Crafts of the Inner Court: The Artistry of Korean Women*. Page 128. Seoul: The Museum of Korean Embroidery.

Heo Yeong-hwan [Huh, Yeong-han] 허영환
1994. Choson Landscape and Genre Painting. In *Korean Cultural Heritage, vol. 1: Fine Arts (Painting, Handicrafts, Architecture)*, pages 54–61. Seoul: The Korea Foundation 한국국제교류재단.

Hinsley, Curtis M. Jr.
1981. *Savages and Scientists: The Smithsonian Institution and the Development of American Anthropology 1846-1910*. Washington, D.C.: Smithsonian Institution Press.

Hoam Art Museum 호암미술관, editor
1983. *Minhwa geoljak-jeon* 民畫傑作展 (MGJ) [The Hoam Art Museum Anniversary Special Exhibition Catalog: Masterpiece Folk Paintings]. Pages 124–125; plates 7, 43. Seoul: Samsung misul munhwa jaedan 三星美術文化財團.

1998. *Kkum gwa sarang: maehok ui uri minhwa 55: 56 (KGS) (Auspicious Dreams: Decorative Paintings of Korea)* [Exhibition Catalog]. Page 46. Seoul: Samsung misul munhwa jaedan 三星美術文化財團.

Hong, Ung-seon 洪雄善, and Yi Hun-jong 李勳鍾, editor
1955. *Gugeo hakseup dobo* 국어학습도보 [A Pictorial Glossary of Korean Terms]. Pages 48, 50. Seoul: Daeyang chulpan-sa 大洋出版社.

Houchins, Chang-su
1982. Smithsonian Mi gungnip bangmul-gwan sojang Hanguk minwha 스미소니안美國立博物館所藏 韓國民畫 (The Smithsonian Collection of Korean Folk Paintings). *Misuljaryo* 美術資料 (National Museum Journal of Arts), No. 30, pages 56–63. Seoul: The National Museum of Korea 國立中央博物館.

1995. *Artifacts of Diplomacy: Smithsonian Collections from Commodore Matthew Perry's Japan Expedition (1853-1854)*. Page 105. Washington, D.C: Smithsonian Institution Press.

Hough, Walter
1888. The Preservation of Museum Specimens from Insects and Dampness. In *The Smithsonian Institution Annual Report (SI-AR) for 1887, part 2*, pages 549–558. Washington, D.C.: Government printing office.

1892. The Bernadou, Allen, and Jouy Korean Collections (HKC), in the U.S. National Museum. In *The U.S. National Museum Annual Report (USNM-AR) for 1891*, pages 429–488. Washington, D.C.: Smithsonian Institution.

1899a. Korean Clan Organization. *The American Anthropologist, New Series, vol. 1*, pages 150–54. New York: G. P. Putnam's Sons.

1899b. Notes and News: Korean Crossbow and Arrow-tube. *The American Anthropologist, New Series, vol. 1*, page 200. New York: G. P. Putnam's Sons.

Huhm, Halla Pai
1980. *Kut: Korean Shamanist Rituals*. Pages 55–59, 64. Elizabeth, New Jersey, and Seoul: Hollym International Corp.

Hwang, Hye-seong 黃慧星
1980. Sik-saenghwal 食生活 [Diet]. In *Doseol Hanguk ui minsok* 圖說韓國의 民俗 (DHM). (The Folkcrafts of Korea), pages 415–426. Seoul: Gyeomong-sa 啓蒙社.

Im, Yeong-ju 林永周
1986. *Jeontong munyang jaryo-jip* 傳統紋樣 資料集 [Collection of Traditional Korean Decorative Design Patterns]. Pages 57, 68, 77–85. Seoul: Mijin-sa 미진사.

Jang, Su-yeong 장수영
1982. 1883 nyeon ui gyeon-Mi sajeoldan gwa suhaengwon Byeon Su 1883 년의 견미사절단과 수행원 변수, KSEA (The Korean Scientists and Engineers Association in America) Letters, vol. 11, No. 3, (November-December), pages 51–54. Rockville: The Korean Scientists and Engineers Association in America. Inc.

1983. Gu-Han mal yeokdae jumigongsa wa geudeul ui hwaldong 구한말 역대 주미공사와 그들의 활동, KSEA

(The Korean Scientists and Engineers Association in America) Letters, vol. 11, No. 6, (May-June), pages 36–42. Rockville: The Korean Scientists and Engineers Association in America. Inc.

Jang, Suk-hwan [Chang, Sook-hwan] 장숙환
1992. Choson sidae ui jangsingu 조선시대의 장신구 [Choson Period Personal Ornaments]. In *Hanguk jeontong saenghwal ui mi* 한국 전통생활의 미 (Korean Costumes and Textiles) [Exhibition Catalog and English Text for IBM Gallery of Science and Art, New York], pages 22–23; illustration pages 50–71. Seoul: Hanguk IBM.

Jang, Suk-hwan 장숙환, editor
1999. *Damin boksik misulgwan gaegwan ginyeom dorok* 澹人服飾美術館 개관기념도록 *(The Inaugural Exhibition Catalogue of the Chang Pudeok Memorial Gallery).* Pages 18–33, 58, 61, 66–69, 76–79, 110–111, 128–131, 149–157, 167–173, 87–188; illustration numbers 65, 69–70, 82–85, 180, 185, 188–190, 194–196, 215–217. Seoul: Ewha Women's University 이화여자대학교.

Jenings, Foster H.
1904. Korean Headdresses in the National Museum. *Smithsonian Miscellaneous Collections, vol. 45,* pages 149–167. Washington, D.C: Smithsonian Institution.

Jeong, Yang-mo [Chung, Yang Mo] 정양모
1993. The Art of Everyday Life. In *Korean Arts of the Eighteenth Century: Splendor & Simplicity,* pages 59–77. New York: The Asia Society Galleries.

Jo, Heung-yun [Cho, Hung-youn] 趙興胤 and Gernot Prunner
1984. Gisan pungsok-do cheop 箕山風俗圖帖 *(Ki-san-Genremalereien)* [Gisan's Genre Painting Album, text in both Korean and German]. Seoul: Beomyang chulpan-sa 汎洋出版社.

Jo, Hyo-sun [Cho, Hyo-soon]
1995. Korean Clothes and Fabrics. *Koreana: Korean Art and Culture, vol. 9, No. 3,* pages 12–19. Seoul: International Cultural Society of Korea.

Jo, Ja-yong [Zozayong] 趙子庸
1970. *Korean Art Series, vol. 1: The Humour of Korean Tiger.* Pages 8–15. Seoul: Emille Museum [에밀레 美術館].

1972. *Korean Art Series, vol. 2: Spirit of the Korean Tiger.* Seoul: Emille Museum [에밀레 美術館].

1974a. Geonchuk gwa hoehwa 建築과 繪畫 [Architecture and Painting]. *Geonchuk Hanguk* 建築韓國, (September, 1974), pages 49–51.

1974b. *Tora no bijutsu* 虎の 美術 [Art of Tiger]. Pages 20, 51. Tokyo: Dai nippon kaiga kogei bijutsu kabushiki kaisha 大日本繪畫巧芸美術株式會社.

1983. Segye sok ui hanminhwa 世界 속의 韓民畫 [Korean Folk Paintings in the World]. In *Minhwa geoljak-jeon* 民畫傑作展 (MGJ) [The Hoam Art Museum Anniversary Special Exhibition Catalog: Masterpiece Folk Paintings], pages 107–129. Seoul: Samsung misul munhwa jaedan 三星美術文化財團.

Jo, Seon-mi [Cho, Sunmie]
1994. Faces from the Past: Portrait Paintings. In *Korean Cultural Heritage, vol. 1: Fine Arts (Painting, Handicrafts, Architecture),* pages 76–83. Seoul: The Korea Foundation 한국국제교류재단.

Jouy, Pierre Louis
1888a. The Collection of Korean Mortuary Pottery in the U.S. National Museum. In *The U.S. National Museum Annual Report* (USNM-AR) *for 1888,* pages 589–596. Washington, D.C: Smithsonian Institution.

1888b. The Korean Potter's Wheel. *Science,* page 144. Washington, D.C.

Ju, Wol-yeong [Chu, Woul Young]
1985. *From Traditional Korean Cuisine.* Pages 104–106. Los Angeles: The Korea Times L.A.

Kim, Cheol-sun 金哲淳
1979a. Minhwa ran mueosinga 民畫란 무엇인가 [What is Folk Painting]. In *Hanguk ui mi vol. 8: Hanguk minhwa* 韓國의 美 8: 韓國民畫 [Korean Aesthetics vol. 8: Korean Folk Paintings], pages 183–203. [First published in 1978]. Seoul: Joongang ilbo 中央日報.

1979b. Dopan haeseol 圖版解說 [Plate Caption]. In *Hanguk ui mi vol. 8: Hanguk minhwa* 韓國의 美 8: 韓國民畫 [Korean Aesthetics vol. 8: Korean Folk Paintings], pages 212–220. [First published in 1978]. Seoul: Joongang ilbo 中央日報.

Kim, Dong-uk 金東旭
1976. Danen fuzoku gacho 檀園風俗畫帖 [Danwon's Genre Paintings]. In *Etonosu* えとのす *(Ethnos in Asia),* vol. 7, pages 12–13. Tokyo: Shin Nippon Kyoiku tosho kabushiki kaisha 新日本教育圖書株式會社.

Kim, Hong-nam 김홍남, editor
1993. *Korean Arts of the Eighteenth Century: Splendor & Simplicity.* Pages 34–42. New York: The Asia Society Galleries.

1996. *Yet gagu ui areumdaum* 옛 가구의 아름다움 *(The Beauty of Old Korean Furniture)* [Exhibition catalog of a special exhibition organized in celebration of the 110th anniversary of Ewha Women's University]. Page 29. Seoul: Ewha Women's University 이화여자대학교.

Kim, Jaewon [Chewon], and G. St. G. M. Gompertz, editor
1961. *Korean Arts, vol. 2: Ceramics.* Pages 92–93. [Seoul]: The Republic of Korea, Ministry of Foreign Affairs.

Kim, Kyeong 金卿
1988a. *Kankoku dentō no bi - kami kōgei-ten* 韓國傳統の 美 - 紙工藝術 [Traditional Korean Esthetics Exhibition of Korean Paper Crafts]. [Titles in both Japanese and Korean]. Unpaged. Fujinomiya-shi 富士宮市: Fuji bijutsukan 富士美術館.

Kim, Samdaeja 金三代子
1992. Munbang jeogu 文房諸具 [Various Stationery Items]. In *Choson sidae munbang jeogu* 118 *(The Elegant Beauty of Choson Studies),* pages 164–218; illustrations pages 81–85, 112–121. Seoul: The National Museum of Korea 國立中央博物.

Kim, Sul-sik [Kim, Soolshik] 金逑植
1972. Garakji 가락지 (Rings). Minhak 民學 *(Folkism),* vol. 1, pages 106–108. Seoul: Emille Museum 에밀레 美術館.

Kim, Ui-suk 김의숙
1994. Jonggyo uirye 종교의례 [Religious Rituals]. In *Hanguk minsok-hak ui ihae* 한국 민속학의 이해 [Understanding Korean Folk Studies], edited by

Minsok hakhoe 민속학회 [Korean Society of Folk Studies], pages 180–189. Seoul: Munhak Academy.

Kim, Won-mo 金源模, editor
1984. *Yeoksa-hak chongseo 1: Geundae Hanguk oegyo-sa yeonpyo* 歷史學叢書 1: 近代韓國外交史年表 (GHOY) [Chronology of Modern Korean Diplomacy]. Seoul: Dandae chulpan-bu 檀大出版部.

1991. *Gu-Han mal gyeokdonggi bisa Allen ui ilgi* 舊韓末 激動期 秘史 알렌의 日記 [A Secret History of the Turbulent End of the Choson Kingdom]. Seoul: Dangook University Press 檀國大學校 出版部 [Allen's diary and newspaper materials in English are included].

Kim, Yeong-suk 金英淑, editor
1988b. *Dohae Hanguk boksik-sa sajeon* 圖解 韓國服飾史辭典 *(An Illustrated Dictionary of Korean Costumes).* Pages 1, 18, 28, 36, 45, 57, 59, 64, 111–112, 114–115, 120, 124, 139, 149, 156–157, 161, 162, 164, 168–169, 194, 198, 212, 216, 217, 220–221, 234–235, 242–243, 252, 257, 258, 266–268, 269, 280, 290, 293, 301–302, 314, 324–325, 348, 375–376, 383, 399, 412–413, 418–419, 426, 443, 446, 448–449, 450–451, 455, 482, 490, 492, 494, 496, 505, 511, 514, 515, 524, 526, 529, 563–564, 572. Seoul: Minmungo 民文庫.

Kim, Yeong-yun [Kim, Young-yun] 金榮胤, editor
1978. *Hanguk seohwa inmyeong saseo* 韓國書畫人名辭書 *(A Biographical Dictionary of Korean Painters and Calligraphers).* Seoul: Yesul chunchu-sa 藝術春秋社.

Kim, Yu-kyeong [Kim, Yoo-kyung] 김유경
1995. Clothes, Ornaments, and Artisans who make them. *Koreana: Korean Art and Culture, vol. 9, No. 3,* pages 26–39. Seoul: International Cultural Society of Korea.

Kunz, George F.
1884. Korean Curios. *Science, vol. 4, No. 82,* pages 172–173. Washington, D.C.

Legeza, Laszlo
1987. *Tao Magic: The Secret Language of Diagrams and Calligraphy.* Pages 21–24, 27. [First published in 1975]. New York: Thames and Hudson Inc.

Lowell, Percival
1886. *Chosôn: The Land of the Morning Calm: A Sketch of Korea.* Pages 314–315. Boston: Ticknor and Company.

Malone, Dumas, editor
1935. *Dictionary of American Biography (Published under the auspices of the American Council of Learned Societies), vol. 16.* New York: Charles Scribner's Sons.

Martin, Samuel E., Yi [Lee] Yang-ha, and Jang [Chang] Sung-un, editor
1967. *A Korean English Dictionary.* Pages 1148, 1578. New Haven and London: Yale University Press.

Mason, Otis T.
1886. Corea by Native Artists. *Science, vol. 8, No. 183,* pages 115–118. Washington, D.C.

1888. Corea by Native Artists. *Scientific American,* (July 14), pages 20–21.

McCune, Evelyn B.
1983. *The Inner Art: Korean Screens (Hanguk ui byeongpung* 한국의 병풍), translated by Soyoung Kim Sohn [Kim Seo-yeong] 김서영. Pages 14–15.

Berkeley, California: Asia Humanities Press and Seoul: Pochin-chai, Co. Ltd.

Minjok munwha yeongu-so 民族文化研究所 [Research Institute of Korean Culture]
1982. *Hanguk minsok daegwan* 韓國民俗大觀 (HMD) *(Survey of Korean Folk Culture)*. 6 volumes. Seoul: Minjok munwha yeongu-so 民族文化研究所, and Korea [Koryo] University 高麗大學校.

Miyoshi, Masao
1979. *As We Saw Them: The First Japanese Embassy to the United States (1860)*. Page 50. Berkeley, Los Angeles, and London: University of California Press.

Moes, Robert
1983. *Auspicious Spirits: Korean Folk Paintings and Related Objects*. Pages 87, 116. Washington, D.C: International Exhibitions Foundation.

Mun, Myeong-dae 文明大
1981. *Hanguk ui bulhwa* 韓國의佛畵 [Korean Buddhist Paintings]. Pages 32, 113. Seoul: Yeolhwa-dang 悅話堂.

Nam, Yeong-sin 남영신, editor
1987. *Urimal bullyu sajeon, vol. 1: Ireumssi-pyeon* 우리말분류사전, vol. 1: 이름씨편 [Dictionary of our Language by Subject Categories, vol. 1: Nouns]. Pages 57, 59, 60, 64. Seoul: Hangang munhwa-sa 한강문화사.

National Cyclopaedia of American Biography
1936. Hough, Walter. In *The National Cyclopaedia of American Biography, vol. 25*. page 277. New York: James T. White Company.

Nihon Dai-jiten Kankokai 日本大辭典刊行會
1972-1976. *Nihon kokugo daijiten* 日本國語大辭典 (NKDJ) [Encyclopedia of Japanese Language]. 20 volumes. Tokyo: Shōgakukan 小學館.

Noble, Harold J.
1929. The Korean Mission to the United States in 1883, the First Embassy sent by Korea to an Occidental Nation. *Transactions of the Korea Branch of the Royal Asiatic Society, vol. 18*, pages 1–21. Seoul.

Onyang minsok bangmul-gwan 溫陽民俗博物館 [Onyang Folk Museum]
1980. *Doseol Hanguk ui minsok* 圖說韓國의 民俗 (DHM) *(The Folkcrafts of Korea)*. Pages 166, 174–175, 182, 186, 194, 196, 198, 203, 211, 330, 331; illustration numbers 323, 324. Seoul: Gyemong-sa 啓蒙社.

Pak, Du-i 박두이
1990. Sangnye-bok ui gujo wa guseong weoli 喪禮服의 構造와 構成原理 [Funerary Costumes and their Symbolism]. In *Yeongwonhan mannam: Hanguk sangjang-nye* 영원한 만남: 韓國 喪葬禮 *(Eternal Beauty: Korean Funeral Customs)* [Exhibition Catalog], pages 159–172. Seoul: National Folk Museum 國立民俗博物館.

Pak, Yeong-sun 朴永橓
1982. Ji gongye 紙工藝 [Paper Manufacture]. In *Hanguk minsok daegwan* 韓國民俗大觀 (HMD) *(Survey of Korean Folk Culture), vol. 5: Minsok yesul, saengeop gisul* 한국민속대관, vol. 5: 민속예술, 생업기술 [Folk Art and Crafts and Industries], pages 598–602. Seoul: Minjok munwha yeongu-so

民族文化研究所 [Research Institute of Korean Culture], and Korea [Koryo] University 高麗大學校.

Papinot, Edmond
1972. *Historical and Geographical Dictionary of Japan*. Page 321. Rutland, Vermont, and Tokyo: Charles E. Tuttle Company. [The original 1910 edition in English is a translation of the earlier *Dictionnaire d'histoire et de géographie du Japan*, 1906.]

Rockhill, W. W.
1891. Notes on Some of the Laws, Customs, and Superstitions of Korea. *The American Anthropologist* [Published under the auspices of the Anthropological Society of Washington], vol. 4, (April), pages 177–187. Washington, D.C: Judd & Detweiler, Printers.

Ross, John, Rev.
1891. *History of Corea*. London: Patenosta Row.

Rubin, David S.
Ms. John Baptiste Bernadou, A Smithsonian Ethnographer in Korea. Unpublished Manuscript, unpaginated [1982].

Sakai, Atsuharu
1947. *We Japanese, vol. 2*. Page 148. Yokohama: Yamagata Press. [Written for Fujiya Hotel, Ltd. in Miyanoshita, Hakone, Japan and first published in 1937.]

Salwey, Charlotte M.
1894. *Fans of Japan*. Page 67. London: Kegan Paul, Trench, Trubner, & Co., Ltd.

Sayers, Robert and Ralph Rinzler
1987. *The Korean Onggi Potter (Smithsonian Folklife Studies No. 5)*. Pages 72–73; figure 19. Washington, D.C.: Smithsonian Institution.

Seok, Ju-seon [Suk, Joo-sun] 石宙善
1979. *Minsok-hak jaryo 1: Hyungbae* 民俗學 資料 第一輯: 胸背 *(Folk Art Research Collection Series 1: Yi Dynasty Upper Garment Insignia Patterns)*. Pages 23–98, 134. Seoul: Suk Joo-sun Memorial Museum of Korean Folk Arts, Dangook University 檀國大學校 附設 石宙善 記念 民俗博物館.

1981. *Minsok-hak jaryo 2: Jangsingu* 民俗學 資料 第二輯: 裝身具 *(Folk Art Research Collection Series 2: Personal Ornaments in Yi [Choson] Dynasty)*. Pages 95–98, 170; illustration numbers 74, 79–82. Seoul: Suk Joo-sun Memorial Museum of Korean Folk Arts, Dangook University 檀國大學校 附設 石宙善 記念 民俗博物館.

1985. *Minsok-hak jaryo 3: Ui* 民俗學 資料 第三輯: 依 *(Folk Art Research Collection Series 3: Clothes of Joson [Choson] Dynasty)*. Page 112. Seoul: Suk Joo-sun Memorial Museum of Korean Folk Arts, Dangook University 檀國大學校 附設 石宙善 記念 民俗博物館.

1992a. *Hanguk boksik-sa* 韓國 服飾史 [History of Korean Costumes]. [First published in 1971]. Pages 21, 41, 46, 51, 73, 143, 192, 193, 209, 217–219, 228, 249, 262, 263, 266–268, 317, 510–511, 559–561, 703; illustration numbers 16, 38. Seoul: Bojinjae 寶晉齋.

1992b. Hanguk boksik ui byeoncheon 한국복식의 변천 [Korean Costumes]. In *Hanguk jeontong saenghwal ui mi* 한국 전통생활의 미 *(Korean*

Costumes and Textiles) [Exhibition Catalog and English Text for IBM Gallery of Science and Art, New York], pages 20–21; illustration pages 27–51. Seoul: Hanguk IBM.

Shinmura, Izuru 新村出, editor
1982. *Kōjien* 廣辭苑 (KJE) [Dictionary of the Japanese Language]. [First published in 1955]. Tokyo: Iwanami shoten 岩波書店.

Smith, Judith G., editor
1998. *Arts of Korea*. New York: The Metropolitan Museum of Art.

Smithsonian Archives, editor
1983. *Guide to the Smithsonian Archives*. Washington, D.C: Smithsonian Institution.

Smithsonian Institution
1884-1885. *The Smithsonian Institution Annual Report* (SI-AR) *for 1882, 1883, and 1884*. Washington, D.C.: Government printing office.

1890. *The U.S. National Museum Annual Report* (USNM-AR) *for 1889*. Washington, D.C.: Smithsonian Institution.

1937. *The U.S. National Museum Annual Report* (USNM-AR) *for 1936*. Washington, D.C.: Smithsonian Institution.

Storm, Carl
1973. The Philosophy of Pillows. In *Minhak* 民學 *(Folkism), vol. 2*, pages 28–30. Seoul: Emille Museum 에밀레 美術館.

Tanaka, Umekichi 田中梅吉
1926. Chōsen no gan'gu mokuroku 朝鮮の玩具目錄 [Catalog of Korean Toys]. *Minzoku* 民族 *(The Japanese Journal of Folklore and Ethnology), vol. 2, No. 1*, pages 183–196.

The National Center for Korean Traditional Performing Arts
1998. *A Study of Musical Instruments in Korean Traditional Music* (SMI). Pages 42–43. Seoul: The National Center for Korean Traditional Performing Arts.

Who Was Who in America
1966. Bernadou, John Baptiste. In *Who Was Who in America, vol. 1*, (1897–1942). Chicago: Marquis Publications.

Wilkinson, W. H.
1894. Chess in Korea. In *Pall Mall Budget* (December 27), pages 30–31. London.

Williams, C.A.S.
1976. *Outlines of Chinese Symbolism and Art Motives*. [Revised edition: first published in 1931 under the title, *Outlines of Chinese Symbolism*]. Pages 186, 295, 300–301, 322–323. New York: Dover Publications, Inc.

Yang, Jae-yeon 梁在淵, Im Dong-gweon 任東權, et al
1974. *Eulyu mungo 73: Hanguk pungsok-ji* 乙酉文庫 73: 韓國風俗誌 [Survey of Korean Ethnology]. [First published in 1971]. Seoul: Eulyu munhwa-sa 乙酉文化社.

Ye, Yong-hae 芮庸海
1969. *Ingan munhwajae* 人間文化財 [Intangible Cultural Properties]. [First published in 1963]. Pages

293–298. Seoul: Eomungak 語文閣.

Ye, Yong-hae 예용해, Jeong Yang-mo [Chung Yang Mo] 정양모, and Kim Gwang-eon 김광언
1989. *Miguk bangmul-gwan sojang Hanguk munhwajae* 미국박물관 소장 한국 문화재 (MBM) *(The Korean Relics in the United States)*. Pages 137–139, 142, 148–150; illustration numbers 21–23, 27, 38, 59, 61–67. Seoul: International Cultural Society of Korea 한국 국제 문화협회.

Yi, Du-hyeon 李杜鉉
1984. *Hanguk minsokhak nongo* 韓國民俗學論考 [A Treatise on Korean Folk Customs]. Series: Hanguk ui minsokhak yeongu 11 韓國의 民俗學 研究 11 [Studies on Korean Folk Customs, No. 11]. Seoul: Hagyeon-sa 學研社.

Yi, Gu-yeol [Lee, Ku-yeol] 李龜烈
1987. Geundae Hanguk-hwa ui sidae-jeok byeonhwa 近代韓國畵의 時代的 變化 [Historical Change of Modern Korean Paintings]. In *Hanguk geundae hoehwa baengnyeon (1850-1950)* 한국 근대 회화 백년 *(Korean Painting: 1850-1950s)* [Exhibition catalog of the National Museum of Korea], pages 210–250. Seoul: Samhwa inswae 三和印刷.

Yi, Gwang-nin 이광린 李光麟
1982a. Hanguin choecho ui Miguk daehaksaeng Byeon Su 韓國人 최초의 美國大學生 邊燧 [Byeon Su, the First Korean Who Became an American University Student]. *Sin Donga No. 218* (October 1982), pages 432–446. Seoul: Donga ilbo-sa 東亞日報社.

1982b. "Ieon" gwa Hanguk ui gaehwa sasang "易言" 과 韓國의 開化思想 [Ieon and the Korean Enlightenment]. In *Hanguk gaehwa-sa yeongu* 韓國開化史研究 [The History of Korean Modernization], pages 19–30. [First published in 1969]. Seoul: Iljo-gak 일조각.

Yi, Gyeong-ja 李京子
1983. *Hanguk boksiksa-ron* 韓國 服飾史論 [History of Korean Costumes]. Page 389. Seoul: Ilji-sa 一志社.

Yi, Hong-jik 李弘稙, editor
1962–1963. *Guksa dae-sajeon* 國史大辭典 (GDS) [Encyclopedia of Korean History]. 2 volumes. Seoul: Jimungak 知文閣.

Yi, Jong-seok [Lee, Jongseok] 李宗碩
1973. Sunchang byeogae subon 李宗碩 (Pillow Designs from Sunchang). In *Minhak* 民學 *(Folkism)*, *vol. 2*, pages 110–113. Seoul: Emille Museum 에밀레 美術館.

Yi, Seong-mi 이성미
1992. *Hanguk jeontong saenghwal ui mi* 한국전통생활의미 *(Korean Costumes and Textiles)* [Exhibition Catalog and English Text for IBM Gallery of Science and Art, New York]. Pages 13, 74–99. Seoul: Hanguk IBM.

Yi, U-hwan 李禹煥
1982c. *Yeolhwa-dang misul seonseo 9: Yi-jo ui minhwa, gujo roseo ui hoehwa* 悅話堂 美術選書 9:李朝의 民畵, 構造로서의 繪畵 [Choson Dynasty Folk Paintings]. [First published in 1977]. Seoul: Yeolhwa-dang 悅話堂.

Yun, Chi-ho 尹致昊
1984. *Hanguk saryo chongseo, No. 19* 韓國史料叢書 第十九: *Yun Chi-ho ilgi* 尹致昊 日記 [Yun Chi-ho's Diary]. [Fist published in 1971]. 4 volumes. Seoul: Guksa pyeonchan wiwon-hoe 國史編纂委員會.

Yun, Yeol-su [Yoon, Yul-soo] 윤열수
1997. *Minhwa iyagi* 민화 이야기 *(Tales of Korean Folk Painting, Minwha)*. Pages 35, 63–65, 74–85, 103, 105–111, 273–277. Seoul: Design House 디자인하우스.

Appendices

I. Bernadou Letter of 2 November 1883, Washington D.C. to Baird
(Source: SI Archives RU 29, Office of the Secretary, 1882-1887, Incoming Correspondence)

WASHINGTON D. C.
Nov 2., 1883

Sir,

As the U.S.S. Alert will leave in a short time (most probably inside of three weeks from San Francisco), I would respectfully request that you mention the fact in your communication to the State Department as a reason for urging speedy action.

> Very Respectfully,
> Your obedient servant,
> J. B. Bernadou,
> Ensign, U.S.N.

Professor Spencer F. Baird,
Director of the National Museum.

II. Bernadou Letter of 10 March 1884, Seoul, Korea to Baird
(Source: SI Archives RU 29, Office of the Secretary, 1882-1887, Incoming Correspondence)

Sèoul, Corea,
Mar 10, 1884

Professor Spencer F. Baird,
Director National Museum,
Washington, D.C.

Sir,

I arrived safely at Nagasaki, Japan, Feb. 24, by the U.S.S. Alert. At that port I transferred my effects to the U.S.S. Juniata bound for Chi-mul-po [Chemulp'o (now Incheon)], Corea, arriving there Mar 1. From Chi-mul-po I proceeded to Seoul, the capital, where I met a warm and courteous reception from General Lucius H. Foote, the U.S. Minister. By him I was given a house on the U.S. Legation ground for use during my stay here. I propose to make Sèoul my headquarters, and mail forwarded here, (care U.S. Consul, Nagasaki) will reach me in the most direct way.

Your letter of Dec 7, and Dec 11 are at hand. One was received by me at Nagasaki, the other upon my arrival here, I forward with this the receipts for articles forwarded (signed), and would state that all arrived in good condition, with the exception of one alcohol tank, which was leaking slightly, causing thereby the loss of a portion of its contents. The gun and equipments were complete and in excellent condition. The blowpipe apparatus needs one or two small articles. These can be sent through the mail and I forward a memorandum.

I cannot imagine any place where a photographic apparatus could be put to a better use than here. The costumes, buildings, memorial arches, bridges, tombs, shops, etc., would furnish work for many. A small camera, plates and developing apparatus would, I think, well pay the investment.

I intend spending the next two months in attempting to acquire a limited knowledge of the language so as to be in a measure independent. To this end I gave all my time on the way out. In the mean time I will take notes of what I may learn or observe.

General Foote will endorse my request that specimens of ores now worked may be furnished me. This will, I think, put much material in my hands that I could not otherwise obtain, as I could not visit so may localities. The marbles of Corea are among the most beautiful that I have ever seen. They are worked into boxes and ornaments, and are exposed for sale here.

As I have just arrived in Seoul, I have, as yet been able to do nothing. My idea, is to make to you, from time to time a general statement of what I may have been able to accomplish; but to submit a final report to you, together with what articles I may have collected after I return to the United States. I think that I can thus systematize matter in the simplest way; but I will be thankful for any suggestions that you may have to make on the subject.

Very respectfully,
J. B. Bernadou
Ensign,U.S.N.

III. Bernadou Letter of 2 September, Seoul, Korea to Baird
(Source: NMNH Registrar's Office accession number 16970)

Söul [*sic*], Corea,
Sept. 2, 1884.
(Care U. S. Legation).

Sir,

Your letter of June 17 has been received. I have intended to send you notes of my progress, and take occasion of doing so in my reply.

In a new country, like this, there are many things to attract one's attention; the field is an open one, and it remains to select a particular line of study. If too many are attempted, but little can be accomplished. I therefore make my plans as follows:

(1) To remain in Seoul during the first part of my stay, to collect such objects as would come under the head of Corean art, that I could obtain; and to study the Corean language in order to become conversant with the people, and thus enable myself to give my attention to Corean ethnology.

(2) To visit the interior of Corea later, to make such general observations as in my power, and to incorporate such matter as might be useful in my ethnological report to you; also, to collect specimens, mineralogical and others. It being impossible with the limited funds at my disposal to travel heavily equipped, I concluded to collect fish chiefly from one point, Chi-mul-po [Chemulp'o (now Incheon)], the seaport of Sôul; and to transfer such as I might find on the way packed in native spirits, adding them to those collected in the tanks on my return.

(3) Later, in the fall, to go to a point whence I could obtain the use of two native hunters to kill game and skin it under my directions. These were promised me by an official of high rank.

(4) To return to Sôul in midwinter, finish my ethnological collection and report, and make preparations for leaving.

It being impossible to obtain much besides natural history specimens without funds, I have concluded to purchase some articles at my own expense, and will give them to the Museum. This I am enabled to do by the relatively low prices, foreign trade having had, as yet, but little influence on domestic rates of exchange.

I will try to briefly summarize what work I have accomplished under the heads given below, commencing with such articles as would come under the general head of Art.

Pottery. Old pottery, though rare and commanding high prices, is obtainable. There is but little in the design of the greater part to commend it to one's interest for this alone. The earlier pieces appear to be less ornamented than the later. One piece, over seven hundred years old, had a rough design of a wreath of leaves. The pottery here known as old dates from six hundred to three hundred years back; that of kingdom of Korai [Japanese for Koryo] — over five hundred years — is the most esteemed. I have obtained one small piece of the Korai period, and fragments of a later date.

Painting. There appears to be no living artist of note in Corea; one whose works have any renown. Coarse portraits of Chinese and Corean heroes, Corean landscapes, and pictures of officials in their robes are common, and are made by the hundreds. The people buy them to decorate the interiors of their houses. Individual efforts, such as are seen in modern picture books, are of greater interest. The work is more akin to the Chinese school than to the modern Japanese; yet seem to occupy an intermediate position in that the perspective is better than in the former, while the execution resembles more the latter. I have a most excellent screen, painted on silk. It is undoubtedly the work of a Corean, but the picture represents a Chinese scene, the presentation of tribute by various nations to the Chinese Emperor of a former dynasty. I have not been able as yet to fix the period, but hope to do so by showing it to several well read Coreans of my acquaintance.

The most valuable object that I have succeeded in obtaining is a picture book between two and three hundred years old representing scenes in Corean domestic life, and general life of the common people. The pictures are faithful to the minutest details; among them are; a marriage procession, students at an examination, a dancing girl and band of musicians, weir fishing, shoeing a horse in a manner I think peculiar to Corea (by throwing him upon his back and tieing his four feet to an upright post). It has been suggested to me that the book might furnish a hint as to the origin of the Japanese realistic school, which is said to be comparatively new.

Metal work and inlaid work. Metal work of much merit comes from Nyong-pyon [Yeongbyeon] in Puing-an-do [Pyeongan-do]. Upon an iron base designs are filled out in copper or silver. At the time of the Japanese invasion, some three hundred years ago, the best of the artificers were taken to Japan. There their descendants, who follow the trade of their fathers, are still to be found. The present Japanese work is much better than that now made in Corea.

In mother o' pearl a number of inlaid dishes, such as are used in the cylindrical pillows in common use.

Furniture. I have several small specimens, one in particular being quite good. It was made by a Corean in Soul. It has, in silver inlaid on copper, the Chinese character, (long life and happiness), repeated a number of times; this is characteristically Corean. The locks, hinges, and panelling are all of good workmanship and peculiar. I have also another piece illustrating the average articles found in the houses of the better classes.

Wood-carving. A bamboo quiver, ornamented with a curious device of deers and pine-trees. The brass work is also good.

Stone work. A number of boxes of Corean marbles. These are more remarkable for material than for workmanship. They are polished rectangular forms.

Books. A number of books in the ern-moun [eonmun (Hangul)] or common writing. There is one common school-book, in which about fourteen hundred Chinese characters are given with the sound and meaning in the ern-moun. Here the native writing supplies a difficulty felt by the Chinese, there being nothing definite in a Chinese character to indicate to a beginner the sound or meaning. There are several books of Corean folk-lore; these by the aid of an interpreter have been put into good English by an European here.

I have given some little time to endeavors to find Sanscrit books. That a knowledge of Sanscrit once existed here is well known. Five hundred years ago, Buddhism was the court religion. It has been replaced by Confucianism.

I have succeeded in obtaining one book in Chinese and Sanscrit; giving the pronunciation of the Sanscrit characters in the ern-moun. It contains a number of prayers, and the meaning of the characters is described in Chinese. I was unable to find a trace of either a Sanscrit dictionary or a grammatical work.

A German, who examined mines for Coreans, had permission to go to a certain well-known Buddhist monastery to enquire for Sanscrit manuscripts. He found none, although armed with considerable power, and after searching through a library of a thousand volumes, returned with a copy of the book now in my possession and one other, a similar one.

I have copies of the inscriptions from a fine Buddhist bell at Sung-do [Songdo (now Kaesong)], in Sanscrit, Pale, and Chinese.

Two months ago I started upon a trip to the interior and have just returned. I went to Song-do, a former capital and then to Peng-yang [Pyongyang], also a former capital, and intended visiting Ooi-tchw [Uiju] on the Chinese frontier. The season was midsummer, hot and rainy, and the trip was a tedious one. Owing to the change of food, I had trouble with my digestion and was compelled to return to Seoul for medical aid. I had projected a trip from Ooi-tchw [Uiju] across to the

Pacific coast, but was compelled to retrace my steps. I made a journey of over five hundred miles, however.

I am now nearly recovered but, by the advice of the doctor will remain in Seoul for the present. As I can talk enough of the language to make myself (generally) understood, I have engaged the services of an intelligent Corean, and am working systematically upon the ethnology. I say systematically, as I will collect and make notes according to the excellent classification given by Dr. Rau in his paper on the archaeological collection in the National Museum. This is for work among savage races, but it will do for half civilized ones.

I am especially desirous that you send me a list of all the Corean articles in the National Museum of ethnological interest. I do not care to duplicate and so am desirous of having the names at an early date.

I have made myself familiar with a number of musical instruments, their names and peculiarities, and hope to have no difficulty in obtaining some of them. I will send to the Museum costumes of the coolie, peasant woman, soldier, gentleman, and, if possible, a court dress.

In minerals, I have been disappointed. I took notes on the nature of the country travelled through. It was not rich, and but few mines were worked in it. And from all that I can hear and learn, I may say that I greatly doubt the story of the great mineral wealth of Corea. I have obtained a very small nugget of gold. The government monopolizes the production of this metal and is suspicious of foreigners, so that although no obstacles were put in my way, yet no assistance was afforded me in this work. I hunted for coal, but could not find any. The German before referred to was similarly occupied in another part of the country and succeeded in finding a vein which he estimated to be about two millimeters in thickness.

I have obtained a number of specimens of plants and insects; this was difficult on the march, and my temporary sickness prevented me from going to Nyeng-pyen [Yeongbyeon], where I had decided to remain two weeks for this purpose.

I have been looking anxiously for some way to obtain a skeleton. This is extremely difficult to do, however, as from their religion, setting such a high value upon human remains, they are averse to disposing of them. As heads are cut off frequently, I might be able to get the remains of some criminal; but the subject is a very delicate one and I would not act until I felt sure that my motive was fully understood.

There are three religions in this country; Confucianism, Buddhism, and a third, a very primitive one apparently that of the mass of the common country people. It is a worship of the spirits of the woods and hills, and appears to embrace some of the superstitions of Shamanism of Northern Asia, and the Shintoism of Japan. I have taken many notes on this subject. In the northern provinces it is less marked by the other creeds. Besides the spirits of the hills and woods, those of Corean heroes are worshipped. I have seen pictures of Buddha in what I knew were not Buddhist temples.

Along the roads throughout the country, in shady spots under large trees and in thickets, piles of stones are made, and on the bushes are tied pieces of garments. On the high hills in many places are built the shrines. The rich, or their friends, commonly make offerings there, pieces of garments or plates containing food.

As my work is planned to my supposed extent of stay, I am specially anxious to remain until next April. So that if you are consulted as regards any change of my orders, I earnestly ask that you request that I be allowed to remain.

I will not forward articles to the Museum until the time of my return to the United States. In case of my wishing to do so, however, as the goods will have to be re-shipped in Japan, I would suggest your writing to Messrs. R. H. Powers and Co., of Nagasaki, who transact my business there. They will re-forward them to the National Museum, care the Alaska Commercial Company.

Please remember to forward me a list of the Corean articles in the ethnological collection.

Very respectfully,
J. B. Bernadou,
Ensign, U.S.N.

Professor Spencer F. Baird,
Director of the National Museum,
Washington, D. C.

I would add that the Corean officials have been very kind to me, affording me every facility for travelling, furnishing me horses at government rates, and giving me lodging on my way, in the official buildings.

IV. Bernadou Letter of 4 October 1884, Seoul to Baird
(Source: SI Archives RU 29,Office of the Secretary, 1882-1887, Incoming Correspondence)

Soul, Oct. 4, 1884

Sir,

I forward herewith an abstract, taken from my journal, of a trip made by me from Söul to Ping Yang [Pyongyang]. As I know that I am the first authorized European that has entered Peng Yang, and as I do not think that an account of such a trip has been before given, I enclose with this the abstract above mentioned and a native map, and both of which I request you to forward to the American Geographical Society No 11 West 29th St., New York.

I prefer sending the manuscript to you, as I am here in the interests of the National Museum; and I have notified the Geographical Society of what I have done.

I have succeeded in getting some pieces of old Corean porcelain, sufficiently good to satisfy myself that once very beautiful articles were once made here. I have also a mourning dress, such as worn for two years after the death of a parent.

I am now collecting fish at Chi mul po [Chemulp'o (now Incheon)] where the tank forwarded me now is.

Upon my leaving Corea, I will be put to some small expense say about twenty-five mexican dollars in packing the articles that I have collected. I think that this should be borne by the Museum; if this amount is place to my credit with Paymaster Jno. C. Sullivan at Nagasaki Japan, I will be able to obtain it without difficulty.

Hoping to hear from you I remain,

Yours, very respectfully,
J. B. Bernadou
Ensign U.S.N.
Professor Spencer F. Baird
Director National Museum

V. Bernadou Letter of 20 April 1885, Chemulp'o, Korea,
USS Ossipee to Baird Accompanying Packing List
(Source: NMNH Registrar's Office accession Number 16970,
transferred to the SI Archives and given the number RU 305)

U. S. S. Ossipee,
Che-mul-p'o, Korea,
April 20, 1885

Professor Spencer F. Baird,
Director U. S. National Museum
Washington, D. C. U.S.A.

Sir,

Your letter of Jan 14 is at hand. On account of the great irregularity in the times of arrival of Japanese Steamers, it becomes impossible to foretell with any certainty the dates of receipt of mail; – I account in this way for the delay of my last.

I enclose herewith a descriptive list of objects collected by me in Korea for the U.S. National Museum. This list is especially made for the purpose of labelling the specimens; – if further information is needed, as will most probably be, I will be pleased to furnish it from my notes.

The articles named in this list will be forwarded to the U.S. Museum from Japan by Mr. Walter D. Townsend, a merchant who is connected with the China and Japan Trading Company. This firm has its headquarters in New York. I have requested Mr. Townsend to forward the boxes to his firm's office in New York, freight to be paid [there on ?] delivery by the agent of the U.S. Museum. Mr. Townsend will have you notified upon their arrival.

With the exception of fish, you will find no specimens in natural history. A second contemplated trip in to the interior was frustrated by the revolution which has just taken place.

I have also in preparation a translation of [William] Imbrie's Japanese-English phrase book. The translation into Corean is finished, - there remains a certain part of the accompanying text to be written. My object in doing this was to furnish a number of parallel sentences in Corean and Japanese with a view of assisting comparative study. There are, I think, philologists who would be interested in the subject, and I do not know of any work that has established the relation of Corean and Japanese or given Corean its position in the list of agglutinative languages.

Very respectfully,
Your obedient servant,
J. B. Bernadou
Ensign, U.S. Navy

VI. Bernadou Collection Packing List

INVOICE
Invoice of goods shipped as specimens to the United States National Museum at Washington, D. C, United States of America. Forwarded by me through Messrs. R. H. Powers & Co., to Mr. Walter D. Townsend of Kobe, Japan, to be re-forwarded by Mr. Townsend to the U. S. National Museum, Washington, D. C., U. S. A.

J. B. Bernadou
Ensign, U. S. Navy.

Box marked A.
1.   Wooden cabinet.
2.   Disk of wood ornamentd with mother o'pearl.
3.   Set of Corean playing cards.
4.   Coarse comb of wood.
5.   Fine comb of wood.
6.   Headband part of mourning dress.
7.   Disk of wood ornamented in mother o'pearl.
8.   Painted disk of wood.
9.   Brap [Brass] tweezers.
10.   Small pocket looking glass.
11.   Brass pipe.
12.   Comb cleaner.
13.   Head band, part of Corean dress.
14.   Money bag and cord.
15.   Pocket knife.
16.   Slip of bone for adjusting head-band.
17.   White metal pipe.
18.   Hair pin of lead.
19.   Set of Corean dominoes.

Box marked B.
1.   Wooden cabinet.
2.   Corean Official cap.
3.   Koan - Corean cap.
4.   Set of Corean table crockery
5.   Rough bowl of clay.
6.   Box made of red stone.
7.   Corean court hat.
8.   Corean hat.
9.   Bottle of chinaware.
10.   Writing materials.

BOX MARKED C.

1.   China ware water jar.
2.   Set of Corean chessmen.
3.   Specimen of Corean fabric, silk.
4.   "   "   "   ", grass-cloth.
5.   Specimen of Corean fabric, hemp.
6.   "   "   "   ", hemp.
7.   "   "   "   ", cotton.
8.   "   "   "   ", cotton.
9.   Specimen of Corean fabric, silk.
10.   "   "   "   ", silk and grass.

ARTICLES CONTINUED IN BOX MARKED C.

11.   Specimen of Corean fabric, grass.
12.   Specimen of Corean fabric, Silk and grass.
13.   Specimen of Corean fabric, cotton & silk.
14.   Specimen of Corean grain.
15.   "   "   "   "
16.   Gown of silk as worn by women.

Set of articles making a complete set of clothing as worn by women, viz.

17.   Drawers, of cotton stuff.
18.   Under skirt.
19.   "   "   "   "
20.   Waist band.
21.   Outer dress
22.   Inner jacket.
23.   Stockings.
24.   Outer jacket.
25.   Hairpin of lead.
26.   Finger rings of lead. Articles of men's clothing.
27.   Long gown.
28.   Outer garment of similar shape.
29.   Trousers.
30.   Stockings.
31.   Leggings.
32.   Cuffs.
33.   Girdle.
34.   Silk strings for fastening bottoms of trousers.

Articles of child's clothing:

35.   Child's jacket.
36.   " stockings.
37.   " leggings.
38.   " small-coat.
39.   " trousers.
40.   " over-trousers.
41.   " outer garment.
42.   " hair ribbon.
43.   " head dress of ribbon.
44.   " winter hood.
45.   Cap part of men's mourning apparel.
46.   Men's outer girdle out of silk.
47.   Dose of medicine and prescription.
48.   Brass ricebowl and lid.
49.   Men's short jacket.

BOX MARKED D.
1. Printing block of wood.
2. Roll of Corean pictures.
3. Hat cover with strings.
4. Embroideries (2) .
5. Brass spoon and chopsticks.
6. Koul kon or mourning hat.
7. Article of mourning apparel.
8. Mourning robe.
9. Hempen girdle,- part of mourning dress.
10. Leggings, part of mourning dress.
11. Mourning screen.
12. Screen picture of Corean lady.

ARTICLES CONTINUED IN BOX MARKED D.
13. Sheet of oiled paper.
14. Sheet of examination paper.
15. Small iron for ironing clothes.
16. Sticks of wood used in washing clothes.
17. Men's shoes.
18. Women's shoes.
19. Mourning hat.
20. Coolie's hat.
21. Wooden shoes.
22. Oiled paper raincoat.
23. Outer mourning robe.
24. Mourning shoes.
25. Bamboo cuffs.
26. Bamboo shirt.
27. Straw shoes.
28. Hempen shoes.

BOX MARKED E.
1. Circular saucer of Corean pottery.
2. Wine cup of Corean pottery.
3. Dish of Corean potter.
4. " " " "
5. Bottle " " " "
6. Bowl " " " "

ARTICLES IN BOX MARKED F.
1. Chinese Corean book.
2. Picture book.
3. Picture book.
4. Picture book.
5. Fan of oiled paper.
6. Sanscrit - Onmoun book.
7. Small paper fan.
8. Specimen of Corean grain.
9. " " " "
10. " " " "
11. " " " "
12. " " " "
13. " " " "
14. Peacock's feather ornament.
15. On-moun book.
16. Portable mineralogists blowpipe case.

ARTICLES IN BOX MARKED G.
1. Stone pencil jar of yellow and green marble.
2. Silver inlaid box.
3. Copper inlaid box.
4. Disk of yellow marble.
5. Pot of black stone, with furnace.
6. Slab of marble.

ARTICLES CONTAINED IN BOX MARKED H.
1. One Winchester rifle.
2. One Colt double barrel shot gun.
3. One set shot gun loading tools; change leader & recapper.
4. Pillow end of silk embroidery.
5. Examination cap of black cotton stuff.
6. Pongotji or soldier's cap.
7. Ornament for 6.
8. Coolie's straw hat.
9. Black Corean hat of bamboo.
10. Chair coolie's hat of black felt.

ARTICLES CONTINUED IN BOX MARKED H.
11. Specimens of guiseng (ginseng).
12. Chinese book, 3 vols.
13. Map of Soul.
14. Old Corean screen.
15. Corean flint and steel.
16. Fan of oiled paper.
17. Feather fan.
18. Red stone ornament.
19. Corean musical instrument.
20. Specimen of grain.
21. " " " "
22. " " " "
23. Bamboo window screen.
24. Specimen of Corean matting.
25. Straw image.

BOX MARKED I
Containing three copper tanks of alcohol, in which are natural history specimens of fish.
I certify the above to be a correct statement of the contents of boxes above enumerated.

J. B. Bernadou
Ensign, U.S. Navy

VII. BERNADOU LETTER OF 5 AUGUST 1885, CHEMULP'O (NOW INCHEON), KOREA TO BAIRD
(Source: SI Archives RU 29, Office of the Secretary, 1882-1887, Incoming Correspondence)

Direct to U.S.S. Alert, care postmaster, Yokohama
Bernadou, J.B.

U.S.S. Alert
Chemulp'o, Korea
8/5/1885

Professor Spencer F. Baird,
Director National Museum,

Sir,

Yours of the first part of June (I think 8th just received). Herewith I forward certain papers in Sanskrit or Thibetan, obtained from Korean Buddhists. They are Tarani or charms, used by the common people, and placed under the garments of the dead with a view of promoting their future wellfare.

The writing is interesting, and I am very anxious to find out what the text is. Would like them placed in the hands of a good Sanskrit Scholar.

As some of the writing is Chinese, I think that Mr. Goodrich would be a suitable person in whose hands to place them.

Will write again in full. Steamer being now on point of departure.

Respectfully,
J. B. Bernadou
Ensign U.S. Navy.

Index